Praise for *Core 52*

"*Core 52* is simply one of the best daily guides in print to strengthen your faith. Mark Moore condenses decades of learning into a succinct and powerful book. Mark is not only brilliant, but he's also a brilliant communicator of ideas. *Core 52* will transform both your Bible IQ and your life."

—Jud Wilhite, author of *Pursued* and senior pastor of Central Church

"Whether you are someone who reads the Bible on a regular basis, has never read it, or has started and stopped reading it multiple times, *Core 52* is the resource for you! This is an easy-to-use and engaging tool that will strengthen your understanding of God's Word."

— Jon Weece, lead follower at Southland Christian Church and author of *Jesus Prom*

"There is no question that Bible engagement is the single greatest predictor of spiritual growth. That's why I'm so excited about *Core 52.* Mark has provided not only a clear on-ramp to understanding the Bible better but also a guide to applying it to your life."

—Ashley Wooldridge, senior pastor of Christ's Church of the Valley

"*Core 52* will allow you to bridge the gap between your biblical training and your professional impact. If you want to speak confidently on biblical topics while helping to lead others on their faith journey, this resource is for you!"

—Kirk Cousins, pro quarterback

"When it comes to knowing and teaching the fundamental insights of Christ, Mark Moore is a maven. In *Core 52,* you will gain the tools you need for living the life God has called you to. His innovative ideas and colorful illustrations will grab your attention and motivate your will to know Christ and make him known. Start today with chapter 1, be diligent through chapter 52, and you will be satisfied."

—Kyle Idleman, senior pastor of Southeast Christian Church and author of *Not a Fan* and *Don't Give Up*

"As a women's Bible study leader, my heart is to help women know God's Word better so they can learn to connect their everyday frantic lives with their faith in Jesus. *Core 52* is a godsend and a perfect tool to help them do just that. Anything I can offer that will help women get the most out of their time in God's Word is a precious gift indeed. That is what *Core 52* does for me as a teacher and for the women I lead. What a gift this is from a notable teacher I have come to trust as an invaluable resource."

—Lisa Laizure, Bible study teacher at WomensBibleStudy.com

"Through his earlier books, Mark has taught me more about the Bible than any other author. His clear teaching and sly wit always make me read more pages than I plan to. *Core 52* is his best yet. Move it to the top of your daily reading list."

—Phil Smith, coauthor of *Created to Flourish* and creator of *Eyewitness Bible Series* videos

"With a pastor's heart, a scholar's mind, and a sage's pen, Mark Moore has given us a gift in *Core 52* to help us understand God's words, be changed by them, and live them out!"

—Caleb Kaltenbach, author of *Messy Grace* and *God of Tomorrow*

"My wife saw *Core 52* on the counter and looked it over. Her verdict: 'This is so good. Why didn't anyone think of this before? I really like it. A lot.' I think she said it all, except 'This book will help you raise your Bible IQ faster than anything I know.' By the way, all my children love listening to Mark Moore because he combines the understanding of a scholar with the communication of a pastor. So that makes *Core 52* multigenerationally approved."

—Haydn Shaw, author of *Generational IQ: Christianity Isn't Dying, Millennials Aren't the Problem, and the Future Is Bright*

"As a film and television actor, I find myself in different states and countries and in the company of diverse crews and castmates. Often, when people find out that I'm a Christian, they ask about my faith and the Bible. I love sharing what Jesus has done for me, but I wish I was more confident in my knowledge of the Bible. That's why I'm so grateful for *Core 52*. It provides a platform for me to have more spiritually meaningful conversations that will help others take their next step toward faith."

—LaMonica Garrett, film and television actor known for *Designated Survivor, Sons of Anarchy,* and *The Last Ship*

"Paul tells young Timothy to be diligent 'to present yourself to God as one approved, a worker who has no need to be ashamed, rightly handling the word of truth' (2 Timothy 2:15). Pastor Mark has provided a clear path to make that presentation. This is seminary in a bottle."

—Dr. Darryl DelHousaye, president/chancellor of Phoenix Seminary

"I value being able to discipline myself with a resource that will challenge me and allow me to dive in and study the Word better. *Core 52* not only met this challenge, but it also exceeded all my expectations. Mark's background as a professor, preacher, and teacher is very evident in the strategy behind his book. I travel almost every week, and *Core 52* allows me to study God's Word, memorize his Word, interpret his Word, and implement it in my daily walk with God. Thank you, Mark, for challenging me to be a better Christ follower!"

—Doug Crozier, CEO of the Solomon Foundation, Parker, CO

"As a leader, I believe there are very few things that are worth investing your time and energy into on a daily basis. Learning the many different stories and insights of the Bible is definitely one of them. The issue is that many of us have no clue where to start. With his book *Core 52,* Mark has created a clear path to greater biblical literacy that, with a little time and effort, anyone can follow.

—Carey Nieuwhof, founding pastor of Connexus Church
and author of *Didn't See It Coming*

CORE 52

CORE

A FIFTEEN-MINUTE DAILY GUIDE TO BUILD YOUR BIBLE IQ IN A YEAR

MARK E. MOORE

WATERBROOK

Core 52

Italics in Scripture quotations reflect the author's added emphasis.

Trade Paperback ISBN 978-0-525-65325-7
eBook ISBN 978-0-525-65326-4

Cover design by Mark D. Ford

Published in the United States by WaterBrook, an imprint of the Crown Publishing Group, a division of Penguin Random House LLC, New York.

Library of Congress Cataloging-in-Publication Data
Names: Moore, Mark E. (Mark Edward), 1963- author.
Title: Core 52 : a fifteen-minute daily guide to build your Bible IQ in a year / Mark E Moore.
Other titles: Core fifty-two
Description: First Edition. | Colorado Springs : WaterBrook, 2019.
Identifiers: LCCN 2018047782 | ISBN 9780525653257 (pbk.) | ISBN 9780525653264 (electronic)
Subjects: LCSH: Bible—Textbooks.
Classification: LCC BS605.3 .M66 2019 | DDC 220.3—dc23
LC record available at https://lccn.loc.gov/2018047782

Printed in the United States of America
2019—First Edition

10 9 8 7 6 5 4 3 2 1

To Larrie Fraley and Jason Beck

Though a man might prevail against one who is alone, two will withstand him—a threefold cord is not quickly broken.

—Ecclesiastes 4:12

Contents

Introduction

Do you want to know the Bible better?

You're not alone. You're not even in the minority. Eighty percent of people in church want to know the Bible better. Surprisingly, the desire may be even stronger in those outside the church. In a recent survey here in Phoenix, 60 percent of those who said they were interested in the Bible were not connected with any church.

There's a reason so many people want to know the Bible better: they know the Bible will make *them* better.

The positive impact of Scripture on individuals, families, and society has been proved time and again. One study involving one hundred thousand people over eight years showed dramatic results. This research (by Arnold Cole and Pamela Caudill Ovwigho of the Center for Bible Engagement) showed that those who engage the Bible four or more times a week experienced far less destructive behavior: 62 percent less drunkenness, 59 percent less pornography use, 59 percent less sexual sin, and 45 percent less gambling. These results were not from guilt manipulation but were rather the mark of personal transformation. The positive message of Scripture allowed individuals to reduce bitterness by 40 percent, destructive thoughts by 32 percent, isolation by 32 percent, inability to forgive by 31 percent, and loneliness by 30 percent.[1]

Bible engagement improves your self-esteem, family structure, and social interactions. It's "the single most powerful predictor of spiritual growth."[2] So if you want to know the Bible better—you'll be better for it.

Since so many people who want to know the Bible better are not in church, we can't rely on pastors as the sole delivery system for Scripture. Lay leaders must take responsibility for bringing biblical truths to their networks at work, at home, and in the community. That's the purpose of this book. It's not designed to make you smart; it's designed to make you effective. Those who move from Bible curiosity to Bible confidence are far more likely to engage their gifts in service to others for God's glory. Bible confidence fosters social engagement, acts of compassion, and community transformation.

Why do so many want to know the Bible better and so few actually succeed? You likely already know the answers: (1) we're too busy, and (2) we don't know where to start.

What if you could remove both of those barriers? What if you had a clear plan that could easily fit your frantic schedule? That's precisely what's offered in this book. If you can carve out fifteen minutes a day, five days a week, for one year, you'll know the vast majority of what every preacher preaches. That sounds like a pretty audacious claim, but it's well within reach. We have simply applied the Pareto principle (or the 80/20 rule) to the Bible. This rule states that 20 percent of your effort yields 80 percent of the results in virtually every endeavor in life. That's true with the Bible as well.

You hold in your hand fifty-two of the most powerful passages in the Bible—and a faithful representation of the Bible's full message. By grasping these "vital few" verses, you'll wrap your mind around the entire Bible with minimal time and effort. Each of these verses is like a trajectory that runs the length of the Bible. By understanding any single verse in this collection, you'll be able to master dozens of other verses that reflect the same spiritual principle. If you understand the primary passage, dozens of others will fall into place.

Let me introduce myself. For twenty-two years I was a New Testament professor at Ozark Christian College. My job was to train pastors. In 2012 I traded my title Professor Moore for that of Pastor Mark—at Christ's Church of the Valley in Phoenix. It's one of those ridiculously large churches that are often more comfortable for those who've never been to church than for those who grew up in church. I serve as a teaching pastor, helping those far from God navigate that large and intimidating book called the Bible.

This book in your hands is really a culmination of my two professional roles. For decades I dug deep into Scripture. Now I want to bring to the surface the freshest water from the deepest well. People's buckets hold only so much, so I've chosen specific passages with the highest ROI ("return on investment") and the greatest potential for practical application. With this core, you can go further faster, moving from curiosity to confidence. Think of me as your personal trainer for spiritual growth. Each exercise is a punctuated moment (I want to respect your time) with a massive upside potential. With the help of the Holy Spirit, you'll make the most of your strategic investment in Scripture to exponentially increase your impact on society.

Here's the three-pronged strategy I followed for putting this project together:

1. Identify fifty-two of the most influential texts in the Bible.
2. In a brief essay (one for every week of the year), show the trajectory each text takes and how it can affect our lives practically.
3. Augment each essay with four specific tools to help connect the dots and extend the impact of the text: (1) a Bible passage that illustrates the core text, (2) trajectory verses for meditation, (3) an action step for application, and (4) a further resource for exploration.

So here's the strategic plan for helping you master the entire Bible in a single year—fifteen minutes a day, five days each week:

- **Day 1:** *Read the essay.* Following the essay are three key points to check for comprehension. If any of them are unclear, reread those portions of the essay. (You may find it helpful to read the key points first and then read the essay to know what to look for.)
- **Day 2:** *Memorize the core text* and review verses from the previous two weeks.
- **Day 3:** *Read a story or other passage from the Bible* that illustrates the text of the week. By reading these stories in light of the core text, you'll notice how the key principle was expressed in the real lives of God's people.

  By the way, not all these stories apply directly to the text of the week. So why read through them? Because they represent the core biographies that give the best context for the theology embedded in the core verses. The combination of the core verses and the foundational passages will increase your Bible IQ.

- **Day 4:** *Read through the three trajectory passages,* meditating on their implications and connections. You might begin by reviewing the core text from memory.
- **Day 5:** *Put it into practice* by scheduling a time for the action step. No exercise should take more than thirty minutes, and each should be accomplished that same week to embed the principle in practical application.
- *Additional options:* You'll see for each week an "overachiever challenge"—an additional key passage to consider memorizing. (Learn them all, along with the core verses, and the total in your arsenal will be over a hundred verses!) There's also a weekly reference to a helpful book you may want to explore as a "bonus read."

Welcome to the journey from curiosity to confidence. You can do this! By mastering the core, you'll build a firm framework for being an ambassador of Jesus Christ to a world hungering for truth that transforms.

You're more needed now than ever. Our culture is reeling from the demise of biblical literacy. As you gain confidence, you'll find yourself at the epicenter of God's solution in your own circle of influence. God has designed you uniquely for such a time as this.

1

Creation

In the beginning, God created the heavens and the earth.

—Genesis 1:1

Question: Why are we here?

We live in an immense universe on an extraordinary little blue ball. There's no question it's a masterpiece, and at its center is the human species. Yet each of us, treading across this sacred space, wonders why we're here. What's our part to play in this theater of life?

That all depends on the answer to the following three questions.

Who Created This World?

All artists leave fingerprints on their work. So knowing the creation gives a glimpse into the nature of the creator. The Bible teaches that God is actually three in one: Father, Son, and Spirit. Though the clearest glimpses of this "Trinity" are in the New Testament, all three peek from behind the curtain as early as Genesis 1:1–3.

God the Father is the architect. That's how the Bible begins: "God created." Specifically, God created the elements out of nothing. This sounds simple, even obvious. Yet every other creation story from the ancient Near East assumes that what's eternal is physical matter, not God. The gods merely fashioned preexisting matter into the existing world, like children shaping Play-Doh.

The Bible, however, asserts that God alone is eternal. Hence, the universe is an extension of God, not vice versa. This Christian worldview stands in opposition to all worldviews that assert matter as eternal rather than God. This includes polytheism (multiple gods) and pantheism that sees god in inanimate objects such as wind, waves, or animals. The Christian worldview is also in opposition to Darwinian evolution that replaces the eternal God with eternal "stuff."

The idea that God created the earth is a common belief among the monotheistic religions: Judaism, Islam, and Christianity. However, there's a factor added by Christians that's absent from other religions: *the Holy Spirit is the engineer*. As we read in Genesis 1:2, "The earth was without form and void, and darkness was over the face of the deep. And the Spirit of God was hovering over the face of the waters." This Hebrew word "hovering" expresses a vibration. The Spirit "quaked" to bring order out of chaos. It's not dissimilar to a frantic hostess thirty minutes prior to dinner guests arriving. The Spirit was intent on ordering the creation so it would be a life-giving garden.

The Hebrew word for "breath" is also translated "spirit." For example, the breath of God animated Adam in Genesis 2:7. In Genesis 7:22, the word for "breath" is the very word translated "spirit": "Everything on the dry land in whose nostrils was the breath of life died."

This is also true of animals, according to Psalm 104:30: "When you send forth your Spirit, they are created, and you renew the face of the ground." Every animal that has breath is sustained by the Spirit. The Spirit is the ongoing force of God that gives life, breath, and sustaining energy on earth. He's relentlessly, intimately, and perpetually involved in the very fabric of our earthly environment. God the Father *created;* God the Spirit *creates.*

There's a telltale sign when people ignore the Spirit in creation. Namely, the environment becomes a resource to be exploited rather than a gift to be nurtured. The elements become mute, no longer declaring the glory of God (Psalm

19:1–3). We miss God in the thunderstorm and wind, the bloom of a flower, and the majesty of the mountains. Our environmental insensitivities betray our ignorance of the Spirit's continued care for every element of our earth. Consequently, Christians restrict worship to a building on Sunday rather than worshipping daily in the expanse of the universe, where broader culture has replaced the love of the Spirit with the law of the jungle.

We *need* to acknowledge the Spirit in creation.

God the Father is the architect. God the Spirit is the engineer. *Jesus is the builder.* He did the heavy lifting during creation. This is seen in Genesis 1:3: "God said, 'Let there be light,' and there was light." If we lay that alongside John 1:1–3, we see the mechanics of creation: "In the beginning was the Word, and the Word was with God, and the Word was God. He was in the beginning with God. All things were made through him, and without him was not any thing made that was made." This Word, as we learn in verse 14, is none other than Jesus. Even before he came to earth in human form, he was fully God, the embodiment, as it were, of God's spoken word. When God gave the command, Jesus—the Word—turned the command into creation.

The apostle Paul confirmed this:

> He is the image of the invisible God, the firstborn of all creation. For by him all things were created, in heaven and on earth, visible and invisible, whether thrones or dominions or rulers or authorities—all things were created through him and for him. (Colossians 1:15–16)

What happens when we ignore the role of Jesus in creation? Typically, salvation becomes a future spiritual state in heaven rather than an actual earthly reality. We do, of course, have a future in heaven. Nonetheless, Jesus the creator is equally interested in your eternal life here and now.

So there you have it: the Trinity embedded in the first three verses of Genesis. God is the architect, the Spirit is the engineer, and Jesus is the builder. All three are unique and essential to creation. If any of these are ignored, we'll misunderstand not only the nature of creation but also our own nature and the dignified role God intends for us.

Why Did God Create This World?

Some suggest that God created because he was lonely. That's impossible to prove and pretty hard to swallow. God had angels in abundance who could communicate, perform, and do who knows how many other things to entertain, serve, and otherwise delight God. Furthermore, God had himself. God is a community—Father, Son, and Spirit. They love, communicate with, and enjoy one another. There's nothing lacking in God's own person that required him to create someone to keep him company.

So why *did* God create?

We need look no further than Psalm 102:18 for an answer: "Let this be recorded for a generation to come, so that a people yet to be created may praise the Lord." Every generation that God created—from our primal parents in Eden to our own unborn children—has a singular divine purpose: to bring God glory. This shouldn't come as a shock. The fingerprints of God in our own souls will drive us in the same direction. Why do we dress fashionably? To look good. Why do we decorate our homes? To impress company. Why do we present a gourmet meal with such panache? To please others and receive praise. Isn't it our internal impulse to create for others' pleasure and for our own praise? God creates with the same impulse. We're here for the express purpose of bringing God glory.

When we look at our own genetic complexity, we're awestruck. The fingerprints of an infant, the structure of our eyes, the electrical synapses of the brain—our bodies are works of art. From Olympic spectacles to ballet, from the NBA to National Geographic, we're stunned by God's handiwork.

David expressed it well: "You formed my inward parts; you knitted me together in my mother's womb" (Psalm 139:13). Without speaking a word, even inanimate objects like mountains and rivers and stars and rainbows acclaim their Creator (89:12; 148:3–10). Creation itself is primary proof of God's existence (Romans 1:20, 25). By seeing his fingerprints in the world, we're drawn to his self-portrait in the Bible.

Here's where it gets most majestic. We were made to manage the creation of God: "We are God's handiwork, created in Christ Jesus to do good works, which God prepared in advance for us to do" (Ephesians 2:10, NIV). We continue God's act of creation. What makes this more amazing—and what raises the stakes—is that God is personally and perpetually involved in creating and re-creating this masterpiece of a world with the help of humans. God created the heavens and the earth—he leaves it up to us to make of it a world even more wonderful.

How Did God Restore Creation?

This world is a wreck. It all went south in Genesis 3, when Eve was seduced by the serpent. That moment of indiscretion released a cascade of consequences. None of this took God by surprise. But it did take his breath away. He was distraught over the condition of the creation he so cherished.

This flows into the story of the Flood (Genesis 6–8), when God hit "reset" on the world. God knew this wasn't a permanent fix. As the first couple fell in the garden, so Noah's family failed after the Flood. So, too, Abraham's nation rebelled. But the plan of God all along was to bring a fallen creation back. Notice he began with a couple, then a family, then a nation. And today his mercy extends to all the earth—every tongue, tribe, and nation. The recovery of Eden is the story of the Bible.

The finale, of course, is the story of Jesus. By his blood, Jesus would re-create the human spirit by renewing us through his own Spirit. "If anyone is in Christ, he is a new creation. The old has passed away; behold, the new has come" (2 Corinthians 5:17). We're re-created for good works in Christ (Ephesians 2:10). It's not a quick fix nor an easy solution.

This restoration is not merely for humans but for all creation. Paul expressed it like this:

The creation waits with eager longing for the revealing of the sons of God. . . . For we know that the whole creation has been groaning together in the pains of childbirth until now. (Romans 8:19, 22)

Key Points

- Each member of the Trinity plays a vital role in creation.
- God created for the same reasons we do: for others' pleasure and our own praise.
- Just as God *created* the earth, we're to continue to *re-create* a world, reflecting his love.

This Week

- ☐ **Day 1:** Read the essay.
- ☐ **Day 2:** Memorize Genesis 1:1.
- ☐ **Day 3:** Read Genesis 1–2.
- ☐ **Day 4:** Meditate on John 1:1; Ephesians 2:10; Colossians 1:15–16.
- ☐ **Day 5:** Identify one small thing you could do today to help restore Eden where you live.

Overachiever Challenge: Memorize John 1:1.

Bonus Read: Guillermo Gonzalez and Jay W. Richards, *The Privileged Planet: How Our Place in the Cosmos Is Designed for Discovery.*

2

Our True Identity

God said, "Let us make man in our image."

—Genesis 1:26

Question: What does it mean that I'm created in God's image?

After God created the heavens and the earth, the seas and its creatures, the birds and the beasts, he capped off creation by shaping a human being from the dust of the earth. This singularly important moment in history is described in detail in Genesis 1:26–27:

> God said, "Let us make man in our image, after our likeness. And let them have dominion over the fish of the sea and over the birds of the heavens and over the livestock and over all the earth and over every creeping thing that creeps on the earth."
>
> So God created man in his own image,
> in the image of God he created him;
> male and female he created them.

As human beings, we have divine attributes. That's not to say we have God's abilities, but we do share many of his attributes. This simple observation has extraordinary implications. It will change how we view virtually every human activity. So let's dissect this week's core verse to discover who we really are.

God said, "Let *us* make man in our own image." Though the Trinity is a mystery we'll never fully grasp, the least we can say is that God is in community. Though it's tempting to get sidetracked with the spiritual physics of "three in one," let's focus on the subject at hand—not God's nature but human nature. Since God is in community, so are we.

Young adults often leave their families, communities, and traditions to "find themselves." This can get one lost. We'll never know our true selves in isolation. We know ourselves to the extent that we are known. All of us are the sum of our relationships. Though our characteristics are unique, our character is forged on the anvil of our community.

Why does this matter? Because we live in a world that champions individualism in achievements that seldom bring the satisfaction they promise. In terms of the church, this matters because we mistakenly try connecting with God only personally, when we were designed to experience him in community.

Here are some examples of how we've missed the mark:

1. We ask people to accept Jesus as their "personal" Lord and Savior, but the Bible calls us to a kingdom, being built into the body of Christ.
2. Communion becomes the most individualistic event at church, even though the name itself indicates a communal celebration.
3. Bible reading is practiced as a solitary discipline, when in fact the majority of the books in the Bible were written to communities, not individuals.
4. We're often called to pray with "every head bowed and every eye closed." In the Bible, however, prayer was primarily communal. This was true for the church in Acts, for the prayers printed in the epistles, and for the psalms sung in the temple.

Our radical individualism is a denial of our identity. God created us to be *in* community and *for* community. Without the circles God placed us in, we'd have a shrunken view of self and a self-absorbed view of our purpose and place.

A second idea that looms large over this week's core passage is God's *image.* What precisely might that mean? God is spirit, not flesh, so what kind of characteristics has he placed in us that form our identity?

In order to tease this out with integrity, let's identify the five primary life forms in the cosmos: divine, angelic, human, animal, and plant. Each has its own set of attributes and abilities. We can, for now, ignore the plants and angels since they aren't the direct comparison at this point. The chart below, though incomplete, shows a range of characteristics that are partially shared across three life forms.

Divine	Human	Animal
emotion	emotion	emotion
	body	body
	cravings	cravings
	shame	shame
	guilt	
honor	honor	
time	time	
beauty	beauty	
language	language	
love	love	
rule	rule	

Animals, humans, and God all share emotions: joy, affection, sorrow, compassion, etc. Animals and humans share a number of attributes, such as a body that has cravings and the ability to feel shame when not living up to others' standards. The feeling of guilt, however, is unique to humans. God certainly feels no guilt. Neither do animals since they cannot meditate on the past. Dogs, for example, might feel shame for disappointing their master but not feel guilt for violating their conscience. Then there is a range of perceptions that humans share with God but not with animals: honor, time, beauty, language, love, and rule.

This, I believe, encompasses the "image of God" in us. For the sake of clarity, let's explore those listed capacities (while recognizing there are certainly others).

Honor is the underlying factor of virtually all our attractions, distractions, and vocations. It's why we dress up, work hard, and brush our teeth. We *need* (I don't use this word lightly) to be honored. This should come as no surprise, since the driving force of God's creation was his desire for honor. This inherent drive gone bad is the fountainhead of all sin. We call it pride. Our divine nature, gone rogue from God's will, always results in idolatry.

Time is another human construct that derives directly from the nature of God. Though he's eternal, God brokers in time. That's why he has aspirations, patience, and strategies. He is aware of the past and has his eye on the future, perhaps experiencing both simultaneously. Therefore, when we execute a vision, schedule something, look at a watch, or anticipate an event, we're exercising the divine nature in us.

Beauty derives from the divine. From colors to shapes, from sight to taste to sound to smell, we breathe beauty as a spiritual experience. We're the only animals that make art, set a table for dinner, or rearrange the furniture. No other animal sings. Birds and whales call; they don't create music. Not only do we create beauty; we also *constantly* create it. We change styles of hair and dress. We write new songs, create new instruments, and invent novel genres. We don't just tell stories; we create new mediums for those expressions in books, film, plays, musicals, cartoons, sitcoms, etc. Look around you. Unless you're in the wild, there's art in some form right now at your fingertips. We seem to be incapable of living without it—as the human archaeological record attests.

Language is another uniquely human feature. From poetry to prose, mathematics to legal debates, we utilize abstract language. A child can imagine a friend who isn't there and invent a conversation. This ability is why we talk about babies yet unborn. This is the engine driving companies into the future. It inflames our passions, runs our printing presses, and creates romance. Our imagination is a direct reflection of the divine spark in us.

Then there's *love.* Now, some will argue that animals love, and they're not wrong. Of course an animal can protect its young. Pets can bond with owners.

But no animal would sacrifice its life for someone it has never met. No animal has ever given sacrificially to victims of an earthquake. No animal empathizes with the loss of a stranger. The noblest feature of our divine humanity is our capacity to love the stranger, the alien, and our enemy.

Finally, the word *rule* expresses humanity's obligation to govern creation. King David composed an entire song about it:

> O Lord, our Lord,
> how majestic is your name in all the earth! . . .
>
> When I look at your heavens, the work of your fingers,
> the moon and the stars, which you have set in place,
> what is man that you are mindful of him,
> and the son of man that you care for him?
>
> Yet you have made him a little lower than the heavenly beings
> and crowned him with glory and honor.
> You have given him dominion over the works of your hands;
> you have put all things under his feet. . . .
>
> O Lord, our Lord,
> how majestic is your name in all the earth! (Psalm 8:1, 3–6, 9)

We're caretakers of God's garden. Our created purpose is to enhance what God made. We add our creativity to his creation. We've done that in many ways—through agriculture, art, industry, education, medicine, and technology. God's creation was an environment perfectly designed by him for us, but it wasn't complete without us.

Each of us has a gift, a vision of how to delight God by adding to the creation of the cosmos. Our every creative act—whether musical, architectural, athletic, or intellectual—is thus innately theological. We participate with the Father, who's the architect, by utilizing his raw resources to a greater end. We participate with the Spirit by engineering environments that sustain and celebrate life. We participate with the Son by building places and spaces where people are restored to God and his creation.

When we fail in this vocation as stewards of God's earth, we find ourselves gravitating to our animalistic attributes of lust, greed, fear, and violence. Consequently, through addiction, poverty, pain, and alienation, we're ruled by the earth rather than being rulers of it. It's for this reason and in this context that Hebrews 2:6–8 cites Psalm 8 in reference to Jesus. He's not only the Savior of the world; he's also the model man who redeemed creation itself. In a sense, he gave us a second lease in Eden to fulfill our divine destiny. Even the Fall couldn't obscure the divine nature!

We can exult over this before God, as David did: "I praise you, for I am fearfully and wonderfully made. Wonderful are your works; my soul knows it very well" (Psalm 139:14).

Human beings are divinely designed to steward the earth in partnership with God. That's our birthright, which Jesus restored to us by becoming one of us.

Key Points

- Our true identity is found in community, not in individualism.
- God's divine nature in us is exercised in the simplest acts of conversation, art, planning, shared meals, etc.
- Our divine design enables and requires us to participate with God in the ongoing act of creation.

This Week

- ☐ **Day 1:** Read the essay.
- ☐ **Day 2:** Memorize Genesis 1:26.
- ☐ **Day 3:** Read Ephesians 1.
- ☐ **Day 4:** Meditate on Psalm 8:4–5; 139:13–14; Hebrews 2:6–8.
- ☐ **Day 5:** Identify one area of your life where you're living too individualistically, and then invite someone into that area of your life.

Overachiever Challenge: Memorize Psalm 8:4–5.

Bonus Read: John Piper, *Desiring God: Meditations of a Christian Hedonist.*

3

The Fall

When the woman saw that the tree was good for food, and that it was a delight to the eyes, and that the tree was to be desired to make one wise, she took of its fruit and ate, and she also gave some to her husband who was with her, and he ate.

—Genesis 3:6

Question: What is my problem?

We've all felt the effects in our souls, like an odor in the room we can't identify or remove. It's called sin in the Bible; it's called psychosis in society.

We all have this brokenness we can't shake or justify. Its effects are justified in the locker room, made legend in movies, and prosecuted in courts of law. From personal offenses to systemic evils, sin has stained the fiber of humanity.

It all started in a garden.

The story is told in Genesis 3. It begins with a naked woman, a talking serpent, forbidden fruit, and a passive husband idly standing by. Eve knew the fruit was off limits. Yet the serpent's seduction won the day. She took the bait in a bite, while her husband stood dumb but not deaf beside her. Her eyes were open to evil, to her naked body, and to the coming curse.

From that ground zero, death crept slowly across humanity.

Irresistible Temptation

Eve's failure in the garden is neither far removed nor uncommon. This is the shared experience of humanity. So we should probably slow down long enough to ask, "What's my problem?"

First, we should ask what captured Eve's attention, because it's the same thing that captures ours. Eve "saw that the tree was good for food, and that it was a delight to the eyes, and that the tree was to be desired to make one wise" (Genesis 3:6). What seduced her was Satan's half-truth in the previous verse: "You will be like God." That's it! This is the temptation of self-determination—the promise that we can direct our own affairs and determine our own destinies. Pride becomes our Achilles' heel.

Pride isn't merely *a* sin; it's *the* sin. It's the genesis of every murder, theft, lie, adultery, and addiction. Every time, it's at the root of why we prioritize our will over everyone else's good, even God's. That's why the Bible reiterates warnings about pride: "Pride goes before destruction, and a haughty spirit before a fall" (Proverbs 16:18). "Whoever exalts himself will be humbled, and whoever humbles himself will be exalted" (Matthew 23:12). "God opposes the proud but shows favor to the humble" (James 4:6, NIV; 1 Peter 5:5, NIV; paraphrasing Proverbs 3:34). "Humble yourselves before the Lord, and he will exalt you" (James 4:10). The Bible is full of warnings about pride and stories illustrating its catastrophic results. This is a subplot of nearly every book of the Bible, because it's the source of our human condition. Then again, we probably don't need to read it in a book when we all see it in the mirror.

For this reason, we're called to carry a cross, to lay down our lives, and to be crucified with Christ. Self-improvement, self-respect, or self-management won't rescue us from the grip of sin. It's self-extermination—the annihilation of our pride—that can bring us freedom. Perhaps this grates against our culture, which validates pride. But to affirm a disease that ravages one's soul is a cruelty.

No matter how the social pundits spin the freedom of sin, the downward spiral will accelerate until we overcome our pride and submit to the power of God's love.

The story of Eve was summarized thousands of years later by Jesus's best friend, John:

> Do not love the world or the things in the world. If anyone loves the world, the love of the Father is not in him. For all that is in the world—the desires of the flesh and the desires of the eyes and pride of life—is not from the Father but is from the world. (1 John 2:15–16)

These three temptations—fleshly desires, visual cravings, and social position—are the core of Satan's arsenal, abetted, of course, by our pride. These are the prides of passion, possession, and position.

These weren't just Eve's temptations (and ours); they enticed Jesus in the wilderness (Luke 4:1–13). He was tempted by Satan to turn a stone to bread, a form of the lust of the flesh. He was offered all the world's empires for the price of a simple bow; hence, he was tempted by the lust of the eyes. Finally, he was challenged to throw himself off the pinnacle of the temple so God would rescue him in the presence of the religious elite, securing their adoration and satisfying the pride of life.

This is not to suggest that our temptations are the same as Jesus's. After all, Satan was giving Jesus the chance to bypass the cross, escaping human suffering. Yet Jesus's temptations do mirror ours in that Satan's arsenal consistently contains (and is consistently limited to) the lust of the flesh, the lust of the eyes, and the pride of life. By understanding Satan's schemes, we can more confidently face his attacks.

Just reading such a solution on paper seems easy. Face to face, however, Satan's deceptive arguments seem convincing.

Strategic Deception

Satan lied to Eve. He said she wouldn't die if she ate the forbidden fruit. Did she die?

Actually, no—at least not at that moment. Would she die? Sure. We all do—because of Eve's choice. The point is that what Satan communicates is seldom entirely fabrication. That would hardly be effective. He's not going to say squares are round. Any fool could see through that. Rather, he misdirects, misinforms, and misrepresents through half-truths. When he promises pleasure in a bed or a bottle, he holds up his end of the bargain. In the short run, Satan seems sincere. What he holds close to his chest is the trump card of long-term consequences. There's pleasure in the pursuit of money, in the buzz of a drug, and in the frenzy of popularity. Make no mistake—Satan seldom makes promises he doesn't initially and partially keep. What he keeps hidden is the price tag. By the time we've signed the agreement, the charges on the ticket leave us bankrupt, breathless, and ashamed.

Ask my friend Rick. After multiple affairs while serving in ministry, his secret was exposed and his world was shattered. Only then did he start, in his own words, "turning over the price tags." One tag had the name of his wife; another, his daughter; another, his ministry; another, his circle of friends. The price tags extended to his grandchildren, his second wife, his calling by God. Had Satan shared with him up front even one or two of the price tags, Rick would never have fallen for such meaningless moments of gratification. In the heat of passion, he never imagined the consequences. Nor do any of us when faced with cheating, pornography, a bad party, a shady business deal, or a simple theft. Only with a decade of hindsight can we recognize the full terms and conditions. The price is as high as our God is holy.

Divine Retribution

God cursed Adam and Eve, both guilty of mutiny. That's right—it wasn't merely theft; it was mutiny. God's wrath rages not for the loss of property but for the full frontal assault on his position. He created this wondrous universe in a matter of days. The loss of one fruit from one tree is hardly a damnable offense. His concern was not trespassing but mutiny.

Eve, eyeing the prospect of becoming like God, took the bait and bit. In that momentary indiscretion, it was her divorce from the divine that was so egregious. This lump of flesh, freshly drawn from Adam's side, had the audacity to challenge God's eternal wisdom, his divine plan, his creational genius, and his spiritual authority.

We also commit outrageous sedition when we declare ourselves sovereign. In reality, no human has the capacity to manage deification. This is why, of course, emperors and dictators, not to mention local celebrities, implode under the weight of their own arrogance.

For their mutiny, Adam and Eve would have to wear the burden of God's curse along with their new vestments of animal skins. The serpent would slither in the dust and ultimately be snuffed out by the seed of the woman (Genesis 3:14–15). The woman would experience intense pain when she bore children and be at odds with her husband with little chance of prevailing (verse 16). The man would earn a living only by the sweat of his brow (verses 17–19). Though this may seem harsh, in reality this is discipline more than punishment.

For mutiny, what can we expect but exile? Adam and Eve were exiled from the garden for their own good (verses 22–24). The garden is not our goal; the heart of God is. It does no good to live in the luxury of utopia if we are bereft of character, relationships, and connection to the Creator. It's God himself, not his garden, that's our home. His gifts of procreation and working the garden are meaningless without the fellowship of God in the cool of the day.

We sense this desperate need to fill a spiritual void. Our exile from Eden makes our souls cry for reconnection with our Creator. The curse is the very thing that calls us back to our original destination. We return to God through repentance, retracing our steps to submission to our Creator.

Here's the good news, a two-sided golden coin. First, our Creator sent his own son to pay the price to remove the curse. Second, the Son of God sent his Holy Spirit to support us so we can do better than Adam and Eve. Here's the promise: "No temptation has overtaken you that is not common to man. God is faithful, and he will not let you be tempted beyond your ability, but with the temptation he will also provide the way of escape, that you may be able to endure it" (1 Corinthians 10:13).

Key Points

- The core of all sin is pride—that is, the desire for self-determination.
- Sin seduces us in one of three ways: pride of passion, pride of possession, or pride of position.
- Satan deceives with half-truths, not blatant lies.

This Week

- ☐ **Day 1:** Read the essay.
- ☐ **Day 2:** Memorize Genesis 3:6.
- ☐ **Day 3:** Read Genesis 3:1–4:16.
- ☐ **Day 4:** Meditate on Proverbs 16:18; James 4:6; 1 John 2:15–16.
- ☐ **Day 5:** If you have unconfessed sin, seek out an accountability partner or a mentor. This is the first step back to Eden.

Overachiever Challenge: Memorize James 4:6.

Bonus Read: John Owen, *Overcoming Sin and Temptation: Three Classic Works by John Owen*, ed. Kelly M. Kapic and Justin Taylor.

4

Covenant

[Abram] believed the Lord, and he counted it to him as righteousness.

—Genesis 15:6

Question: **How can I become a part of what God is doing in this world?**

Jesus of Nazareth is, without peer, the most influential figure in history. There is, however, one man whom more people look to as the father of their faith. He was an ancient titan named Abraham who became the father of both Judaism and Islam. By extension, he's also the father of the Christian faith. To put that in perspective, 31 percent of the world claims to be Christian; 24 percent, Muslim; and 0.2 percent, Jewish.[1] Hence, nearly three in five people on the planet look to Abraham as the father of their faith.

As Genesis 15:6 says, "[Abram, later renamed Abraham] believed the Lord, and *he counted it to him as righteousness.*" This mantra became the refrain of Abraham's biography (Romans 4:1–25; Galatians 3:6; James 2:23). Abraham is the model of faith for every follower of the monotheistic faiths. A synopsis of his story shows why.

God called this man from ancient Iraq to leave his family and his land. Because Abram trusted God, he left Mesopotamia and immigrated to Israel, following nothing but the next clue God gave about his future. And there wasn't much to go on. Furthermore, Abram—already in his nineties—had neither biological offspring nor a single square foot of real estate. Yet God promised to make Abraham's descendants a great nation, and Abraham believed that God would be true to his word. Eventually, and against all odds, God fulfilled his promise to Abraham, whose son Isaac had a couple of kids who had a gaggle that became a horde.

A golden strand—a promise—runs the length of Abraham's biography. That's important today because Christians grasp the other end of that golden strand when we put our faith in Jesus. This promise (in the Bible it's called a covenant) is a legally binding agreement. The concept of covenant undergirds virtually every relationship God ever had with any human. It's essential to understand if you intend to have a working relationship with God. Our faith in Jesus, our connection to the Holy Spirit, our belonging in the body of Christ are all contingent on a covenant.

Here's how it works and how it has always worked with God. A covenant, or testament, is basically an agreement between two parties. Among the ancients was a kind of contract known as a suzerain treaty. The rules were simple: (1) The greater of the two parties established the conditions. (2) These conditions specified the rewards if the contract was kept and the punishment if it was broken. (3) The covenant was typically ratified by a blood sacrifice showing how serious it was. The two parties could walk together between the bisected carcass as a pledge of loyalty to the contract. This appears to be a symbol that the fate of the animal could become the fate of the one who broke the agreement (Jeremiah 34:18).[2] It had a bit more bite than a handshake. That's precisely what God did with Abraham in Genesis 15:7–21.

Major Covenants in the Bible

The two most important covenants in the Bible make up the Old and New Testaments. The first came through Moses; the second, through Jesus. The Old

Testament includes four other major covenants that were made with Adam, Noah, Abraham, and David. Obviously, many more details could be added, but this is a sufficient summary:

Covenant	Condition(s)	Blessings	Curses
Adam	abstain from one tree	fellowship with God	death and exile
Noah	build an ark	survival	annihilation
Abraham	circumcision	offspring and land	cut off
Moses	Ten Commandments	land and kingdom	exile
David	fidelity to Yahweh	throne in Israel	divided kingdom
New	fidelity to Jesus	eternal life	damnation

With this template in mind, let's look specifically at Abraham's covenant. This will help us mentally map our own covenant in Christ. God made this promise to Abraham:

> I will make of you a great nation, and I will bless you and make your name great, so that you will be a blessing. I will bless those who bless you, and him who dishonors you I will curse, and in you all the families of the earth shall be blessed. (Genesis 12:2–3)

Look again at the last sentence. It guaranteed that Abraham's offspring would have a global impact. The question is, How? Most of the Jewish rabbis understood the promise to mean that nations who adopted Israel, who came to her and repented, would be blessed because of their conversion. It was an inward-focused perspective on religion: come to Israel, become Israel, and you'll be blessed with Israel.

There were some rabbis, however—Jesus among them—who understood the promise of Abraham to be outward focused. Outsiders don't come to us, but we are to go to them. The earth would be blessed because we leave our homes to go where God leads and to say what God has said. This act of extending the fame of our God would result in the inclusion of all cultures, not the protection of a single culture. The best Old Testament example of this is Jonah. The prophet Jonah wanted to be inward focused; God forced him to go beyond his own boundaries.

In Romans 11:29 Paul stated, "The gifts and the calling of God are irrevocable." God was honor bound to bless Abraham's son. So when Abraham had a child through Hagar, his wife's handmaiden, God honored his promise. This is why Ishmael secured a heritage similar to Isaac's. Both proceeded from the loins of Abraham, the fount of God's blessings. Even though the Messiah would not come through Ishmael's lineage, the blessing of God did. God told Abraham,

> As for Ishmael, I have heard you; behold, I have blessed him and will make him fruitful and multiply him greatly. He shall father twelve princes, and I will make him into a great nation. But I will establish my covenant with Isaac, whom Sarah shall bear to you at this time next year. (Genesis 17:20–21)

This has meant a bloody tension ever since. The descendants of Ishmael are one of the peoples most opposed to Jesus the Messiah—the Islamic states of the Middle East. Abraham's single act of unbelief had permanent consequences we contend with yet today.

When we keep the covenant God's way, good things happen. When we try to impose our will on God's, devastating consequences can ensue.

Why Does All This Matter?

In practical terms there are three major implications of all this.

First, *we're in a covenantal relationship with God.* This implies both responsibility and community. God calls us to be part of a nation, a heritage, a people. We call it the church, but it's bigger than that. We're members of a global enterprise—a kingdom—that spans every time zone and all eras. The lineage of this kingdom goes back to our father Abraham, whom we follow as an example of faith.

There's more "we" than "me" in our adventure with Jesus. When we lose sight of the covenant, our discipleship can easily deteriorate into rules we keep for God rather than responsibilities we fulfill for the good of his household.

Second, *Jesus fulfills all the previous covenants.*

- The curse of Adam's covenant was removed when Jesus fulfilled the prophecy against the serpent (the devil) that God spoke in Genesis 3:15: "He shall bruise your head, and you shall bruise his heel."
- Noah's ark was a mere shadow of our salvation imaged in immersion: "Baptism, which corresponds to this, now saves you, not as a removal of dirt from the body but as an appeal to God for a good conscience, through the resurrection of Jesus Christ" (1 Peter 3:21).
- Abraham was asked to sacrifice his promised son, Isaac. At the last second, an angel intervened and God provided a ram, so Abraham named the place "The Lord will provide" (Genesis 22:14). This pointed forward to Jesus, the lamb whom God provided.
- Inherent to David's covenant is the promise that his heir will always sit on his throne. Jesus, quoting David's own words, argued that he himself was the king to come: "The Lord said to my Lord, 'Sit at my right hand'" (Matthew 22:44).
- The night before Jesus died, he connected the covenant of Moses with the new covenant. The Passover lamb was a foreshadowing of "the Lamb of God, who takes away the sin of the world" (John 1:29). Matthew 26:27–28 memorializes the moment: "He took a cup, and when he had given thanks he gave it to them, saying, 'Drink of it, all of you, for this is *my blood of the covenant,* which is poured out for many for the forgiveness of sins.'"

Third, *the condition of every covenant is faith.* Most people define faith as mere belief, particularly irrational belief. According to the Bible, however, faith is not a leap in the dark but a walk in the light. Because God had demonstrated his fidelity, Abram gave his loyalty. That's faith!

Here's a simple exercise that could transform your vision and practice of faith. Every time you read the word *faith* in the Bible, replace it with the word *faithful.* This will make the passage clearer almost every time. For example, let's go back and reword this week's core verse: "[Abram] *was faithful to* the LORD, and he counted it to him as righteousness" (Genesis 15:6).

Or think in terms of a husband and wife (another covenant relationship): if a husband says, "I have faith in my wife," it's a compliment; if he says, "I'm faithful to my wife," it's a commitment.

Faith fluctuates with our emotions and our circumstances. Faithfulness stands unflinchingly on promises. We keep our promises because of the love we have for the character of the one to whom we pledged our loyalty. Your character is only as deep as the covenant you keep. That's true in business, in marriage, in foreign policy, and certainly in our relationship with God. Keep the faith!

Key Points

- Abraham's trust (faith) in God is the model of fidelity for Christians today.
- A covenant is an agreement between two parties that includes conditions, terms, and consequences.
- Every previous covenant in the Bible is fulfilled by Jesus.

This Week

☐ **Day 1:** Read the essay.

☐ **Day 2:** Memorize Genesis 15:6.

☐ **Day 3:** Read Genesis 21:1–22:18.

☐ **Day 4:** Meditate on Genesis 12:1–9; Romans 4; Galatians 3:6.

☐ **Day 5:** Read Romans 3:21–31, replacing the word *faith* with *faithfulness.*

Overachiever Challenge: Memorize Galatians 3:6.

Bonus Read: Mont W. Smith, *What the Bible Says About Covenant.*

5

Holiness

I am the LORD who brought you up out of the land of Egypt to be your God. You shall therefore be holy, for I am holy.

—LEVITICUS 11:45

Question: How can I live up to God's moral standards?

There's hardly a word in the English language that elicits more religious images than *holiness*. That's appropriate, since the word *holy* is used in the Bible for all kinds of religious objects: the temple, priests, sacred vestments, anointing oil, sanctuary utensils, animal sacrifices, etc. Virtually everything a priest touched in order to carry out his religious duties was labeled as holy somewhere in the Bible. Even so, equating "holiness" with "religious purity" is a bit misleading. At its root, the word *holy* doesn't primarily designate "sacred" as much as "selected." This is an important distinction that ultimately will affect how you view yourself.

The Proclamation of Holiness

What makes an object or a person "holy"? Holiness happens when God takes ordinary objects and claims them for his purpose. For example, an ordinary plot of ground can become sacred if God shows up there. An ordinary animal, set aside for sacrifice, suddenly becomes consecrated. A person elected by God becomes a priest or a prophet. These become sacred, not because their nature becomes different but because their purpose becomes different. In one moment, they were ordinary, openly accessed by anyone. In the next moment, God claims them for his own purposes. They're still the same "stuff," and none of their physical properties have magically transformed.

Holiness happens when God proclaims, not when a person performs. Our holiness is God's gift to us, not our gift to him. Holiness is received, not achieved. This simple truth will transform how we view our position with God. Is holiness something you practice? Is it a description of your actions? Well, of course it is. However, our practice of holiness is a result of God's proclamation of holiness, not the other way around. It's only when God's declaration of our holiness—our set-apartness—sinks into our souls that our actions are transformed to align with his character and nature.

The idea that holiness is received, not achieved, shouldn't come as a shock. Every one of us does the same thing with ordinary objects. Take a toothbrush, for example. It's an ordinary object that has dozens of potential uses. Yet once you put it in your mouth, you're protective of anyone else using it for anything else. Or take an ordinary bolt of white linen fabric, fashion it into a garment, drape it on a bride, and it becomes unthinkable to wear it on a morning jog. Why? Because when ordinary objects are sanctified for special service, they become "out of bounds"—or to use biblical terminology, "holy."

Just to ensure we're on the same page before moving on, let me restate this as clearly as I can: *You are holy not because of your performance but because of God's proclamation.* You don't become holy though religious rites. You don't develop holiness through sheer discipline. You become holy the millisecond God places his hand on you and says "Mine."

With that in mind, let's look at our key verse. In Leviticus 11:45, God said, "I am the Lord who brought you up out of the land of Egypt to be your God. You shall therefore be holy, for I am holy."

Notice that the declaration was based on God's selection, not Israel's action. Of all the nations on earth, God placed his hand on Israel and said "Mine." From that moment on, Israel was set apart for his service, chosen as his people. That declaration made them holy. As Exodus 19:6 says, "You shall be to me a kingdom of priests and a holy nation." Were they holy in behavior? Not so much. Israel did indeed have thousands of priests, but the common Israelite wasn't involved in sacred service. Why? Because they expected someone "special" to stand between them and God as a mediator. Surely the average person can't just waltz up to God and pray! Surely the commoner can't offer a sacrifice!

If holiness is based on our own actions, then they were correct. If, however, holiness comes from God's election, then they were sadly mistaken.

God always intended for all his followers to have personal access and a sacred purpose. In the New Testament, after Jesus's death and resurrection, one of his key leaders, the apostle Peter, repeated the decree from Exodus—only this time he applied it to the church: "You are a chosen race, a royal priesthood, a holy nation, a people for his own possession, that you may proclaim the excellencies of him who called you out of darkness into his marvelous light" (1 Peter 2:9).

What does this mean? Has God replaced Israel with the church? No—emphatically no. The church hasn't replaced Israel; she has fulfilled Israel's ultimate destiny. We who call Jesus "Lord" have been grafted into Israel and thereby adopted into Abraham's lineage. Our God-given access in prayer, through the blood of Jesus, is merely an acceptance and fulfillment of the original intention of God to grant sacred status to every Israelite who follows him.

This is the ultimate destiny of the church as portrayed in Revelation 20:6: "Blessed and holy is the one who shares in the first resurrection! Over such the second death has no power, but they will be priests of God and of Christ, and they will reign with him for a thousand years." (See also Revelation 1:6; 5:10.)

The Practice of Holiness

Holiness happens when God shows up. It's first his presence and then his proclamation that make us holy. Afterward, our actions align with God's declaration. Our lives represent the nature of the God who set us apart. When we get that backward, we attempt to earn God's grace rather than allowing his grace to transform us. Conversely, when the practice of holiness results in gratitude and when awe is our natural response to God choosing us, then our holiness becomes obedience marked by humility.

This is the heartbeat of 2 Timothy 1:9, where Paul said that God "saved us and called us to a holy calling, not because of our works but because of his own purpose and grace, which he gave us in Christ Jesus before the ages began." This kind of holiness is attractive, even enviable, to a watching world.

So what does this kind of holiness look like?

Have you ever watched a young man fall in love? Video games give way to romantic walks. Microwaved meals are replaced with candlelit dinners. You get the picture. You don't have to guilt-trip or strong-arm a lover. He alters his behavior out of affection.

Jake was one of those. He was a naturally likable kid. Something in his personality made him a blast to be around. Unfortunately, his father wasn't around. This didn't make him bitter, just unwise. So throughout high school he always opted for the shortest route to immediate pleasure. Because he was the life of the party, he preferred the party life. As one might expect, sports, girls, and drugs all came easy, which doesn't make life easy. Jake spent most of his high school days in a low-grade buzz that became a raging rave on the weekends.

His story is not uncommon. His meeting with Jesus was common. Nothing in the details is dramatic. After graduation, his former high school soccer coach invited him to church. He heard the simple message of the gospel with a clear head. Jake decided to follow Jesus. He was immediately marked and eternally sanctified. As his circle of friends changed, so did Jake's pleasures and pastimes. Again, this isn't one of those crazy grace stories with a miraculous intervention. It's simply the normal process of meeting someone who wins your heart. For Jake, his choice to give up partying, drugs, and drinking was not a hard-fought struggle. It was like pushing aside a salad when the steak comes to the table.

Paul put it this way:

> I appeal to you therefore, brothers, by the mercies of God, to present your bodies as a living sacrifice, holy and acceptable to God, which is your spiritual worship. Do not be conformed to this world, but be

> transformed by the renewal of your mind, that by testing you may discern what is the will of God, what is good and acceptable and perfect. (Romans 12:1–2)

Sometimes holiness is a challenge. Sex tonight or a strong marriage later? Speak my mind now or build a relationship later? Steal now or keep my dignity later? These aren't hard decisions. The difficulty is in the delay—that nagging "later." When we wrestle with holiness, it's not because we really believe what the world has to offer is better. It's because we don't believe that either the presence or the proclamation of God is reality.

This bears repeating. We make each decision to abandon the practice of holiness because we don't believe that God is present now or because we don't believe he'll show up later. This is why Paul urged holiness in light of God's promises: "Since we have these promises, beloved, let us cleanse ourselves from every defilement of body and spirit, bringing holiness to completion in the fear of God" (2 Corinthians 7:1).

In the light (and heat) of our current culture, the call to holiness seems somewhat prudish and restrictive. From the eternal perspective, however, in light of God's own holiness, any sacrifice we make of temporal satisfaction is trivial. True, we sacrifice now in order to receive a future reward. Yet more importantly in this present life, (1) God's ways are better ways, leading to the greatest happiness a person can experience on earth; and (2) God's election of us deserves our best representation of him.

Key Points

- Holiness is in your election, not in your action.
- Israel was called to be a kingdom of priests. The church fulfilled that vocation when Israel failed.
- Righteous behavior is the appropriate and natural response for one who is called to a noble life given to God's purpose.

This Week

- ☐ **Day 1:** Read the essay.
- ☐ **Day 2:** Memorize Leviticus 11:45.
- ☐ **Day 3:** Read 2 Samuel 11; Psalm 51.
- ☐ **Day 4:** Meditate on Exodus 19:6; 2 Corinthians 7:1; 1 Peter 2:9.
- ☐ **Day 5:** Seek out a place to serve voluntarily so you can tap into God's purpose for you.

Overachiever Challenge: Memorize Exodus 19:6.

Bonus Read: Jerry Bridges, *The Pursuit of Holiness.*

6

Jesus and Moses

> I will raise up for them a prophet like you from among their brothers. And I will put my words in his mouth, and he shall speak to them all that I command him.
>
> —Deuteronomy 18:18

Question: Did Jesus fulfill the promise to replace Moses?

God promised that the Messiah would be someone like Moses. This prophecy wasn't wasted on the rabbis. They viewed Moses as the model for the future Messiah. Christians took their cue from them, portraying Jesus as the new Moses. Both were liberators, lawgivers, and shepherds. Both were rescued as infants in Egypt, tested in the wilderness, and suffered for the nation.

To compare any Jew to the founder of the nation was an outrageous claim. Such a bold claim is better demonstrated than merely stated. Hence, most of the comparisons of Jesus to Moses in the New Testament are allusions rather than assertions. Even so, the sheer volume offers a compelling case that Jesus fulfilled this messianic prophecy.

So let's do a flyover of the New Testament to see how these allusions stack up. We can start with Jesus himself. In the Sermon on the Mount, six times we read something to the effect of "Moses said . . . but I say" (Matthew 5:17–48). Pretty gutsy, given the religious climate. Jesus clearly saw himself not merely as an authoritative interpreter of the Mosaic law but as one who could fulfill and even extend that divine law.

Matthew seemed to agree, shaping his entire book in the shadow of Moses. Beginning with his birth, Jesus mirrored Moses. In Egypt he was saved from a tyrannical despot. He survived his testing in the wilderness after passing through water. Jesus's five major sermons mirror the Torah, the five books of Moses. Both Jesus and Moses were known as humble leaders (Numbers 12:3; Matthew 11:29; 21:5). Moses and Jesus have a conversation on top of a mountain during the transfiguration (17:3). Finally, Jesus's Last Supper was during the Passover meal that Moses established (26:17–29). Clearly, Moses foreshadowed Jesus.

For Luke, it's clearly not enough to equate Jesus with Moses. Jesus, in his view, is greater by far than Moses. First, at the transfiguration, Luke recorded God's voice: "Listen to *him*" (Luke 9:35)—over Moses. Jesus is the unparalleled son of God. Later, Luke recorded this vivid declaration by Paul about Jesus: "By him everyone who believes is freed from everything from which you could not be freed by the law of Moses" (Acts 13:39).

Turning from Luke to John's gospel, we see the same superiority of Jesus the Messiah over Moses the prophet. In John 3:14–15, Jesus alluded to Numbers 21:4–9, when deadly vipers went on a rampage, striking the rebellious Israelites. Moses pleaded with God to relent. His solution was to have Moses place a bronze serpent on a pole and lift it up. Anyone who looked at the raised serpent by faith was healed of the venomous bite. Jesus compared his crucifixion to the bronze serpent of Moses: "Just as Moses lifted up the snake in the wilderness, so the Son of Man must be lifted up, that everyone who believes may have eternal life in him" (John 3:14–15, NIV).

Two chapters later, we find Jesus debating with the religious leaders. Moses was called to testify:

> Do not think that I will accuse you to the Father. There is one who accuses you: Moses, on whom you have set your hope. For if you believed Moses, you would believe me; for he wrote of me. But if you do not believe his writings, how will you believe my words? (5:45–47)

Thus, in both chapters 3 and 5 of John, Jesus is superior to Moses, not his equal. Not only does Jesus fulfill the prediction of Moses; he also supersedes the person of Moses.

In the very next chapter of John, there's a whole discussion about manna (6:26–58). Jesus said, "Truly, truly, I say to you, it was not Moses who gave you the bread from heaven, but my Father gives you the true bread from heaven. For the bread of God is he who comes down from heaven and gives life to the world" (verses 32–33). Clearly, Jesus claimed to be superior to Moses. He wasn't merely God's messenger; he was God's gift, the very bread of life (verse 48). Furthermore, the Israelites under Moses ate manna and died, but Jesus is the bread from heaven that provides eternal life (verses 48–51). This text exalts Jesus well above Moses.

Paul, likewise, drew a parallel between the first and second redeemers. For him, Jesus is far superior. This is clearly seen in his allegory in 1 Corinthians 10:1–4 about the wilderness wanderings of Moses. Here Jesus isn't compared to Moses the liberator (which seems like an obvious enough connection). Instead, Jesus is the rock from which the Israelites drank: "All drank the same spiritual drink. For they drank from the spiritual Rock that followed them, and the Rock was Christ" (verse 4; see Exodus 17:6). In other words, Moses was God's messenger to Israel, but Jesus was God's gift to Israel.

John 6 focused on manna and the bread of life; 1 Corinthians 10 focused on the rock and the water of life. Both exalt Jesus above Moses.

Another example comes from 2 Corinthians 3:13–18 when Paul recalled the incident in Exodus 34:33. After Moses met with God on Mount Sinai, his face shone because he had been in the presence of God. He somehow absorbed a bit of God's glory. The effect was not long lived, however. Moses veiled his face after speaking to the crowd so they wouldn't see the glory fading. Who knows how many times he repeated this cycle: talk to God, talk to the crowd, cover his fading face.

When Paul compared Moses with Jesus, he compared the fading glory of Moses with the unfading glory of Jesus on the Christian: "We all, with unveiled face, beholding the glory of the Lord, are being transformed into the same image from one degree of glory to another. For this comes from the Lord who is the Spirit" (2 Corinthians 3:18). Here the glory of the law was allegorically compared to the fading glory of the face of Moses. It was fading because Jesus would replace it. Notably, Moses was compared not to Christ but to the Christian. Christ is the unfading glory itself, the embodiment of the new law that replaced the old.

In summary, Jesus is not Moses. Instead, he is the manna, the water, and the glory of God. Moses, the messenger, gives way to Jesus, the means of connecting with God.

This is precisely the point of Hebrews 3:3–6:

> Jesus has been counted worthy of more glory than Moses—as much more glory as the builder of a house has more honor than the house itself. (For every house is built by someone, but the builder of all things is God.) Now Moses was faithful in all God's house as a servant, to testify to the things that were to be spoken later, but Christ is faithful over God's house as a son. And we are his house, if indeed we hold fast our confidence and our boasting in our hope.

Nearly every author of the New Testament compared Moses with Jesus. This isn't surprising, since Abraham, Moses, and David are the three key figures of Israel's history. What's surprising is the ease with which the early believers portrayed Jesus as superior to Moses. Moses instituted the Passover; Jesus is the sacrificial lamb of God. Moses offered manna; Jesus is the bread from heaven. Moses miraculously provided water from the rock; Jesus is that rock.

Don't miss the gravity of this. Moses was revered in Israel. In fact, in a number of Jewish texts and traditions, he's given semidivine status. He was a Jewish superhero. To assert that a peasant carpenter outmatched the founder of the nation was an assault on religious sensibilities. What tectonic shift allowed such an unprecedented exaltation of Jesus? How could they exalt Jesus over Moses against all cultural expectations? How did the early followers of Jesus convince crowds to believe such an assertion?

Only two things can account for this tidal shift. First, Jesus's incomparable moral life demonstrated the power of God on human soil. Second, his irrefutable resurrection testified to God's vindication of his son. Without Jesus's life, death, and resurrection, there's no valid explanation for how he could claim to have fulfilled the prophecy of Moses, let alone surpassed his status.

Key Points

- Moses, along with Abraham and David, made up the trinity of Hebrew heroes. Therefore, any comparison of Jesus with Moses would have raised more than eyebrows. It would have raised religious ire.
- Nearly every author of the New Testament compared Jesus with Moses. Jesus is not merely like Moses. He's superior to this Hebrew superstar.
- Any explanation of Jesus's superiority to Moses must be grounded in the impeccable moral life of Jesus and in his resurrection.

This Week

- ☐ **Day 1:** Read the essay.
- ☐ **Day 2:** Memorize Deuteronomy 18:18.
- ☐ **Day 3:** Read Exodus 2–3.
- ☐ **Day 4:** Meditate on John 5:45–47; Acts 13:39; 1 Corinthians 10:1–4.
- ☐ **Day 5:** Ask someone at work or school what the current president of the United States would have to do in order to be remembered as greater than George Washington. After he or she answers, share this concept of Jesus being greater than Moses, and use it as an opportunity to make Jesus famous in that person's eyes.

Overachiever Challenge: Memorize Acts 13:39.

Bonus Read: Dale C. Allison Jr., *The New Moses: A Matthean Typology.*

7

Kingdom of God

Do not look on his appearance or on the height of his stature, because I have rejected him. For the LORD sees not as man sees: man looks on the outward appearance, but the LORD looks on the heart.

—1 SAMUEL 16:7

Question: What does it take to be a great leader?

The original plan for the nation of Israel was that Yahweh (the Jewish name for God) would be their only king. This vision of God as the exclusive ruler of Israel undergirds Hebrew history: "The LORD is our judge; the LORD is our lawgiver; the LORD is our king; he will save us" (Isaiah 33:22).

Israel's Desire for a King Was a Rejection of God's Rule

This idea that God ruled Israel was so strong that the establishment of a Jewish monarchy was seen as rejecting Yahweh. Samuel, Israel's first major prophet, was appalled by Israel's request for a king. He warned them about the cost of having an earthly monarch. A king would take their sons as soldiers, daughters as servants, and crops as taxes (1 Samuel 8:11–15). Even though God agreed with

Samuel, he told his prophet, "Obey the voice of the people in all that they say to you, for they have not rejected you, but they have rejected me from being king over them" (verse 7). Though this was a long time ago, we all know what it's like to trust something other than God—money, power, relationships, or sex.

Samuel repeated his warning three times to no avail (1 Samuel 10:19; 12:15, 20). Israel was infatuated with human monarchs.

What Israel really wanted in a king was military protection. They trusted a human warrior more than an invisible God, even though Yahweh historically had proved himself a formidable protector. But God's invisible monarchy had seemingly led also to visible anarchy. Twice we read, "In those days there was no king in Israel. Everyone did what was right in his own eyes" (Judges 17:6; 21:25). This was the subtext in Judges. It became clear a king was needed to rule Israel.

That God's rule wasn't enough for them should have made them uneasy. God permitted a king because the people rejected him. This had inevitable consequences.

Saul, a Man the People Sought

Israel's first experience with monarchy was with a king named Saul. From a human perspective, he had all the right qualifications. Saul was tall, strong, attractive, and from a wealthy family (1 Samuel 9:1–2). If you look at his actions, however, he had several fatal flaws.

Saul did the exact thing God told him *not* to do. We see this when his troops got restless after the battle of Gilgal. Saul overstepped his authority by personally performing the sacrifice before Samuel arrived (13:8–9). Because of this insubordination, God stripped Saul of his kingdom, even though he sat on the throne for nearly forty more years. His dynasty was cut off with these words: "Now your kingdom will not endure; the Lord has sought out a man after his own heart and appointed him ruler of his people, because *you have not kept the Lord's command*" (verse 14, niv).

Following this incident, Saul made a vow he neglected to keep. Granted, it was a foolish vow he never should have made. When his son Jonathan put the Philistines to flight, Saul rashly pledged to kill any soldier who ate any food before putting an end to his enemies (14:24). Because Jonathan was ahead of the troops in hot pursuit of the Philistines, he knew nothing of the vow. He dipped his staff in a honeycomb to energize himself for battle (verse 27). When Saul heard of it, he was committed to keeping his vow by executing his own son. His soldiers intervened and talked him out of it, as they should have (verses 43–45).

We then see Saul neglecting to do what God had specifically commanded. We see this after he was told to eradicate every living thing among the Amalekites. This was God's justice in response to the Amalekites attacking the wandering Israelites on their way to the promised land (Deuteronomy 25:17–19; 1 Samuel 15:2–3). Saul *claimed* to have kept God's command (1 Samuel 15:13). However, as Samuel heard the bleating of Amalekite sheep, he knew Saul was a liar (verse 14). Saul tried to excuse his disobedience by saying that the people saved the best livestock to sacrifice to God (verse 15), but Saul's actions betrayed him.

That was the last straw. God said to Samuel, "I regret that I have made Saul king, for he has turned back from following me and has not performed my commandments" (verse 11).

Looking at this brief biography, we observe fatal flaws in Saul. First, people's opinions were more important to him than God's command. Each time he failed, it was because popular opinion went against God's clear command. Second, Saul promoted himself through manipulation rather than resting on God's approval. Saul forced the results he wanted rather than waiting for God to provide. Third, when Saul failed, he blamed someone else. When a leader cannot take responsibility for failure, he's doomed to repeat his mistakes.

Why are we talking so much about Saul when David is the subject of our key passage? Because without understanding Saul's failure, one cannot appreciate David as his replacement.

God's response to Saul was to send Samuel the prophet to anoint a new king. Saul was the right man from a human perspective—tall, strong, capable. Yet none of those qualities qualified him in God's eyes. God looks for leaders of a different fabric. God instructed Samuel, "Do not look on his appearance or on the height of his stature, because I have rejected him. For the LORD sees not as man sees: man looks on the outward appearance, but the LORD looks on the heart" (1 Samuel 16:7; see 13:14; Acts 13:22).

David, a Man After God's Own Heart

David became the model leader of Israel precisely because he left leadership in the hands of Yahweh, Israel's ultimate king. He was merely God's servant to point God's people to God's laws. David's goal was God's fame, not his own. He battled for God's honor, not his own reputation. That's the kind of leader God is looking for. This is, in fact, what he wants from you in your own realm of influence.

David sought God's heart. That's why he became the ideal king. However, he wasn't a perfect king. In fact, he was flawed on multiple levels, as we all are. This is why Israel needed a Messiah—a king who would lead with God's heart, not just chase after it. For this, we needed Jesus Christ. David's flaws didn't disqualify him from being a leader, but they did disqualify him from ruling God's kingdom permanently.

David, though imperfect, became the model after which the messianic hopes would be fashioned. His life and legacy point to Jesus. First Samuel 16:7 is a powerful reminder to us to look at the heart of the man, not his appearance.

How Might Jesus Have Thought About Kingship?

Jesus knew he was the ultimate king of Israel. And in many ways, he must have looked to his predecessor David as the model for his own leadership. Though

Jesus claimed a kingdom (Matthew 4:17), he never overtly claimed the title of king. He never gathered a military force or passed laws. He never sat on a throne. Why? Because Jesus thought of himself as king without asserting himself as king during his life on earth. There are two major reasons for this.

First, God is the only true king. There was always a question whether the monarchy was a good idea. The Scriptures themselves describe it as a deviation from God's original political order. Jesus must have been suspicious of any leadership role that resembled the ancient kings of Israel. No question, there had to be a Davidic ruler to establish God's kingdom (2 Samuel 7:12). But what should he look like? Perhaps a "judge," akin to Moses, would have struck Jesus as a better model.

Since Jesus's primary message was about the kingdom of God, it seems obvious that he was more interested in God's rule than his own. He was well aware of the Israelite tradition that criticized the monarchy.

Second, if Jesus were to rule Israel, he would have to be different from all the other kings in at least four ways. First, he had to promote and defend the exclusive rule of Yahweh (1 Samuel 12:12–15). Second, he had to live by and enforce God's rules given in the Torah (Deuteronomy 17:18–19). Third, he would live with and for his fellow Israelites, because all are created in the image of God (verses 15, 20). And fourth, he would use power selflessly to enact justice for the poor (Jeremiah 22:3–4). This is, in fact, exactly what we see in Jesus's ministry.

The monarchy was not God's original political structure for Israel, and it came with both birth pains and permanent scars. Although God permitted it, the monarchy appears to have been a necessary evil. Yes, Jesus was a Davidic descendant with a regal role to play. Yet his brand of leadership had to be characterized by submission and sacrifice.

If that's the kind of kingship Jesus envisioned, the Gospels have captured it with precision. For this reason, we can say that 1 Samuel 16:7 is more a description of Jesus the Messiah than of David the king. It should characterize our own ambitions as well, if we're to follow in the footsteps of both.

Key Points

- Kingship in Israel was never ideal because it contradicted God's sole rule of Israel.
- Saul's self-promotion forced God to replace him with David, a man who sought God's heart.
- The reason Jesus was the rightful king is that he deflected authority back to Yahweh, the only true king of Israel.

This Week

- ☐ **Day 1:** Read the essay.
- ☐ **Day 2:** Memorize 1 Samuel 16:7.
- ☐ **Day 3:** Read 1 Samuel 15–16.
- ☐ **Day 4:** Meditate on Judges 21:25; 1 Samuel 8:1–18; 13:14.
- ☐ **Day 5:** Take this essay to a friend or mentor. Read the three fatal flaws of Saul and the four characteristics of Jesus's leadership. Ask your friend or mentor to point out your greatest strength in imitating Jesus and your greatest risk of turning out like Saul.

Overachiever Challenge: Memorize 1 Samuel 13:14.

Bonus Read: Gene Edwards, *A Tale of Three Kings: A Study in Brokenness.*

8

Jesus and David

> When your days are fulfilled and you lie down with your fathers, I will raise up your offspring after you, who shall come from your body, and I will establish his kingdom.
>
> —2 Samuel 7:12

Question: Was Jesus a king literally or spiritually?

David was a national hero for ushering in the "golden age" of Israel both politically and spiritually. He was a giant-killer, famous musician, nation-builder, and passionate lover of God, women, and friends. He stands next to the Hebrew titans, Abraham and Moses. These three form the trinity of Hebrew heroes. It's therefore hardly surprising that the Scriptures record the people's longing for David's return. Why not? Israel hit a high mark under his rule.

God's Promise of a New David

God promised that David would always have an heir on the throne: "When your days are fulfilled and you lie down with your fathers, I will raise up your offspring after you, who shall come from your body, and I will establish his kingdom. He shall build a house for my name, and I will establish the throne of his kingdom forever" (2 Samuel 7:12–13). This promise is repeated in a prayer by the psalmist Ethan the Ezrahite:

> You have said, "I have made a covenant with my chosen one;
> I have sworn to David my servant:
> 'I will establish your offspring forever,
> and build your throne for all generations.' " (Psalm 89:3–4)

And through the prophet Isaiah, God said, "There shall come forth a shoot from the stump of Jesse, and a branch from his roots shall bear fruit" (11:1).

This longing for David's return was recorded in a number of Jewish writings outside the Bible. The Psalms of Solomon include this prayer: "Thou, O Lord, didst choose David (to be) king over Israel, and swaredst to him touching his seed that never should his kingdom fail before Thee."[1] Similarly, one of the Qumran scrolls found at the Dead Sea predicted that King David's heir would reign forever.[2] Later, the Talmud (about AD 500) declared David's son would come with thunder and great warfare.[3]

This longing for a return to the glory days of David was present throughout all strands of Judaism. Imagine how shocking it must have been when the gospel writers applied this promise to a peasant carpenter. When all the relevant passages are stacked together, it's a small mountain.

God's Fulfillment of the Promise in Jesus

The New Testament opens with a genealogy that many perceive as just plain boring—until we see what Matthew is up to. This former tax collector proves quite clever in how he arranged his list of names in three groups of fourteen generations, as he himself summarized for us: "All the generations from Abraham to David were fourteen generations, and from David to the deportation [exile] to Babylon fourteen generations, and from the deportation to Babylon to the Christ fourteen generations" (Matthew 1:17).

Perhaps you've never taken the time to check Matthew's math. Upon careful examination, we discover that the second group includes only thirteen names, not fourteen. Did Matthew miscount? While that's possible, it wouldn't be the first thing to suspect of a tax collector. Perhaps he rounded up for convenience? Actually, that's not the case. We can compare Matthew's genealogy with the parallel genealogical record in 1 Chronicles 3. There we discover Matthew actually had seventeen names to draw from, and he omitted four. Why?

Apparently, Matthew crafted the central group to have thirteen names, not fourteen. In our modern mechanized society, that makes no sense, because numbers are supposed to be precisely counted. For the Jews, however, numbers had symbolic value, not merely numeric value. In this instance, Matthew was doing what every Jewish father did when dispensing his inheritance. He gave a double portion to the eldest brother. In Matthew's listing, the older brother, figuratively speaking, is David. If we count David twice—giving him double honor—then we have precisely three groups of fourteen names. David is the most important figure because he was the center of the Old Testament as king of the Jews. Look again at Matthew 1:1 and you'll find an embedded clue to David's importance. He's listed first, even before Abraham, who lived a thousand years before him.

Moreover, if we can think like a Jew for a moment, we would see something that jumped out at every rabbi: the number fourteen. You see, Jews counted with letters, not numbers. Each letter of a person's name had a numerical value. In Hebrew, David is spelled with just three letters, corresponding to *DVD* in English. *D* is the fourth letter of their alphabet and *V* is the sixth. Adding together those values for David's name—*D* plus *V* plus *D*—we have 4 + 6 + 4 = 14. The very numbers in the genealogy testify to the supremacy of David, who's given a double portion. Hence, from the opening paragraph of the New Testament, a reader wearing a yarmulke would put the pieces together. The promise

God made to David that a descendant would forever sit on his throne was ultimately fulfilled in Jesus.

Even Luke, a Gentile, understood Jesus's connection with King David. The angel Gabriel promised Mary concerning her son, "He will be great and will be called the Son of the Most High. And the Lord God will give to him the throne of his father David" (Luke 1:32). This was the whole reason the Messiah had to be born in Bethlehem, the city of David (Luke 2:4, 11). It's also why this Son of David entered Jerusalem, the capital city, riding a donkey as other kings did during their coronations (Matthew 21:2–9, 15).

In the very first sermon Peter preached after Jesus's resurrection, he reminded his audience that Jesus was David's heir; Peter spoke of David as "being therefore a prophet, and knowing that God had sworn with an oath to him that he would set one of his descendants on his throne" (Acts 2:30).

Another critical moment of church history was the Jerusalem council (Acts 15:1–29), when the very nature of salvation was up for debate. Did Gentiles have to convert to Judaism before they could become Christians? Ultimately the answer is no. They didn't practice Judaism, but they were nonetheless nationalized (through conversion) into the Davidic kingdom. Jesus's brother James affirmed the house of David as the destined dwelling of Gentiles, quoting God's words to the prophet Amos: "After this I will return, and I will rebuild the tent of David that has fallen; I will rebuild its ruins, and I will restore it" (Acts 15:16; paraphrasing Amos 9:11).

The great apostle Paul, a former rabbi, opened his magisterial book of Romans by describing Jesus in these words: "who as to his earthly life was a descendant of David, and who through the Spirit of holiness was appointed the Son of God in power by his resurrection from the dead: Jesus Christ our Lord" (Romans 1:3–4, NIV). In his last letter, Paul continued to highlight Jesus's Davidic ancestry: "Remember Jesus Christ, risen from the dead, the offspring of David, as preached in my gospel" (2 Timothy 2:8).

We see it also in John's words in Revelation: "One of the elders said to me, 'Weep no more; behold, the Lion of the tribe of Judah, the Root of David, has conquered, so that he can open the scroll and its seven seals'" (5:5). Jesus himself affirmed this: "I, Jesus, have sent my angel to testify to you about these things for the churches. I am the root and the descendant of David, the bright morning star" (22:16).

Why Didn't Jesus Claim to Be King?

Since the New Testament makes it clear that Jesus was David's heir, why did Jesus never overtly make the claim during his years on earth? Sure, the political theater of the Triumphal Entry and the cleansing of the temple clearly asserts his royal role (Matthew 21:1–16). Likewise, Jesus's calling of twelve apostles looks like a political cabinet over Israel's twelve tribes. These actions were clear enough to get him crucified as a would-be king of the Jews. Pilate, the Roman procurator, even inscribed that title on the cross (John 19:19). But Jesus never clearly claimed to be king. Why?

This is where the previous lesson on 1 Samuel 16:7 comes into play. The true king of Israel is God. Any vassal who sits on Israel's throne must never usurp Yahweh's rule. The very claim to the throne is a dangerous step in the wrong direction. The rightful heir to the throne would be anointed by God without ever asking to be. He would be installed in God's timing rather than through his own campaigning. This is precisely where the kings of past—especially Saul—went wrong. Their attempts to promote and protect themselves destroyed their reigns.

It's in Jesus's self-abnegation that he truly modeled David's heart for God. David was anointed king years before actually sitting on the throne. During those days he was rejected and maligned, abused and attacked, until Saul's self-destruction inaugurated David's rule over Israel. So, too, for Jesus: suffering was the prelude to enthronement, because he did *not* assert his rule.

> God has highly exalted him and bestowed on him the name that is above every name, so that at the name of Jesus every knee should bow, in heaven and on earth and under the earth, and every tongue confess that Jesus Christ is Lord, to the glory of God the Father. (Philippians 2:9–11)

Key Points

- God promised David an heir to sit on his throne forever.
- The New Testament claims that Jesus fulfilled that promise.
- Because Jesus is the king on David's throne, Christians are citizens of his nation, Israel.

This Week

- [ ] **Day 1:** Read the essay.
- [ ] **Day 2:** Memorize 2 Samuel 7:12.
- [ ] **Day 3:** Read Matthew 21–22.
- [ ] **Day 4:** Meditate on Matthew 1:1; Philippians 2:9–11; Revelation 5:5.
- [ ] **Day 5:** Ask your pastor what practical difference it should make that you're a citizen of a kingdom, not merely members of a church.

Overachiever Challenge: Memorize Philippians 2:9–11.

Bonus Read: Norman Perrin, *The Kingdom of God in the Teaching of Jesus.*

9

Finding Happiness

Blessed is the man
    who walks not in the counsel of the wicked,
nor stands in the way of sinners,
    nor sits in the seat of scoffers;
but his delight is in the law of the Lord,
    and on his law he meditates day and night.

He is like a tree
    planted by streams of water
that yields its fruit in its season,
    and its leaf does not wither.
In all that he does, he prospers.

—Psalm 1:1–3

Question: Does God want you to be happy?

Before answering this question, we'd better recognize that happiness is a universal human quest. Happiness is a desire as strong as food, sex, and sleep. That's why people tend to determine their ethics by their happiness. If a particular action, habit, or relationship makes me happy, it must be moral. Right?

Perhaps we should think this through.

Should we really determine what's right by what feels right? It's common for people to use happiness as their metric of morality. Yet no parent applies this rule to children. Why? Because it can destroy them. To an eight-year-old boy, happiness is jumping off the roof on a skateboard into the pool. Not okay. Toddlers are fascinated with electrical outlets and power tools. Not okay. Parents know that moments of happiness can bring decades of regret. Yet we keep hearing that as long as you're happy, that makes it right. Sheryl Crow memorialized the sentiment by singing, "If it makes you happy, it can't be that bad." When we download her lyrics into our theology, it sounds like this: "God wants me happy."

But does he?

Before I give an answer, let me share my experience as a pastor. One hundred percent of the time when people say, "God wants me happy," they're about to make a tragic mistake, usually in their marriage. A husband explains to his wife, "God wants me happy. *You* don't make me happy. That woman at the office makes me happy." Is your happiness God's greatest priority? No! On the other hand, when someone says, "God must *not* want me happy" (usually as a response to some difficult situation), we should respond, "Of course God wants you to be happy! Now get up, go out, and do something about it!"

Here's the paradox of happiness in the context of Christianity: those who claim God wants them happy are usually wrong, and those who claim God doesn't want them happy are also usually wrong.

So what's right?

God Wants You to Be Happy

What father doesn't want his kids to be happy? Perhaps you've heard, "God doesn't want you to be happy; he wants you to be holy!" On the surface that sounds reasonable. However, it contains a fatal flaw. It assumes happiness and holiness are opposites. They aren't mutually exclusive. Holiness and happiness go hand in hand most of the time.

The Bible hasn't been particularly timid on the topic: "Delight yourself in the LORD, and he will give you the desires of your heart" (Psalm 37:4). "Rejoice in the Lord" (Philippians 3:1). "Rejoice always" (1 Thessalonians 5:16). "We consider those blessed [happy] who remained steadfast" (James 5:11). The entire book of Ecclesiastes is a treatise on happiness, and Proverbs is a happiness handbook of sorts. So it can be misleading at best to say God desires your obedience more than your happiness. Obedience to God fosters our happiness!

Regarding happiness, there's one passage that towers above the rest. Before looking at the Bible, however, let's take a peek at our bodies. Science shows that we're designed for happiness.

Science of Happiness

When God constructed your brain, he lubricated the synapses with three specific chemicals of happiness. They're the happy juices of your brain.

Oxytocin is the chemical that gives a sense of comfort. It's released through a handshake or a hug. Oxytocin creates a sense of safety and trust.

Dopamine is the chemical of adventure. It's released when your mind is buzzing with activity and creative energy. When you invent a new product, write a song, solve a problem, or learn something new, you get a dopamine drip. It drives productivity, travel, and adventure.

Serotonin is the chemical of respect. It's released when someone asks your opinion, treats you with respect, or applauds your performance.

Now, several things are important to understand. First, these chemicals are highly addictive. That may sound negative, but it's not. God gave you these insatiable cravings for a reason—he craves your happiness. His design drives you toward it.

Second, these chemicals are short lived. You get a little squirt that dissipates quickly. Hence, God didn't create you to remain in a long-term state of happiness. Rather, he designed you for brief moments of happiness that require repetition. Why? Because happiness is dependent on persistent habits that release the minibursts of chemicals. As a result, God's design leads to long-term habits that build positive communities. It's an ingenious design.

Third, happiness is a chemical cocktail that you can control. This deserves a bit of explanation.

In addition to these three chemicals are three other sources of happiness for every human being: genetics, circumstances, and choices. Which of these three do you think accounts for the greatest variance of our happiness?

Some people are naturally perky. They're optimists by nature. Others are more pessimistic (or realistic, if you ask them). In other words, all of us have a "set point" for happiness. For some the baseline is a bit higher; for others it's a bit lower. But all of us have some degree of biological propensity to happiness. According to substantial scientific research, genetics accounts for about half the variation in our happiness.

A second source of happiness is circumstances. Most of us expend a lot of energy trying to change our circumstances to bring happiness, even though they're a fractional part of the equation. Circumstances can vary our happiness a mere 10 percent. What's more is that the highs and lows of circumstances are not long lasting. On average, any circumstance affects happiness for only ninety days. In one fascinating study, researchers measured the happiness of lottery winners and of paraplegics or quadriplegics. Paraplegics and quadriplegics obviously considered the accident a negative event, and lottery winners rated winning as a positive event. However, neither event was rated as positively or negatively as one would expect, and when asked how happy they expected to be in a couple of years, both groups projected similar levels of happiness.[1] People are apparently happy or sad not because of what has happened to them but because of the choices they make.

Choices like diet, rest, and relationships account for 40 percent of the variance in our happiness.[2] That's statistically huge. You can't control your genetics any more than you can control your circumstances. However, you can control your choices, accounting for nearly half your overall happiness. To put this in perspective, if you could control 40 percent of the stock market swing, you would be stupid rich.

With that in mind, what does the Bible have to say about choices affecting happiness?

Scripture on Happiness

Psalm 1 is the single most important passage in the Bible on happiness. It opens with the key word *blessed*—the Bible's term for "happy": "Blessed is the man who walks not in the counsel of the wicked, nor stands in the way of sinners, nor sits in the seat of scoffers" (verse 1). If your ambition is a blessed life, Psalm 1 is the starting line.

Our relationships account for the bulk of our happiness. When we build godly relationships, our happiness increases. Friends and family are the best source of oxytocin. Therefore, above all, choose companions that lead to healthy choices. That's step one.

Step two is to increase dopamine, the discovery chemical. Verse 2 points the way, as it speaks of the person "whose delight is in the law of the LORD, and who meditates on his law day and night" (NIV). While there are many ways to release dopamine, meditation is up toward the top. Meditation has been the focus of much of the research on happiness. Not just from Eastern mysticism, but even from a Christian perspective. Caroline Leaf, a neuroscientist, revealed how we can rewire our brains. Because proteins hold our thoughts, our thoughts literally take up real estate in our brains. So the more we meditate on a positive thought, the larger it grows. As we meditate, we release the addictive dopamine that determines happiness.[3]

Step three is serotonin, the chemical of significance. Being helpful is the key to releasing serotonin. As we serve others, we gain significance. The process is described in verse 3: "That person is like a tree planted by streams of water, which yields its fruit in season and whose leaf does not wither—whatever they do prospers" (NIV). When we're fruitful, we find significance—whether we're helpful to a president or a pauper. Consequently, we don't have to climb the corporate ladder or win an Olympic event to be drenched in serotonin. Simple acts of kindness to people around us will be just as effective in giving you the chemical rush of happiness.

Psalm 1 rightly addresses our own choices as more important than our circumstances. Written three thousand years ago, it gives us a clear process for building the blessed life: (1) Foster relationships with people who honor the Lord. (2) Create space in your brain for truths of God's Word. (3) Serve others in significant ways.

It's that simple and that effective. Furthermore, because these chemicals come in microbursts, it doesn't take a Herculean effort to release them. The small things you do today can increase happiness. A note of gratitude to a friend, five minutes of meditation, or a random act of kindness can release chemicals of happiness in your brain. The secret to happiness is in micromoments that turn into habits. Habits, continued over a lifetime, become a biography with a very happy ending.

Key Points

- Your happiness is a chemical cocktail you can control by practicing habits that release oxytocin, dopamine, and serotonin.
- While genetics accounts for 50 percent of the variability in happiness, circumstances account for only 10 percent—leaving a whopping 40 percent of our happiness to the choices we make.
- Psalm 1 offers wise counsel about building happiness.

This Week

- ☐ **Day 1:** Read the essay.
- ☐ **Day 2:** Memorize Psalm 1:1–3.
- ☐ **Day 3:** Read Job 1–2.
- ☐ **Day 4:** Meditate on Psalm 37:4; Philippians 3:1; 1 Thessalonians 5:16.
- ☐ **Day 5:** Plan five minutes today to deliberately practice one simple action listed in Psalm 1 to release a shot of happiness.

Overachiever Challenge: Memorize Psalm 37:4.

Bonus Read: Jonathan Haidt, *The Happiness Hypothesis: Finding Modern Truth in Ancient Wisdom.*

10

Prophecy

You are my Son;
today I have begotten you.
—Psalm 2:7

Question: Is there proof that Jesus was God's son?

The book of Psalms contains several royal psalms sung in honor of the king. Yet each king, to various degrees, disappointed Israel, and each king died. These royal songs were repeatedly sung by Israel in expectation of the long-awaited day when the Messiah they sang about would become the king they knelt before.

Seeing the Messiah in Psalm 2

The crescendo of this royal poem is seen in the words of our core verse. God himself paraphrased this verse twice during Jesus's ministry. The first time was at his baptism, when God spoke in a voice audible to the crowd. The Holy Spirit affirmed God's declaration by descending in the form of a dove (Matthew 3:16–17). It was a *big* deal. The second time God cited Psalm 2:7 was in the middle of Jesus's three-year ministry, when he was transfigured on a high mountain in the presence of Moses and Elijah (Matthew 17:1–8). In one sense, this event marked the apex of Jesus's earthly existence. It was the closest he ever got to sharing God's glory on this globe.

This wasn't merely a declaration of approval. It was an affirmation of Jesus's regal heritage as the rightful heir to the throne of Israel. A thousand years before Jesus was born, the Bible predicted a coming Messiah. The word *messiah* means "anointed one," in reference to a king's coronation. Israel's Messiah was to sit on David's throne, rescue Israel as Moses did, and bless all nations as Abraham's offspring. That, after all, was the duty of the highest political official whom God chose to represent him.

Psalm 2:7 is just one of dozens of major messianic prophecies that identified who the Savior-King would be and what he would do. They told where he would be born (Micah 5:2), how he would die (Isaiah 53:3–5), the price of his betrayal (Zechariah 11:12), and the nature of his ministry (Isaiah 61:1). Christians have always seen Jesus as the figure to fulfill this broad array of prophecies. No one else fulfilled these predictions. In fact, there's not even a close second. Before Jesus, no individual had ever been touted as the Messiah. After Jesus, supporters for any other "Messiah" were few and fading. For example, in the first century, the Jewish historian Josephus actually suggested the Roman emperor Vespasian was the Jewish Messiah.[1] No one bought it! In the second century, a famous rabbi named Akiva promoted a rebel leader named Bar Kokhba as the messianic savior of the nation. However, Bar Kokhba's defeat and death in AD 135 deflated any further messianic claims.[2]

This leaves Jesus as the only individual in the past two thousand years to successfully claim the title of Messiah. With that in mind, let's return to Psalm 2. This psalm has not just one messianic prophecy but three. First, verses 1–2 are cited in the believers' prayer in Acts 4:25–26 as a commentary on Jesus's trials. The very people listed by King David—nations, peoples, kings, and rulers—are interpreted in verse 27 as the players in the drama of Jesus's passion: Gentiles, Jewish people, Herod, and Pilate. While many rabbis would deny that this was the correct interpretation, they could hardly deny that the descriptions fit.

Second, verse 7 of Psalm 2 is paraphrased in all three synoptic gospels (Matthew, Mark, and Luke) at both the baptism (Matthew 3:17; Mark 1:11; Luke

3:22) and the transfiguration (Matthew 17:5; Mark 9:7; Luke 9:35). This holds even more weight, given the fact that God spoke audibly only three times during Jesus's ministry, and twice he paraphrased this verse.

Third, Psalm 2:9 is cited three times in Revelation (2:27; 12:5; 19:15) to describe Jesus's regal rule: "You will break them with a rod of iron; you will dash them to pieces like pottery" (NIV). That's a surprising description of the man we call the Good Shepherd, who said from the cross, "Forgive them, for they know not what they do" (Luke 23:34). The least one can conclude is that the meek and mild Son of Man will return with a vengeance glimpsed only during the cleansing of the temple (John 2:13–17). He is not to be trifled with or taken for granted.

This incredible poem, standing in tandem with Psalm 1, opens the book of liturgy for Israel and the church. Psalm 2 concludes with the same word—*blessed*—that began Psalm 1. These psalms are the twin pillars of authentic worship: right relationships with our fellow people (Psalm 1) and right reverence for our Messiah (Psalm 2). When our community develops habits of godliness and when we honor Jesus as Lord, our prayers, singing, and service will deepen our understanding of God and our connection to him.

Per square inch, there's hardly a passage with more messianic meaning than Psalm 2. That's why we can use this poem as a springboard into the world of messianic prophecy. There are many passages pregnant with messianic promises (such as Psalm 110; 118; Isaiah 53; Daniel 7; Zechariah 11–12).

Other Messianic Predictions

Throughout the Old Testament, there are more than sixty major prophecies concerning the coming Messiah. One might suppose that God had to be that detailed and specific. After all, hope for a Messiah can be clouded by doubt in the daily grind during seasons of suffering. God wants you to have all the evidence you need to give your loyalty to Jesus.

This is especially important when Jesus doesn't meet our expectations, which he seldom does. Even in his own day, he wasn't the Messiah the Jews hoped for. He was not a warrior king who conquered his enemies but a suffering Savior who died for them. Where they hoped for liberation, God granted salvation. They wanted their borders secured, but God wanted their borders abolished so all people could have access to him. When they expected God to send help, he saw fit to send himself. Such an earth-shattering shift would require overwhelming evidence. That's exactly what we have in the Old Testament prophecies. Because they're so specific and because many could not be fulfilled by human effort alone, they're compelling evidence that Jesus is the Messiah.

For example, these seven prophecies tell us this about the Messiah:

1. He would be born in Bethlehem (Micah 5:2).
2. He would be preceded by a forerunner (Malachi 3:1).
3. He would enter Jerusalem riding a donkey (Zechariah 9:9).
4. He would be betrayed by a friend, which would result in his hands being wounded (Zechariah 13:6).
5. He would be sold for thirty pieces of silver, which would be given to a potter (Zechariah 11:12–13).
6. He would stand silent before his oppressors (Isaiah 53:7).
7. He would die by crucifixion (Psalm 22:16).

Some of these predictions are very specific and unexpected. Most would be impossible to manipulate or prearrange (such as where you're to be born). Therefore, their cumulative weight is substantial.

Peter Stoner, in his book, *Science Speaks,* calculated the probability of these passages being fulfilled by one man to be only 1 in 100,000,000,000,000,000—that's one in *one hundred quadrillion*![3]

One hundred quadrillion is an incomprehensibly large number. To put it in perspective, Stoner calculated this number to be equivalent to covering the state of Texas two feet deep in silver dollars. If we painted one of those silver dollars red and asked a blindfolded vagabond to meander across the state and randomly select one of the coins, his odds of picking the red one are the same as the odds of Jesus randomly fulfilling just these seven predictions.[4]

However, Jesus didn't fulfill just seven. There are another fifty major prophecies about Jesus's life and death and dozens of minor references. With each added prophecy, the infinitesimally small probability is reduced exponentially to the point of virtual impossibility. Hence the title of Josh McDowell and Sean McDowell's book, in which they referenced the probability from Stoner: *Evidence That Demands a Verdict*.[5] If we're going to deny that Jesus is the Messiah, we owe ourselves an explanation as to how one man can randomly fulfill so many detailed prophecies.

Perhaps you're a skeptic. Fair enough. So let me be clear: predictive prophecy is but one evidence for Jesus the Messiah. In fact, the earliest witnesses leaned far more heavily on the resurrection of Jesus and the character of his life (two topics for another time). Psalm 2 opens to us a slew of messianic prophecies. Any single prophecy could be explained away, I suppose. But the cumulative effect, the weight of the whole, is a thick foundation on which to stand.

Key Points

- Only Jesus has successfully claimed to be the Messiah.
- Psalm 2 is a particularly influential messianic prophecy because of its three separate predictions cited in the New Testament and because of its introductory position in the book of Psalms.
- Messianic prophecies are compelling evidence for Jesus because they're so specific and because so many are impossible to intentionally fulfill.

This Week

- ☐ **Day 1:** Read the essay.
- ☐ **Day 2:** Memorize Psalm 2:7.
- ☐ **Day 3:** Read Psalm 22; 110; 118
- ☐ **Day 4:** Meditate on Psalm 22:1; 118:22–29; Revelation 19:15.
- ☐ **Day 5:** Take one of the seven predictive prophecies above and share it with a friend as something exciting and incredible you just learned. See what your friend's reaction is.

Overachiever Challenge: Memorize Psalm 22:1.

Bonus Read: John Ankerberg, Walter Kaiser, and John Weldon, *The Case for Jesus the Messiah: Incredible Prophecies That Prove God Exists.*

11

Good Shepherd

The LORD is my shepherd; I shall not want.
He makes me lie down in green pastures.
He leads me beside still waters.
He restores my soul.
—PSALM 23:1–3

Question: If the Lord is my shepherd, what's my obligation to those I lead?

Next to John 3:16, Psalm 23 is likely the most well-known passage of the Bible and is the most common passage at funerals. It has a mystical power to comfort in the midst of life's greatest tragedies—almost as if the words of this poem breathe deeply into a weary breast. It embraces the mourner, welcomes the vagabond, soothes the broken, and casts a ray of hope on the outcast.

"The Lord Is My Shepherd" is David's most famous poem. Whispers of its theme are heard as far back as Abel (Genesis 4:4) and Jacob after him (48:15). It reverberates through the psalms and prophets (Psalm 28:9; 78:52; 79:13; 80:1; 95:7; 107:41; Isaiah 40:11; Jeremiah 31:10; Ezekiel 34:15; Zechariah 9:16). These descriptions of a caring, loving God bring comfort to his people. "He is our God, and we are the people of his pasture, and the sheep of his hand" (Psalm 95:7). "He will tend his flock like a shepherd; he will gather the lambs in his arms" (Isaiah 40:11). Even in the valley of the shadow of death, even under the discipline of his rod, even in the presence of our enemies (Psalm 23:4–5), we sense that God is up to good.

Leaders as Shepherds

When God delegates his authority to kings, priests, and prophets, he expects them to lead like shepherds. For Yahweh, "shepherd" is no mere metaphor; it's the divinely authorized method of exercising authority. The leader's power is for protection. His rod and staff are for guidance. The shepherd sacrifices for the sheep, not the sheep for the shepherd. This is obvious in the life of David, the great shepherd-king who penned this psalm and who came to prominence by slaying a giant with a shepherd's sling (1 Samuel 17:40–49).

It turns out that David's time in the field was his best preparation for the throne. We read,

> [God] chose David his servant
> and took him from the sheepfolds;
> from following the nursing ewes he brought him
> to shepherd Jacob his people,
> Israel his inheritance.
> With upright heart he shepherded them
> and guided them with his skillful hand. (Psalm 78:70–72)

The same could be said of Moses (Exodus 3:1; Psalm 77:20; Isaiah 63:11). It was forty years in the wilderness with Jethro's flocks that prepared Moses for his forty years of leading Israel through the desert. And before Moses there was Abraham (Genesis 13:2–6), who was famed for the size of his flocks.

Because the heroes of Israel's past were literal shepherds, leaders throughout her history were compared to shepherds. This was true for kings, governors, prophets, and priests (1 Kings 22:17; Jeremiah 10:21; 17:16). God gave even the pagan ruler Cyrus, who rescued Israel, the title "my shepherd" (Isaiah 44:28).

Bad Shepherds

The honor afforded metaphorical shepherds (leaders) is interesting, given the fact that the actual occupation was one of the most despised. For example, when the sons of Jacob immigrated to Egypt to survive a famine, Joseph took care to isolate them in Goshen. They needed space to separate them from the nationals, or their occupation would offend their new neighbors. Hear Joseph's counsel to his brothers in Genesis 46:34: "You should answer, 'Your servants have tended livestock from our boyhood on, just as our fathers did.' Then you will be allowed to settle in the region of Goshen, for all shepherds are detestable to the Egyptians" (NIV). Clearly, shepherds were on the lower rungs of the social totem pole.

Because shepherds had to move constantly through others' lands and fields, they had a reputation of being thieves. As an occupational hazard, shepherds were physically dirty. More than that, they were ritually unclean, since they slaughtered animals and delivered lambs. All told, they lived on the edges of communities and the underbelly of society.

Paradoxically, literal shepherds were the dregs of society and spiritual shepherds were the heroes. This treatment of shepherds did create space for a pointed critique of spiritual shepherds gone bad. Those leaders who didn't live up to God's standards got a pretty brusque beating in the Bible. For example, Jeremiah (not known for soft-pedaling his critique) gave us these words from God:

> "Woe to the shepherds who destroy and scatter the sheep of my pasture!" declares the LORD. Therefore thus says the LORD, the God of Israel, concerning the shepherds who care for my people: "You have scattered my flock and have driven them away, and you have not attended to them. Behold, I will attend to you for your evil deeds, declares the LORD." (Jeremiah 23:1–2)

Similar censures are found throughout the prophets (Isaiah 56:11; Jeremiah 10:21; 12:10; 25:34–36; 50:6; Ezekiel 34:1–10; Zechariah 10:3; 11:1–17). The most famous of these is Ezekiel 34. It's a full-throttle frontal assault on the rulers of Israel who had used their influence to fleece the flock rather than feed them:

> You eat the fat, you clothe yourselves with the wool, you slaughter the fat ones, but you do not feed the sheep. The weak you have not strengthened, the sick you have not healed, the injured you have not bound up, the strayed you have not brought back, the lost you have not sought, and with force and harshness you have ruled them. (verses 3–4)

The Lord as Shepherd

The problem of poor leaders was pandemic. For the Jewish people this led to a longing for a new David, a new shepherd-king to care for God's flock. A number of prophets embedded this hope in messianic predictions: "I will set up over them one shepherd, my servant David, and he shall feed them: he shall feed them and be their shepherd" (Ezekiel 34:23).

The implication is clear: God leads like a shepherd. His delegates therefore must follow suit. Since they failed, they were terminated, and another shepherd was promised.

Jesus's status as the promised shepherd-king is clear from his birth in Bethlehem (Micah 5:2–4, cited in Matthew 2:6) to his death in Jerusalem (Zechariah 13:7, cited in Matthew 26:31; Mark 14:27; John 16:32).

Jesus said he would judge sheep and goats (Matthew 25:32). In John 10:1–18, he critiqued the false shepherds in the same vein as the prophets of old did. When Mark wrote that the crowds waiting for Jesus were like "sheep without a shepherd" (6:34), he was alluding to Moses's description of Joshua as a leader who would keep Israel from being like "sheep that have no shepherd" (Numbers 27:17). Joshua was to lead Israel into the promised land. That's exactly the kind of national leadership Mark was attributing to Jesus, especially since Jesus's name, in Hebrew, is "Joshua."

Three New Testament authors referred to Jesus's role as the shepherd: "May the God of peace who brought again from the dead our Lord Jesus, the great shepherd of the sheep, by the blood of the eternal covenant, equip you with everything good that you may do his will" (Hebrews 13:20–21). "You were straying like sheep, but have now returned to the Shepherd and Overseer of your souls" (1 Peter 2:25). "The Lamb in the midst of the throne will be their shepherd, and he will guide them to springs of living water, and God will wipe away every tear from their eyes" (Revelation 7:17).

By the end of the Bible, the shepherd of Psalm 23 has a new name, a new face, and a new mailing address. Jesus is Yahweh incarnate and abided among us to lay down his life for the sheep. That's just what the Good Shepherd does.

In fact, in an extraordinary twist, the Good Shepherd is the lamb of God. His sacrifice at Passover permanently replaced the Jewish system of sacrifice. During the first Passover, a lamb belonged to the Lord as a replacement for the firstborn son. Jesus is our substitute to cover all our sins. He is the perfect Passover sacrifice.

That shift in the New Testament is not a new message. It was earlier embedded in Psalms. Psalm 23, the song of the Shepherd, is preceded by Psalm 22, the song of the Lamb—the clearest description of Calvary outside the Gospels.

Leadership is no longer what you get from the sheep but what you sacrifice for the sheep. Consequently, any Christian leader who picks up the staff also accepts the rod of the suffering servant. Apostles, evangelists, and pastors (Ephesians 4:11), along with elders (Acts 20:28–29; 1 Peter 5:2–3), have the privilege of leading and feeding the sheep if they're willing to lay down their lives for the sheep. Paul outlined the specific qualifications for elders in 1 Timothy 3:1–7 using the synonymous title *overseer.* Mark his words: "Here is a trustworthy saying: Whoever aspires to be an overseer desires a noble task" (1 Timothy 3:1, NIV).

Noble indeed. Just as Jesus represents God, so we as leaders represent kings and priests of the past. Either we'll wear the title of leader well, with humility and sacrifice, or we'll repeat the mistakes of past kings and priests and suffer similar consequences. Shepherding is noble only when we suffer. This is a theological twist that's incomprehensible to those who don't know the Good Shepherd—our God who suffered on our behalf.

Key Points

- "Shepherd" is the primary metaphor for God as our leader. His example was to be followed by any who ruled or rules on his behalf.
- Leaders' rampant disregard for the sheep led to a longing for a better shepherd, the promised Messiah.
- Church leaders—apostles, evangelists, pastors, elders—take up the mantle of shepherds.

This Week

☐ **Day 1:** Read the essay.

☐ **Day 2:** Memorize Psalm 23:1–3.

☐ **Day 3:** Read John 10.

☐ **Day 4:** Meditate on Ezekiel 34:3–4; 1 Timothy 3:1; 1 Peter 2:25.

☐ **Day 5:** Identify two practices of shepherding you could implement in one of these areas: (1) raising your kids, (2) leading a team at work, (3) leading a volunteer team at church, and (4) coaching a kids' sports team.

Overachiever Challenge: Memorize 1 Timothy 3:1.

Bonus Read: W. Phillip Keller, *A Shepherd Looks at Psalm 23.*

12

Messiah

The LORD says to my Lord:
"Sit at my right hand,
until I make your enemies your footstool."
—PSALM 110:1

Question: Is there proof that Jesus is the Messiah promised by God?

Psalm 110 is quoted more in the New Testament than any other passage. The first time is by Jesus himself, in Matthew 22:44. It came after a full day of debates when Jesus's opponents sent experts to trap Jesus with questions. He answered each one, then asked a question of his own: "What do you think about the Christ? Whose son is he?" (verse 42).

Who Is the Messiah?

The word *Christ* is a Greek translation of the Hebrew word *Messiah.* These are foreign terms, so let's make sure we understand them.

First, *Christ* is not Jesus's last name. It's his title, meaning "anointed one," and is roughly equivalent to the term *king.* Second, *anointed one* in the Old

Testament always referenced an earthly ruler, not a divine figure. Is Jesus divine? Yes. But that's not the point of the title *Christ* or *Messiah.* Third, the coming Messiah was not a common conversation in Jesus's day. Of the eight hundred documents found in Qumran—the Dead Sea Scrolls—only about a dozen mention the Messiah.[1]

The Old Testament has dozens of messianic predictions, including Deuteronomy 18:15–18; 2 Samuel 7:12; Psalm 2; 22; 118:22; Isaiah 9:1–7; 53; 61:1–2; Daniel 7:13–14; Micah 5:2; Zechariah 9:9; 12:10. Many of these verses are part of the Core 52.

So when Jesus burst on the scene, the Jews of his day already had an idea of what the Messiah would look like, gleaned from their sacred texts. For instance, "He shall strike the earth with the rod of his mouth" (Isaiah 11:4). Some of these texts were in the Bible; some were in the local libraries; all were considered authoritative. Specifically, they anticipated a violent warrior who would destroy their enemies.

Here are a few snippets from their texts: "The Gentiles will be destroyed before the Messiah."[2] "First he will bring them alive before his judgment seat, and when he has reproved them, then he will destroy them."[3] "The last leader of that time will be left alive, when the multitude of his hosts will be put to the sword, and he will be bound, and they will take him up to Mount Zion, and My Messiah will convict him of all his impieties."[4]

This regal warrior and Davidic destroyer was the dominant messianic portrait of Jesus's day. Psalm 110 leans in that direction:

> The Lord sends forth from Zion
>   your mighty scepter.
>   Rule in the midst of your enemies! . . .
>
> The Lord is at your right hand;
>   he will shatter kings on the day of his wrath.
> He will execute judgment among the nations,

filling them with corpses;
he will shatter chiefs
over the wide earth. (verses 2, 5–6)

When Jesus claimed the title without meeting their expectations, heads turned and tempers flared.

Jesus's Use of Psalm 110

Jesus was in the temple in Jerusalem on the Tuesday before he died. His opponents stood in stunned silence as this peasant carpenter stymied their greatest theological minds (Matthew 21:23–22:40). Then it was Jesus's turn to ask them a question, referencing Psalm 110. It should have been easy enough to answer: Who is the Christ? Surely the national religious leaders could explain their position. After all, Psalm 110 was a famous passage.

At this point, it gets a bit complex for those outside Jewish culture. Two points of clarification will help. First, when reading, "The LORD says to my Lord" (verse 1), you might notice in the English translation that the first "LORD" is in all caps. Why? Because it's a different Hebrew word. The Hebrew literally says, "Yahweh (LORD) said to my *Adonai* (Lord)." Clearly *Yahweh* is a reference to God. *Adonai,* however, could refer to either God or a human dignitary. So which is it? Is Jesus claiming to be divine or just the human descendant of David?

This question makes the second point of clarification critically important. In Jewish culture, the father was always greater than the son. So if the Messiah (or Christ) was a descendant of David—who is greater? Even though the forefather was always greater, that's not what David wrote. He said the Messiah was *his* Lord. How is that possible?

That was Jesus's question: "If then David calls him Lord, how is he his son?" (Matthew 22:45). His hearers had no answer: "No one was able to answer him a word, nor from that day did anyone dare to ask him any more questions" (verse

46). They were not only tongue-tied; they were hog-tied (an awkward predicament for a rabbi).

The problem, of course, is that they had no category for incarnation. If God can't become flesh, David's statement is nonsense. Once we admit, however, that God became flesh, the entire poem comes into focus. There are two particular statements that make sense only in the context of incarnation.

The first: "Sit at my right hand" (Psalm 110:1). God's right hand is a position of divine power (Mark 16:19; Matthew 26:64; Acts 7:55). If Jesus is not divine, he could not be placed at God's right hand, where he *always* is after the Ascension: "The Lord Jesus, after he had spoken to them, was taken up into heaven and sat down at the right hand of God" (Mark 16:19; see also Luke 22:69; Acts 5:31; 7:55; Romans 8:34; Hebrews 1:3).

The second statement of Psalm 110 that suggests deity is this: "You are a priest forever after the order of Melchizedek" (verse 4). This strange mention of a mysterious figure harks back to the story of Abraham. He honored Melchizedek, the king of Salem, with a tenth of the spoils of war (Genesis 14:17–20). Melchizedek in Judaism—like Santa Claus in the West—had a real history, but his legend is greater by far. This king of a Canaanite city was somehow also a priest of the Most High God. What's striking is that king and priest were separate vocations in Judaism. The Davidic kings and the Aaronic priests ran on two different tracks. Hence, if a Jewish king were to also be a priest, his qualifications for priesthood would have to come from a completely separate lineage. Enter Melchizedek. Because he had no recorded genealogy, Melchizedek foreshadowed the Messiah.

One of the scrolls of Qumran (11Q13) claims as much: Melchizedek will carry out the vengeance of Go[d's] judgments.[5] In Judaism, Melchizedek is clearly a metaphor for the Messiah. Christianity inherited that idea. The book of Hebrews was written about the time the Qumran scrolls were hidden. In Hebrews 7 we read,

> This Melchizedek, king of Salem, priest of the Most High God, met
> Abraham returning from the slaughter of the kings and blessed him,

> and to him Abraham apportioned a tenth part of everything. He is first, by translation of his name, king of righteousness, and then he is also king of Salem, that is, king of peace. He is without father or mother or genealogy, having neither beginning of days nor end of life, but resembling the Son of God he continues a priest forever. (verses 1–3)

Only Jesus has ever fulfilled Psalm 110. He's a human descendant of David who was anointed as both king in the royal lineage and high priest in the lineage of Melchizedek. Jesus made this claim himself, and Peter repeated it on the Day of Pentecost near the very spot where Jesus had earlier recited the verse: "David did not ascend into the heavens, but he himself says, 'The Lord said to my Lord, "Sit at my right hand, until I make your enemies your footstool"'" (Acts 2:34–35). It was so effective that the crowd asked what they could do to be saved (verse 37). Consequently, three thousand repented and were baptized right after hearing this quote (verse 41).

Paul followed suit. Three times he alluded to Psalm 110, asserting that Jesus is at the right hand of God (Romans 8:34; Ephesians 1:20; Colossians 3:1). The author of Hebrews concurred, placing Jesus on God's right hand as coregent (Hebrews 1:3; 8:1; 10:12; 12:2). So the unanimous voice in the New Testament is that Jesus fulfilled the prophecy of Psalm 110. No other individual fits the description. Jesus alone can claim to be God's son and David's *Adonai*.

Is it any wonder that Peter recognized Jesus as the Messiah? No one else in history had claimed this title. Yet when Jesus asked, "Who do you say that I am?," Peter replied, "You are the Christ, the Son of the living God" (Matthew 16:15–16). This was a watershed moment. Jesus marked the momentous occasion with these immortal words: "Blessed are you, Simon Bar-Jonah! For flesh and blood has not revealed this to you, but my Father who is in heaven. And I tell you, you are Peter, and on this rock I will build my church, and the gates of hell shall not prevail against it" (verses 17–18).

The question "Who is Jesus?" is the single most important question one will ever answer.

Key Points

- The Messiah (or Christ) was an earthly king whom few talked about until Jesus.
- Only the incarnation of Jesus solves the interpretive problems of Psalm 110.
- No other individual in history fits the description of Psalm 110.

This Week

- ☐ **Day 1:** Read the essay.
- ☐ **Day 2:** Memorize Psalm 110:1.
- ☐ **Day 3:** Read John 5–6.
- ☐ **Day 4:** Meditate on Matthew 16:16–18; 22:41–46; Acts 2:34–35.
- ☐ **Day 5:** Pray through Psalm 110 using the words of the passage to shape your acclamation of Jesus.

Overachiever Challenge: Memorize Matthew 16:16–18.

Bonus Read: Donald Guthrie, *Jesus the Messiah: An Illustrated Life of Christ.*

13

Jesus Rejected

The stone that the builders rejected
has become the cornerstone.
—Psalm 118:22

Question: If Jesus was rejected by his own people, why should I accept him?

The simple sentence we see in Psalm 118:22 created quite a splash when Jesus quoted it during his final debate in the temple (Mark 12:10). Peter quoted it in his first defense before the Sanhedrin (Acts 4:11) and later embedded it in his first letter (1 Peter 2:7). Paul referenced it in Ephesians 2:20, describing the foundation of the church. That's quite a superstructure built on this cornerstone passage.

The Parable

Jesus told a story on the Tuesday of the last week before his death. It's an agricultural parable about a vineyard (Matthew 21:33–44). (Vineyards in the Bible were sometimes metaphors for the nation of Israel; see Isaiah 5:1–7.) The basic plot is simple. A rich man invested in a vineyard that he leased to tenants. When harvesttime came, they refused to pay the owner his due. In fact, they murdered the servants sent to collect the fruit.

After two unsuccessful (and MIA) delegations, the master sent his own son. He was certain the tenants would show him the respect he deserved. The wicked tenants, however, assassinated the son. They thought his death would ensure their own inheritance of the vineyard.

It's the kind of story that boils your blood. At the end of it, Jesus asked a follow-up question: "When therefore the owner of the vineyard comes, what will he do to those tenants?" (verse 40). The chief priests and Pharisees knew all too well how God would respond to mutiny. They answered, "He will put those wretches to a miserable death" (verse 41). As the words spilled from their lips, they realized what Jesus was doing. He allowed them to convict themselves with their own words. They were furious (verses 45–46).

Though most parables are pretty cryptic, this one was clear as crystal. God is the owner. The servants are the prophets of old. The assassinated son is Jesus himself. This story publicly exposed the Sanhedrin's plot to murder Jesus. He allowed their own words to reveal their hidden intent. That's the parable. Jesus concluded it with a quote that converts the story from fiction to biography: "The stone that the builders rejected has become the cornerstone" (verse 42; quoting Psalm 118:22). This single sentence, plucked from the prophetic psalm, describes the plan of God. Jesus's execution by the leaders of Israel would result in the nation's salvation. The divine irony is thick.

The Psalm

Psalm 118 was not foreign soil for the scribes. They wrote about it in what they called the Targum—what we would call a paraphrase of the Bible. It records a curious variation that apparently predates Jesus: "The *boy* the builders rejected; he was among the *sons of Jesse* and he was privileged to be appointed as king and ruler."[1] Why on earth would they change "stone" to "son"? Well, these two words in Hebrew are almost identical. "Son" is *ben;* "stone" is *eben.* A simple sound at the beginning of the word turns the boy into a stone. In other words, the Targum makes a play on words that helps interpret the verse. God's foundation stone turned out to be a person, not a rock.

Well, that makes sense. God's kingdom is built on people, not property. Furthermore, the person on whom the nation would stand was to be King David's descendant or, as the Targum phrases it, "among the sons of Jesse."

Therefore, long before Jesus, the rabbis understood that the prophesied Messiah would be rejected in his day. God would, however, reverse the rejection by using it to establish his son in the most important role in the nation. If you were a chief priest in Jesus's audience, this parable would be a gut punch that left you breathless. Not only did Jesus expose their plot, but he also argued from Scripture that this plot was proof he was the Messiah. They planned his death to prove he was *not* the Messiah. Jesus used Scripture to show how his death would prove he *was* the Messiah. This must have been maddening to the Sanhedrin. They just couldn't win with this guy.

Jesus said, "I tell you, the kingdom of God will be taken away from you and given to a people producing its fruits. And the one who falls on this stone will be broken to pieces; and when it falls on anyone, it will crush him" (Matthew 21:43–44). The brilliance of Jesus is evident. He took their attempt to discredit him and turned it into evidence in his favor.

The response of the Sanhedrin is predictable: "When the chief priests and the Pharisees heard his parables, they perceived that he was speaking about them. And although they were seeking to arrest him, they feared the crowds, because they held him to be a prophet" (verses 45–46).

The Apostles and the Psalm

Fast-forward from Jesus's death. A month and a half later, we land in Acts 3–4. Peter and John healed a lame man (3:1–8). He was a simple beggar at the temple gate who became a major witness to the power of the Resurrection. As a result, all three—Peter, John, and the healed beggar—were arrested (4:3).

After staying in jail overnight, Peter and John—these uneducated fishermen—found themselves nose to nose with the religious elite. When asked to defend their actions, Peter replied,

> If we are being examined today concerning a good deed done to a crippled man, by what means this man has been healed, let it be known to all of you and to all the people of Israel that by the name of Jesus Christ of Nazareth, whom you crucified, whom God raised from the dead—by him this man is standing before you well. (verses 9–10)

Peter then followed closely in Jesus's footsteps by citing Psalm 118:22: "This Jesus is the stone that was rejected by you, the builders, which has become the cornerstone" (verse 11). If you were Peter—outgunned and outnumbered—wouldn't *you* mimic Jesus by quoting the very passage he'd used to silence his opponents? It worked! Game, set, match. Although this is hardly a model of how to win friends and influence people. Insulting the judge when you're on trial may not be your best play. Even so, Peter wasn't trying to convince the judge; he was winning the crowd. Jesus's rejection back then is not a reason for anyone to reject him now. The prophetic psalm points out that God saw this coming.

This also explains Paul's use of the psalm. In his letter to the Ephesians, he argued for the unity of all ethnic groups based on the power of Jesus's death and resurrection:

> Through him we both have access in one Spirit to the Father. So then you are no longer strangers and aliens, but you are fellow citizens with the saints and members of the household of God, built on the foundation of the apostles and prophets, *Christ Jesus himself being the cornerstone.* (2:18–20)

Jesus's denigration led to his exaltation. His humiliation resulted in his being uplifted. This is a universal biblical principle: humiliation precedes exaltation. When people humble themselves, God lifts them up (James 4:10). Hence, Gentiles—who'd been humbled—now have a place in the kingdom.

Throughout the Bible, humiliation and exaltation go hand in hand. Just as Jesus's life ended with humiliation as a precursor to exaltation, in his birth we see both humiliation and exaltation. He was born in a humble town to peasant parents and laid in a feeding trough. Yet his conception was through the Holy Spirit. In other words, the humblest birth was predicated on the most divine procreation.

Isaiah predicted as much: "The Lord himself will give you a sign. Behold, the virgin shall conceive and bear a son, and shall call his name Immanuel" (7:14). Look carefully: this special sign is named *Immanuel,* meaning "God with us." The God of the universe robed himself in human flesh. His divinity was shrouded by humanity.

Some believe that this "virgin" in Isaiah was actually a maiden who procreated through the normal human process as a sign in Isaiah's day. The Hebrew word translated "virgin" does mean "unseen" but not necessarily "untouched." However, this prophecy may have had a double fulfillment—one in Isaiah's day and one in Jesus's birth. The second and more important fulfillment brought the Messiah into the world. The New Testament word *parthenos* (Matthew 1:23; Luke 1:31) clearly means "virgin" and not merely "maiden."

This was a unique concept up to that point. It was a startling claim unparalleled in Greco-Roman history. Although the virgin birth wasn't a *necessary* claim (both Mark and John wrote their gospels without including it), it was a compelling claim made by an eyewitness who walked the same streets as Jesus (Matthew) and by a physician (Luke) who knew well the natural processes of procreation. Their testimony is compelling evidence for the divine nature of Jesus despite the humblest circumstances of his birth.

The point is this: God chose to appear as a baby. His humiliation preceded his exaltation. The virgin birth was a reminder that this was no ordinary child and no ordinary promise. Jesus, the son of Mary, is actually the son of God. He paved the way for us to walk. It's the way of humiliation, leading ultimately to exaltation. Just when his enemies thought they'd rid themselves of Jesus, come to find out, the humiliation they caused was essential to establishing him as king of kings.

So, too, with you. As followers of Christ, our path to exaltation is the same rugged road of trials and tears. It's paved with humiliation ordained by God and essential to our exaltation and establishment as keystones in the temple of God—his church.

Key Points

- Jesus's parable of the vineyard is actually Israel's history and a picture of his establishment as king.
- Some rabbis contemporary with Jesus interpreted this stone as the offspring of King David.
- The biblical principle of humiliation as a precursor to exaltation is played out in Jesus's death.

This Week

- ☐ **Day 1:** Read the essay.
- ☐ **Day 2:** Memorize Psalm 118:22.
- ☐ **Day 3:** Read Acts 3–5.
- ☐ **Day 4:** Meditate on Isaiah 7:14; Matthew 21:33–46; Acts 4:11.
- ☐ **Day 5:** Practice one act of deliberate humiliation. See whether those affected treat you with less or more honor.

Overachiever Challenge: Memorize Isaiah 7:14.

Bonus Read: J. Gresham Machen, *The Virgin Birth of Christ.*

14

Wisdom

> The fear of the LORD is the beginning of knowledge;
> fools despise wisdom and instruction.
> —PROVERBS 1:7

Question: How do I become wise?

Proverbs 1:7 is the theme of the entire book. This theme is repeated two more times using almost identical wording: "The fear of the LORD is the beginning of wisdom" (Proverbs 9:10), and "The fear of the LORD is instruction in wisdom, and humility comes before honor" (Proverbs 15:33).

There are two words in this famous statement that beg for an explanation: *fear* and *wisdom*. Common sense seems to suggest that fear is a bad thing while wisdom is a good thing. But there they sit right next to each other. What if it turns out that fear is the very thing we need to gain good wisdom?

If we were to ask people to fill in the blank in "The ____ of the Lord is the beginning of wisdom"—the word *fear* wouldn't likely be people's first choice. Perhaps they would say "The love of the Lord" or "The knowledge of the Lord" or "Obedience to the Lord." As it turns out, *fear, knowledge, love,* and *obedience* are all synonymous in this context. How? Let's begin our investigation by clarifying what the Bible means by *wisdom*.

Wisdom in the Bible

Often the word *wisdom* conjures up images of Yoda or some guru sitting cross-legged and pondering the mysteries of the universe. For the Jews of the Bible, wisdom was more bolted to everyday experience. Wisdom in the Bible is the ability to practically live out God's truths in a way that brings health to you, your family, and your community. It's the skills that a builder needs to construct a house, a general needs to win a war, and a father needs to raise his children.

Here's an example of how the rabbis thought about wisdom: "Keep them and do them, for that will be your wisdom and your understanding in the sight of the peoples, who, when they hear all these statutes, will say, 'Surely this great nation is a wise and understanding people'" (Deuteronomy 4:6). When other nations observed Jewish families, communities, businesses, and ethics, they were drawn to Yahweh. His "rules" worked to make life better.

Jesus stood squarely in that tradition of wisdom in action. Responding to his critics, he said, "The Son of Man came eating and drinking, and they say, 'Look at him! A glutton and a drunkard, a friend of tax collectors and sinners!' *Yet wisdom is justified by her deeds*" (Matthew 11:19).

Biblical wisdom always manifests itself in action. Joshua's wisdom empowered him to lead the people of Israel (Deuteronomy 34:9). Ezra's wisdom enabled him to administrate a community (Ezra 7:25). By wisdom, Daniel lived ethically in exile among enemies (Daniel 1:4).

Of course, the most famous sage was Solomon. When he succeeded his father, David, God offered him a blank check in prayer: "Ask what I shall give you" (2 Chronicles 1:7). Here's what Solomon requested: "Give me now wisdom and knowledge to go out and come in before this people, for who can govern this people of yours, which is so great?" (verse 10). God's answer was a resounding yes: "God gave Solomon wisdom and understanding beyond measure, and breadth of mind like the sand on the seashore" (1 Kings 4:29).

Such precious wisdom is portrayed as a woman:

> Get wisdom; get insight;
>
> do not forget, and do not turn away from the words of my mouth.
>
> Do not forsake her, and she will keep you;
>
> love her, and she will guard you.
>
> The beginning of wisdom is this: Get wisdom,
>
> and whatever you get, get insight.
>
> Prize her highly, and she will exalt you;
>
> she will honor you if you embrace her. (Proverbs 4:5–8)

Because true wisdom comes from God, the Scriptures portray wisdom not just as a woman but as the actual Spirit of God. Wisdom is a gift of the Spirit himself. It's not an inanimate attribute but the living, breathing Spirit with whom we live. Wisdom is when the Spirit of God animates and engages a person for God's good (Deuteronomy 34:9; Isaiah 11:2; Acts 6:3, 10; 1 Corinthians 2:13; Ephesians 1:17; Colossians 1:9).

Take Solomon as an example. When he asked for wisdom, God gave himself in the abiding presence of the Spirit to help Solomon lead on God's behalf.

Was Solomon the wisest man who ever lived? Or would that be Jesus?

In one sense the title fits both of them. However, if we parse it out theologically, Solomon was the wisest man, while Jesus is wisdom itself. While Solomon had wisdom because the Spirit was with him, Jesus *is* wisdom because he shares the same essence as the Spirit. This is why Paul could say that "Christ [is] the power of God and the wisdom of God" (1 Corinthians 1:24) and that in Jesus "are hidden all the treasures of wisdom and knowledge" (Colossians 2:3).

Let's press "pause" here and turn to *fear,* the other key word of Proverbs 1:7.

Fear of the Lord

If God is love, why in the world would we fear him? Doesn't the Bible say that "perfect love casts out fear" (1 John 4:18)?

No Christian should fear punishment, since Christ paid our debt. Nor should we fear failure, since we're empowered by the Holy Spirit. However, fear and love are not opposites. The most obvious example is that we can both fear and adore an earthly father. Remember when you were a kid and your father threw you to the moon? The very strength that launched you into the air also comforted you in the dark.

So it is with our Father in heaven: "As a father shows compassion to his children, so the LORD shows compassion to those who fear him" (Psalm 103:13). *Fear* and *love* are frequently lodged in the same verse: "Behold, the eye of the LORD is on those who fear him, on those who hope in his steadfast love" (Psalm 33:18). "As high as the heavens are above the earth, so great is his steadfast love toward those who fear him" (Psalm 103:11). You can fear someone out of respect for his power without cringing before him because of his capacity for wrath. Yet it requires a right relationship.

The crucial question is not whether fear and other emotions can hold hands. The crucial question is what I should do when I fear someone. That answer is easy: I obey that person. This combination is captured in a single statement: "Now, Israel, what does the LORD your God require of you, but to *fear* the LORD your God, to *walk* in all his ways, to *love* him, to *serve* the LORD your God with all your heart and with all your soul?" (Deuteronomy 10:12). If you both fear and love someone, then honoring that person in obedience is your instinctive response.

This was Solomon's summary of his final book: "The end of the matter; all has been heard. Fear God and keep his commandments, for this is the whole duty of man" (Ecclesiastes 12:13).

If wisdom is the capacity to live life well, its apex is the ability to obey God's commands: "Behold, the fear of the Lord, that is wisdom, and to turn away from evil is understanding" (Job 28:28). "The fear of the LORD is the beginning of wisdom; all who follow his precepts have good understanding" (Psalm 111:10, NIV). This was so central to the Hebrew worldview that fear of God became the hallmark of the faithful Israelite (Acts 13:16, 26; 2 Corinthians 5:11). Conversely, not fearing God was the mark of an unrighteous person (Psalm 36:1, cited in Romans 3:18).

Fear of God is not just what we do; it defines who we are.

The Advantage of Fearing God

"Fear God" isn't the most popular command of the Bible. Yet fearing God offers a number of great gains.

"The *friendship* of the LORD is for those who fear him" (Psalm 25:14). The Hebrew word here for "friendship" could be translated "secret counsel." When you fear him, he lets you into his inner circle.

Fearing God makes you *fearless.* The Bible includes hundreds of verses about fear. One of the golden threads of this theme is that God's people are told to fear only two things: God and nothing. "You shall not fear them, for it is the LORD your God who fights for you" (Deuteronomy 3:22). Again and again we're encouraged to be fearless. Why? Because once you fear God, there's nothing left to fear.

Along with the fear of the Father comes the *comfort* of the Spirit: "The church throughout all Judea and Galilee and Samaria had peace and was being built up. And walking in the *fear* of the Lord and in the *comfort* of the Holy Spirit, it multiplied" (Acts 9:31).

Fear fosters *holiness:* "Since we have these promises, beloved, let us cleanse ourselves from every defilement of body and spirit, bringing holiness to completion in the fear of God" (2 Corinthians 7:1). And fear fosters *health:* "The fear of the LORD prolongs life, but the years of the wicked will be short" (Proverbs 10:27). And again, "The fear of the LORD is a fountain of life, that one may turn away from the snares of death" (Proverbs 14:27).

Finally, fear of God and *praise for God* go hand in hand (Psalm 22:23, 25; 40:3; Revelation 19:5). Fear turns to reverence; and reverence, to awe; and awe, to adoration. Our praise rises to its heights not merely by love but by honor rightly rooted in fear of God's power, majesty, and omnipotence.

The angel of the LORD encamps
around those who fear him, and delivers them.

Oh, taste and see that the LORD is good!
Blessed is the man who takes refuge in him!
Oh, fear the LORD, you his saints,
for those who fear him have no lack! (Psalm 34:7–9)

Key Points

- Wisdom is the practical ability to succeed at life.
- Fear of the Lord is like respect for fathers—it is not antithetical to love.
- Fear of the Lord is demonstrated by obedience to his commands.

This Week

☐ **Day 1:** Read the essay.

☐ **Day 2:** Memorize Proverbs 1:7.

☐ **Day 3:** Read 1 Kings 3; 10–11.

☐ **Day 4:** Meditate on Deuteronomy 10:12; Ecclesiastes 12:13; James 1:5.

☐ **Day 5:** Pray for wisdom where needed: "If any of you lacks wisdom, let him ask God, who gives generously to all without reproach, and it will be given him" (James 1:5).

Overachiever Challenge: Memorize James 1:5.

Bonus Read: Mark DeMoss, *The Little Red Book of Wisdom.*

15

Atonement

He was pierced for our transgressions;
he was crushed for our iniquities;
upon him was the chastisement that brought us peace,
and with his wounds we are healed.
—Isaiah 53:5

Question: How does Jesus's death cover my sin?

"Jesus died for me." That's common coin in Christian circles—in songs, sermons, and conversations. What does it actually mean?

The big theological term is *atonement.* You'll run across that now and again in Scripture and sermons. Over half of its uses in the Bible are in a single book—Leviticus—where it describes the role of a sacrifice to cover the sins of the people. Atonement basically means that you owed a debt and somebody else paid it for you.

According to Scripture, sin carries a penalty of death: "The life of a creature is in the blood, and I have given it to you to make atonement for yourselves on the altar" (Leviticus 17:11, NIV). To recover our relationship with God, there needs to be a blood sacrifice. Perhaps that seems barbaric or archaic. However, I'm not sure our earthly evaluation holds much weight, particularly when we're the ones who broke covenant. We're the ones who marred the good creation. We're the ones poisoned by our own pride and Satan's seductions.

Perhaps our response to this biblical truth should be submission more than critique. In light of that, there are three ideas embedded in Isaiah 53 that will help us better understand this grand theme of atonement in the Bible.

Great Surprise of Isaiah 53 for Modern America

Atonement is corporate, not just individual. The sin of Israel wasn't merely a personal problem. Their sin was a national crisis that led to their exile.

Whether we realize it or not, our own nation is experiencing unprecedented levels of moral bankruptcy. It's not just me who's in need of a Savior; it's "we the people." Our communities, our churches, and our nation could use a good bit of saving.

Isaiah 53 is one of four poetic portions of the book of Isaiah that have been labeled as "suffering servant" songs (42:1–9; 49:1–13; 50:4–11; 52:13–53:12). This chapter describes how the servant suffers on behalf of the nation and brings healing to God's people. Some have identified the suffering servant as the entire nation of Israel—God's people suffering for his cause. The problem with this is that the very ones suffering are those who need a Savior. Since the nation itself was the problem, the nation can hardly be expected to save itself.

In Acts 8 we come across an Ethiopian eunuch on his way home from the temple in Jerusalem. He happened to be reading Isaiah 53 just as he encountered a Christian named Philip, and he asked Philip to explain the passage: "About whom, I ask you, does the prophet say this, about himself or about someone else?" (Acts 8:34). Philip, of course, took the opportunity to proclaim Jesus as the suffering servant.

Moses prefigured Jesus, the suffering servant, when he asked that his own life be blotted out for the sake of the nation (Exodus 32:32):

> *"Because he poured out his soul unto death"*—because he surrendered himself to die, as it is said, *And if not, blot me, I pray thee* etc. "And was numbered with the transgressors"—because he was numbered with them who were condemned to die in the wilderness. "Yet he bare the sins of many"—because he secured atonement for the making of the Golden Calf.[1]

It was clear back then and should be today: we need a Savior. What wasn't clear was that such a Savior would suffer on behalf of his people rather than cause suffering for his enemies.

Enter Jesus. He was a very different kind of Savior. His salvation wasn't merely personal; it was national. He was rescuing not an individual but an entire nation.

Great Surprise of Isaiah 53 for Ancient Israel

This idea that the Savior would suffer turned the normal Jewish perspective on its head. In Judaism, the wicked were supposed to be sacrificed—"a ransom for the righteous" (Proverbs 21:18; see also Isaiah 43:3, 14). The Messiah was to save Israel with power, not suffering. He was to dish out the pain, not absorb it himself. The expectation was that he would conquer Israel's enemies, not lay down his own life.[2]

While Israel expected a king and got a sacrifice, American Christians expect a sacrifice and get a king. Power and sacrifice are not antithetical, as long as a resurrection stands between them.

What Israel had to learn was that their Messiah was a suffering servant. What we must remember is that our Savior is our king.

Great Fulfillment of Isaiah 53 in Jesus

This servant song (Isaiah 52:13–53:12) is full of predictions about Jesus's life and ministry.

- "His appearance was so marred, beyond human semblance" (52:14)—this fits the description of his brutal beatings.
- "He had no form or majesty that we should look at him" (53:2)—this was true of a peasant carpenter.
- "He was despised and rejected by men" (verse 3)—this was true during his execution.
- "He has borne our griefs and carried our sorrows . . . he was pierced for our transgressions . . . with his wounds we are healed . . . the LORD has laid on him the iniquity of us all. . . . like a lamb that is led to the slaughter. . . . stricken for the transgression of my people" (verses 4–8)—these are descriptions of the cross.
- "They made his grave with the wicked and with a rich man in his death" (verse 9)—this is a poetic juxtaposition of the criminals being crucified beside Jesus and of the tomb of Joseph of Arimathea in which Jesus was buried.
- "When his soul makes an offering for guilt, he shall see his offspring; he shall prolong his days; the will of the LORD shall prosper in his hand" (verse 10)—these statements predict the resurrection of Jesus.
- "By his knowledge shall the righteous one, my servant, make many to be accounted righteous, and he shall bear their iniquities" (verse 11)—this describes Jesus's substitutionary atonement.

Given all this obvious overlap, it's stunning that the New Testament authors didn't make more of Isaiah 53. Nonetheless, what's stated is clear enough. Jesus himself quoted verse 12 in Luke 22:37: "I tell you that this Scripture must be fulfilled in me: 'And he was numbered with the transgressors.'" Significantly, Jesus introduced the quote as a fulfillment of prophecy, and he concluded it in the same way: "Yes, what is written about me is reaching its fulfillment" (NIV). The quote is framed with the gravitas of fulfilled prophecy.

Jesus saw himself as the suffering servant of Isaiah 53. In fact, he spelled that out in Mark 10:45 as his vocational purpose, connecting both national leadership and personal sacrifice: "Even the Son of Man came not to be served but to serve, and to give his life as a ransom for many." This echoes Isaiah 53:11: "Out of the anguish of his soul he shall see and be satisfied; by his knowledge shall the righteous one, my servant, make many to be accounted righteous, and he shall bear their iniquities."

Mark 10:45 is no outlier. Every New Testament author (except James and Jude) describes the substitutionary effect of Jesus's death (Matthew 20:28; John 11:49–52; Acts 20:28; Romans 3:23–25; 2 Corinthians 5:14–15; Galatians 3:13–14; 1 Timothy 2:5–6; Titus 2:14; Hebrews 9:22, 28; 1 Peter 1:18–19; 1 John 2:2; Revelation 5:9).

In each of the Gospels, Jesus spoke of his death as beneficial for others (Matthew 20:28; Mark 10:45; Luke 22:19–20; John 12:24, 32). Three prominent New Testament authors are particularly clear about Jesus's victory through suffering.

The apostle Paul famously wrote, "The wages of sin is death, but the free gift of God is eternal life in Christ Jesus our Lord" (Romans 6:23). And,

> The love of Christ controls us, because we have concluded this: that one has died for all, therefore all have died; and he died for all, that those who live might no longer live for themselves but for him who for their sake died and was raised. (2 Corinthians 5:14–15)

The apostle Peter wrote of how Christians "were ransomed from the futile ways inherited from your forefathers, not with perishable things such as silver or gold, but with the precious blood of Christ, like that of a lamb without blemish or spot" (1 Peter 1:18–19).

Finally, the apostle John spoke of Christ as "the propitiation for our sins, and not for ours only but also for the sins of the whole world" (1 John 2:2).

There's a clear and unified voice in the New Testament: through Jesus's suffering and death, the penalty of our sin was paid. We can therefore live in freedom from sin.

Key Points

- Atonement is a necessary sacrifice of blood for our sins.
- Jesus sacrificed his life to save a nation, not merely individuals.
- Sacrifice and victory are not antithetical; sacrifice is the means to victory.

This Week

☐ **Day 1:** Read the essay.

☐ **Day 2:** Memorize Isaiah 53:5.

☐ **Day 3:** Read Exodus 7:14–11:10.

☐ **Day 4:** Meditate on Leviticus 17:11; Romans 6:23; 1 Peter 1:18–19.

☐ **Day 5:** Mark Isaiah 53 in your Bible to read the next time you take communion.

Overachiever Challenge: Memorize Romans 6:23.

Bonus Read: Leon Morris, *The Atonement: Its Meaning and Significance.*

16

New Covenant

This is the covenant that I will make with the house of Israel after those days, declares the LORD: I will put my law within them, and I will write it on their hearts. And I will be their God, and they shall be my people. And no longer shall each one teach his neighbor and each his brother, saying, 'Know the LORD,' for they shall all know me, from the least of them to the greatest, declares the LORD. For I will forgive their iniquity, and I will remember their sin no more.

—JEREMIAH 31:33–34

Question: What advantages do Christians have under the new covenant?

Jeremiah was known as the weeping prophet—and for good reason. First, he constantly suffered for saying what God told him to say. He was beaten, mocked, arrested, and threatened. In one of the most memorable events of his book, Jeremiah was punished for preaching by being dropped into an empty cistern (Jeremiah 38:6).

Another reason for Jeremiah's tears was how deeply he grieved over the fate of his homeland. For decades he predicted the destruction of Jerusalem. With his own eyes he saw it fall to Nebuchadnezzar in 586 BC. It was unparalleled destruction that left her citizens devastated and the temple in ruins.

Many Bible scholars have noted the strong similarities between Jeremiah and Jesus (who also wept over the city of Jerusalem in Matthew 23:37–39). Even during Jesus's day, people compared him to Jeremiah (Matthew 16:14). As he cleansed the temple, Jesus also cited Jeremiah's words, standing on the very spot where they were first uttered (Matthew 21:13; Jeremiah 7:11).

The Need for a New Covenant

Through all Jeremiah's tears and above all his dark prophecies, there was a single ray of light. It's the high point of his career and his most famous prophecy. Jeremiah 31:31–34 predicts a new and better covenant for God's people. If we take a running start at this prophecy, we track through some amazing lyrics.

The chapter opens with a moving poem about God's extravagant love for his people: "I have loved you with an everlasting love" (verse 3); "Again I will build you" (verse 4); "He who scattered Israel will gather him, and will keep him as a shepherd keeps his flock" (verse 10); "I will turn their mourning into joy" (verse 13). These are extraordinarily comforting promises coming from a weeping prophet.

The chapter crescendos in verses 33–34, our core passage, with one of the great jewels of Scripture.

With these words Jeremiah gives expression to one of the deepest longings of Israel. God's people loved God's law but were incapable of keeping it. They kept sinning, kept sacrificing, and kept suffering for their rebellion. They needed a better law and a deeper relationship with God.

This hope for a new covenant wasn't unique to Jeremiah. It's echoed in Ezekiel 36:26–27: "I will give you a new heart, and a new spirit I will put within you. And I will remove the heart of stone from your flesh and give you a heart of flesh. And I will put my Spirit within you, and cause you to walk in my statutes and be careful to obey my rules."

We read it again in Joel 2:28, 32:

It shall come to pass afterward,
that I will pour out my Spirit on all flesh;
your sons and your daughters shall prophesy,
your old men shall dream dreams,
and your young men shall see visions. . . .

And it shall come to pass that everyone who calls on the name of the
LORD shall be saved."[1]

The bottom line is that the Jews felt the failure of the old covenant of Moses.

Just so we're clear, the problem was not with the law but with humanity. The people refused to keep the law. So the promised punishment fell on the nation during Jeremiah's day. The sacrifices multiplied, but the moral failures surpassed them.

Advantages of the New Covenant

Jeremiah gave us a promise of a new covenant. It's different and better in three ways.

First, *everyone would know God personally without a mediator.* There would no longer be a priest or prophet between men and God. All would have equal access to God—men and women, old and young, rich and poor, of all nations, ethnicities, and political affiliations. We're all supposed to be able to approach God with confidence, according to Hebrews 4:16: "Let us then with confidence draw near to the throne of grace, that we may receive mercy and find grace to help in time of need." This was always God's intent. He said so himself: "I will dwell among the people of Israel and will be their God" (Exodus 29:45) and "I will walk among you and will be your God, and you shall be my people" (Leviticus 26:12).

How can this be? Doesn't our sin separate us from a holy God? It does indeed. That's why Israel never fully achieved the confidence to approach God with the intimacy he offered. Christians can, however, because *our sins are forgiven through the perfect sacrifice of Jesus.* Hebrews 10:19–22 expresses it powerfully:

> Brothers, since we have confidence to enter the holy places by the blood of Jesus, by the new and living way that he opened for us through the curtain, that is, through his flesh, and since we have a great priest over the house of God, let us draw near with a true heart in full assurance of faith, with our hearts sprinkled clean from an evil conscience and our bodies washed with pure water.

This is truly an extraordinary passage. Think back to the old covenant when only the high priest could enter the holy of holies. Without our sins forgiven, the presence of God is a terrifying place.

Jesus alluded to Jeremiah's promise of a new covenant during the Last Supper (Luke 22:20). The apostle Paul would later quote those very words in his own instructions to believers about communion (1 Corinthians 11:25). In short, the new covenant is pictured in the blood and bread of the Lord's Supper.

The third difference of the new covenant is *the internalization of God's law.* This happens through the indwelling of the Holy Spirit. While the sacrifice of the Son clears our past, the indwelling of the Spirit assures our future.

Joel 2:28–32 is a parallel promise to Jeremiah 31:33–34. It indicates that anyone of any nation at any time could be forgiven of anything by calling on the name of the Lord and receiving the Holy Spirit. Peter quoted Joel's promise on the Day of Pentecost (Acts 2:17–21). It was then that the Spirit descended on the apostles and empowered them to speak in foreign languages. It was a striking miracle that captured the attention of the crowds. Even more impressive than the miracle, however, was the promise that those three thousand baptized at Pentecost would receive the permanent indwelling presence of the Spirit (verses 38–41).

Right now, those who accept Jesus Christ by faith not only have their past sins forgiven but also receive the indwelling gift of the Spirit to guide them in following God. Do we always obey the guidance of the Spirit? No. Even so, he's always there, prompting, coaching, and correcting.

Can we still be forgiven of sins after our baptism? Of course. The blood of Jesus flows both ways: across our past and toward our future.

Because of our internal connection, the Spirit inside us will guide us to lead different lives in the future. Under the old covenant, the law of Moses was like an electric fence. It jolted everyone who crossed the barrier. It was designed to protect through punishment. Under the new covenant, the Spirit inside us is very different. He's more like a compass than an electric fence. He doesn't limit our movement but frees us by pointing us in the right direction. By the Spirit we have a magnetic pull toward righteousness. Through the Spirit we have a change of heart.

This new way of living is described powerfully in 1 Corinthians 6:19–20: "Do you not know that your body is a temple of the Holy Spirit within you, whom you have from God? You are not your own, for you were bought with a price. So glorify God in your body." Paul put it succinctly in 2 Corinthians 3:6: "The letter kills, but the Spirit gives life." Because of the Spirit in us, there's no need for a law around us. Our behavior is internally motivated rather than externally constrained.

The entire book of Hebrews is an exposition of the superiority of the new covenant. That book can be confusing because it's written from a Jewish perspective to Jewish converts. Nonetheless, the topic was so substantial (and shocking) that it deserved an entire book of the New Testament to answer our question, What advantages do Christians have under the new covenant?

Key Points

- Jeremiah promised a new covenant during the days of Jerusalem's destruction.
- The hope of a new covenant was common in ancient Israel because of their perpetual sin and punishment.
- There are three things promised in the new covenant: personal relationship with the Father, forgiveness of sins through the sacrifice of the Son, and the law of God in our hearts through the Holy Spirit.

This Week

- ☐ **Day 1:** Read the essay.
- ☐ **Day 2:** Memorize Jeremiah 31:33–34.
- ☐ **Day 3:** Read Matthew 3; Luke 4.
- ☐ **Day 4:** Meditate on Luke 22:20; 1 Corinthians 6:19–20; Hebrews 9:14–15.
- ☐ **Day 5:** Read the book of Hebrews, making a list of advantages the new covenant offers Christians.

Overachiever Challenge: Memorize 1 Corinthians 6:19–20.

Bonus Read: Watchman Nee and Witness Lee, *The New Covenant.*

17

Son of Man

> Behold, with the clouds of heaven
> there came one like a son of man.
>
> —Daniel 7:13

Question: Is Jesus really fully human *and* fully divine?

Son of man is a strange turn of phrase. Its precise meaning is a bit of a mystery, so let's start with some clear stats.

The Data

Son of man is found 107 times in the Old Testament. Nincty-three of these are in a single book—Ezekiel—where God calls his prophet "son of man." It's not exactly an insult, but neither is it a compliment, reminding him of his human frailty.

The first time we hear *son of man* is on the lips of Balaam, a pagan prophet speaking on Yahweh's behalf: "God is not man, that he should lie, or a son of man, that he should change his mind" (Numbers 23:19). We also hear it from Job's friend Bildad as he described God's perspective on humanity: "Behold, even the moon is not bright, and the stars are not pure in his eyes; how much less man, who is a maggot, and the son of man, who is a worm!" (Job 25:5–6).

This sounds similar to Psalm 8:4: "What is man that you are mindful of him, and the son of man that you care for him?" Again, not an insult, but it certainly puts people in their place. All told, the term can be friendly, but it's never flattering.

This use of *son of man* is consistent throughout the entire Old Testament, with the single exception of Daniel 7:13. In this unique passage, Daniel had a vision. He saw God ("the Ancient of Days") exalted on his throne (verse 9). There suddenly appeared a divine figure—"one like a son of man" (verse 13)—who is brought into God's presence for a stunning power move: "To him was given dominion and glory and a kingdom, that all peoples, nations, and languages should serve him; his dominion is an everlasting dominion, which shall not pass away, and his kingdom one that shall not be destroyed" (verse 14). This is quite the conundrum. How can a mere mortal attain such exalted status, sharing God's authority?

This was an ongoing conversation among Jewish rabbis. It was extremely difficult for Jewish leaders to accept that any human being could share in God's glory and authority. But Psalm 122:5 had already established a precedent for David's descendant (the Messiah) to share God's glory: "There thrones for judgment were set, the thrones of the house of David." Clearly, God intended for a human being to rule and judge alongside him.

Moving from Daniel to the New Testament, we find yet another perplexity. *Son of Man* shows up eighty-five times, almost always in the Gospels (the only exceptions are Acts 7:56; Hebrews 2:6; and Revelation 1:13; 14:14). Furthermore, every use in the Gospels (with the exception of the crowd's question in John 12:34) is not only *about* Jesus but also *from* him. It's as if only Jesus had the gall to call himself a mere mortal.

We can conclude that only Jesus is the "Son of Man": he was virtually the only person to call himself this, and he called himself almost nothing else. So if the term is one of deprecation (except in Daniel, where it implies extreme exaltation), how does that jive with Jesus? How can Jesus be the exalted Son of Man who humbles himself on the human plane? That is precisely the point of the

Incarnation (Jesus coming to earth in human form). It's the promise of the Old Testament that God would come to his people and change their destiny.

The Big Idea

When we humble ourselves, God exalts us. It's a hard and fast rule in Scripture. Jesus modeled this spiritual law throughout his life. He came in incarnation and rose in resurrection. He was born in poverty and ascended to a throne. He died on a cross and now wears a crown.

Son of Man is therefore the perfect title for Jesus. Identifying himself with frail and fragile humans gives space for God alone to exalt him. As the apostle Paul said, "Therefore God has highly exalted him and bestowed on him the name that is above every name" (Philippians 2:9).

That's why Daniel 7:13 is the only sufficient source for Jesus's self-designation as Son of Man. It's a title of humility, to be sure. Yet it's also the rightful recognition of his role at God's right hand.

This comes into focus when Caiaphas grilled him at his trial. The high priest demanded an answer: "Are you the Christ, the Son of the Blessed?" (Mark 14:61). The question was a setup. If Jesus said yes, he'd be executed for blasphemy. Jesus responded, "I am, and you will see the Son of Man seated at the right hand of Power, and coming with the clouds of heaven" (verse 62). This unique combination of "seated at the right hand of Power" and "coming with the clouds of heaven" is an unmistakable allusion to Daniel 7:13–14. It's also the necessary background for Jesus coming "in the glory of his Father with the holy angels" (Mark 8:38). Because Jesus knew who he was as God's son, he could identify with human beings—and even become one—without losing sight of his role at God's right hand.

This paradoxical combination of deity and humanity permeated Jesus's ministry. It began when he healed a paralytic let down through the roof. Jesus said, "That you may know that the Son of Man has authority on earth to forgive sins" (Mark 2:10). Such authority to forgive sins is reserved for God. In the same chapter Jesus claimed, "The Son of Man is lord even of the Sabbath" (verse 28). Think about that for a minute. The Sabbath was established in Eden, not at Sinai. Jesus was putting a stake in the ground where only God lays claim. He was claiming the same right as the very God who created the world in the beginning.

He also claimed to arbitrate the final judgment (Matthew 13:41; 16:27). More than that, he laid claim to the throne of glory in eternity (19:28). This is audacious in the extreme.

On the other hand, the Son of Man had no place to lay his head (8:20). He came eating and drinking like every other human (11:19). He was betrayed by a friend (26:24, 45) and suffered at the hands of the Sanhedrin (Mark 8:31; 9:12, 31; 10:33; 14:41). He's human in every way—and claims every right and privilege of the divine.

This may seem shocking. Yet how else could the God of the universe relate to, connect with, and communicate with the human population he loved so desperately? God went to extraordinary lengths to have a relationship with you.

The Consequence

After Jesus's resurrection, none of the human limitations of the Son of Man apply anymore. Remember, there are four uses of *Son of Man* after the Gospels. Each portrays him as a divine figure, no longer subject to human frailty.

In Acts 7:56 Stephen saw Jesus exalted at God's right hand. Stephen said, "Behold, I see the heavens opened, and the Son of Man standing at the right hand of God." There it is: the position of authority promised to the Son of Man in Daniel 7:13–14.

The next citation, from Hebrews 2, is a bit more complex. The author quoted a stanza from Psalm 8. According to the psalm, though God alone is exalted in heaven, humans are the pinnacle of his creation on earth. They're appointed to rule over everything else God created. Because of sin, however, humanity lost its dignity and aborted its calling to care for creation. We were incapable of fulfilling God's commission. Therefore, it required a perfect human—a model man—to recover our role by suffering our fate. Jesus took on himself the penalty due to us so he could restore to us the dignity God designed for us.

Revelation 1:13 paints Jesus with the same brushstrokes as the Son of Man in Daniel 7:13. This passage also reveals the image of God with white hair, blazing eyes, and a voice of thunder (Revelation 1:14–15; see also Daniel 7:9–10). He's the incarnation of Yahweh himself.

Finally, Revelation 14:14 also portrays Jesus in his glory: "Then I looked, and behold, a white cloud, and seated on the cloud one like a son of man, with a golden crown on his head, and a sharp sickle in his hand." There's no more human frailty. The Son of Man and the God of creation are one and the same.

For those who grew up in Christian homes, this idea of God becoming a man seems natural and reasonable. For most people, however, this is a nearly impossible idea, especially for Jews and Muslims. If you think about it, they have a point. How could the great God of the universe squeeze himself into the frailty of humanity? But isn't that the point? *God can pull off the impossible.*

Not only is his incarnation possible; it's also practical. Jesus's incarnation is a model for us to follow. It's the best route to success in your work, family, and other relationships. When we humble ourselves, God will exalt us. When we live among and for other human beings, God will restore us to our former dignity as caretakers of creation.

Key Points

- In the Old Testament *son of man* was a title of human frailty.
- Jesus alone is "Son of Man" in the New Testament. It was his own title for himself.
- *Son of Man* is the perfect title for Jesus because it demonstrates his humility, which led to his exaltation. His humility also set a precedent for us to follow.

This Week

- ☐ **Day 1:** Read the essay.
- ☐ **Day 2:** Memorize Daniel 7:13.
- ☐ **Day 3:** Read Daniel 3; 6.
- ☐ **Day 4:** Meditate on Isaiah 9:6; Mark 14:62; Hebrews 2:6.
- ☐ **Day 5:** Ask a friend who's not a Christ follower what he or she thinks God would look like if he came and lived on earth.

Overachiever Challenge: Memorize Isaiah 9:6.

Bonus Read: St. Athanasius, *On the Incarnation of the Word of God.*

18

Blessedness

> Blessed are you when others revile you and persecute you and utter all kinds of evil against you falsely on my account. Rejoice and be glad, for your reward is great in heaven, for so they persecuted the prophets who were before you.
>
> —Matthew 5:11–12

Question: How can I be happy?

Clearly we all want to be happy. There's nothing wrong with that. God wants you to be happy as well. So what is it that will contribute to your greatest happiness? A simple Google search or a stroll through Barnes and Noble will prove what a powerful drive is our desire to be happy—not some of us but all of us! It's a primal human drive. The question is how to achieve it.

Jesus tackled this question head-on in the introduction of his first and most famous speech, known as the Sermon on the Mount. The eight simple statements that open Jesus's sermon are called beatitudes (Matthew 5:2–12). Each statement turns the totem pole of social expectations on its head. They each begin with the word *blessed* (or "happy"; think "fortunate" or "lucky"). But what Jesus said will make us happy is counterintuitive: being poor in spirit, mourning, meekness, hunger, etc.

The Human Quest for Happiness

The Greek philosophers spent a lot of time thinking about the human quest for happiness. According to their highest wisdom, happiness requires *virtue* as well as other good things like *wealth, kinship, status,* and *peace.*[1] Wealth protects us from the ravages of poverty (hunger, cold, and thirst). Kinship connects us to meaningful relationships where we can be valued and loved. Status gives significance at work and in the community. Peace is the result of escaping enemies in business, in the courts of law, and on the battlefield.

Anyone who had these things could live above the pressure and pain of normal human existence. They're supposed to make us happy. Yet we look around and see that many who are wealthy, popular, and powerful only magnify their misery. We all realize that getting the right things in the wrong way will hinder our happiness.

There was a moral side of happiness in Jewish religion as well as in Greek philosophy. Obedience to the law brings blessings: bearing children (Psalm 127:5), a good wife or friends,[2] and vengeance against enemies (Psalm 137:8–9). Blessed are those who show benevolence to the poor (Psalm 41:1) and do justice (Psalm 106:3). Thus, the land is blessed when the rulers are just (Ecclesiastes 10:17). The righteous are also blessed (Psalm 1:1), and those who gain wisdom are blessed (Proverbs 3:13).

But religion hasn't been any more successful at building happiness than philosophy. Perhaps it's because religion is often as self-focused as philosophy. We clearly need a different approach.

The Christian Quest for Happiness

Jesus's beatitudes explode our expectations about happiness. No one but Jesus could have so radically altered the philosophy of happiness. Rather than saying those with money, power, friends, or fame are happy, Jesus effectively said, "Fortunate are the unfortunate."

The beatitudes are disruptive and unexpected but not unprecedented. Each intensifies an idea found elsewhere in Hebrew literature. Simply put, he was amplifying in one poem what others had alluded to in scattered statements. Let's start by seeing how he pulled these ideas from past Hebrew literature.

1. *"Blessed are the poor in spirit" (Matthew 5:3).* "It is better to be of a lowly spirit with the poor than to divide the spoil with the proud" (Proverbs 16:19; see also Psalm 34:6; Proverbs 29:23; Isaiah 57:15; 61:1). Isn't it true that those with a deep connection to God seem to have peace even without prosperity?
2. *"Blessed are those who mourn" (Matthew 5:4).* "Comfort all who mourn" (Isaiah 61:2). Isn't it true that God often seems closer in times of trouble?
3. *"Blessed are the meek" (Matthew 5:5).* "The meek shall inherit the land" (Psalm 37:11). Isn't it true that those with humble and quiet strength eventually outlast the boisterous and brash?
4. *"Blessed are those who hunger and thirst for righteousness" (Matthew 5:6).* "Let justice roll down like waters, and righteousness like an ever-flowing stream" (Amos 5:24; see also 1 Kings 10:9; Job 29:14; Psalm 89:14; Proverbs 29:7; Isaiah 9:7). Isn't it true that the passion for righteousness is more gratifying than the passions of the world?
5. *"Blessed are the merciful" (Matthew 5:7).* In the Old Testament, with rare exceptions, only God is described as merciful. Thus, showing mercy reflects the very nature of God and positions us to receive his mercy. This explains the rabbinic exhortation: "So long as you are merciful, He will have mercy on you."[3] Isn't it true that people of mercy are often more respected than people of power?
6. *"Blessed are the pure in heart" (Matthew 5:8).* "He who has clean hands and a pure heart. . . . He will receive blessing from the Lord" (Psalm 24:4–5; see also Psalm 73:1; Proverbs 22:11). Isn't it true that a pure heart is a reward of its own?

7. *"Blessed are the peacemakers" (Matthew 5:9).* "When a man's ways please the LORD, he makes even his enemies to be at peace with him" (Proverbs 16:7; see also Numbers 25:12; Ezekiel 34:25). Isn't it true that the Nobel Prize goes to peacemakers over warriors?
8. *"Blessed are those who are persecuted" (Matthew 5:10).* One of the books written between the Old and New Testaments declares martyrs to be blessed by God: "By the blessed death of my brothers, by the eternal destruction of the tyrant, and by the everlasting life of the pious, I will not renounce our noble family ties."[4]

Clearly, each individual beatitude has a comparable statement somewhere in Jewish literature. Jesus's beatitudes were therefore not unheard of. Yet no one else had ever stacked together such countercultural statements in a single shocking stanza.

The biggest shock came in the end. Jesus added an explanation for only the final verse: *"Blessed are those who are persecuted."*

Blessed Are the Persecuted

It's not unreasonable to think that God would reward someone who suffered for his name. In Jewish literature between the Old and New Testaments, those persecuted for keeping God's laws were to be rewarded after death. Their fate would be reversed, making their suffering worthwhile after all.

For example, in 165 BC, Eleazar was killed for refusing to eat pork that God forbade. He replied to his persecutor with these words: "We, O Antiochus, who have been persuaded to govern our lives by the divine law, think that there is no compulsion more powerful than our obedience to the law."[5] Seven brothers were also martyred during this era. As one died, he said, "The King of the universe will raise us up to an everlasting renewal of life, because we have died for his laws."[6] The historic heroes of the Jewish revolt under the Maccabees (168–164 BC), as well as the Zealots who were contemporary with Jesus, were held in high esteem. They were promised a glorious reward in the afterlife.

"Blessed are the persecuted" thus became common coin in the centuries between the Testaments. The blessing, however, was specifically for those who suffered for keeping God's law. So imagine standing in the midst of the crowd when Jesus claimed that we'll be blessed if we suffer for his name: "Blessed are you when others revile you and persecute you and utter all kinds of evil against you falsely *on my account*" (Matthew 5:11). Did Jesus seriously just put himself in the sentence where historically Yahweh had stood? He did. Jesus presented himself as God's equal or perhaps more accurately, the embodiment of God's Torah.

Little wonder, then, that Jesus followed the beatitudes with comments on six specific Old Testament laws: "You have heard that it was said. . . . *But I say*" (verses 21–22, 27–28, 31–32, 33–34, 38–39, 43–44). He was showing how his words were more important than God's word through Moses. That was *bold.* The words of Moses were the very words of God. So one might rightly ask, "Who does Jesus think he is?" The beatitudes offer a very clear answer. Moses *received* the law; Jesus *is* the law. When Jesus spoke, it held the same authority as God himself. Hence, those who suffer for following Jesus are on par with those who'd been persecuted for following God.

Don't miss this. True happiness isn't found in the philosophy and ethics of the Greeks or of Israel. True happiness is in Jesus. Loyalty to Jesus offers nothing less than inheritance of the kingdom of God. To know God and follow his commands always leads to the blessed life.

This theme runs the length of the Sermon on the Mount. We see the same teaching at the sermon's end. Jesus began the sermon with a beatitude comparing himself to God's word, then ended the sermon comparing his words to the bedrock of God's word: "Everyone then who hears these words of mine and does them will be like a wise man who built his house on the rock" (Matthew 7:24). Jesus was claiming that his words are the foundation for a happy life.

Is it any wonder the crowds stood stunned at the end of this message? "When Jesus finished these sayings, the crowds were astonished at his teaching, for he was teaching them as one who had authority, and not as their scribes" (verses 28–29).

The sermon's big theme turned culture on its head. Lucky are the unlucky as long as they align themselves with Jesus's words. Christians are part of an upside-down kingdom where losers are winners, the dead live, the poor are rich, and those who pick up a cross experience resurrection.

Why does this actually work? Here's the secret: *happiness comes with having a higher purpose, not possessions or protection.*

Key Points

- Both Hebrews and Greeks were blessed by friends, wealth, and health, as well as the wisdom and morality to live in the right way.
- Jesus, amplifying themes expressed earlier in Jewish literature, altered the normal rules of who was blessed to include the poor, meek, mourning, and beaten.
- In Jewish tradition, martyrs were blessed by obeying God's commands. In Christian tradition, we're blessed by obeying Jesus's commands. He and God are on par.

This Week

☐ **Day 1:** Read the essay.

☐ **Day 2:** Memorize Matthew 5:11–12.

☐ **Day 3:** Read John 3:1–4:42.

☐ **Day 4:** Meditate on James 1:2, 12; 4:10; 1 Peter 4:13–14.

☐ **Day 5:** Go to www.icommittopray.com, the website of the Voice of the Martyrs. Read one story of a Christian suffering persecution. Pray for that person for three consecutive days.

Overachiever Challenge: Memorize James 4:10.

Bonus Read: James Hefley and Marti Hefley, *By Their Blood: Christian Martyrs of the Twentieth Century.*

19

Deeper Morality

I tell you, unless your righteousness exceeds that of the scribes and Pharisees, you will never enter the kingdom of heaven.

—Matthew 5:20

Question: What does it take to be a "good" person?

Jesus made a stunning statement in the Sermon on the Mount. He said that to enter God's kingdom, we have to be more righteous than the Pharisees. This seems impossible, since these religious leaders fasted twice a week, tithed off their garden herbs, and paused for prayer three times a day. If that's what it takes to impress God, we're all failing. Is it really possible to exceed the righteousness of the most faithful faction of Jesus's day? This is an important and practical question. Sometimes sermons make it seem that we can never measure up to God's expectations. We Christians are often paralyzed by our past. Can we really live a life that God considers "righteous"?

The answer is a resounding yes. Not because we can do more personal improvement, but because we can improve our personal motives. Jesus was asking not for a broader righteousness but for one that's deeper. He doesn't expect us to go to church more often, tithe a greater percentage, or pray for more minutes. Rather, he's calling us to righteous motives. How does this work?

The Practice of Deeper Righteousness

The law can measure *actions.* True righteousness grows out of *motives.* If I keep the law by not killing, I'm still liable for destroying a life by gossip. If I love my neighbors, it's likely good for me, but if I love my enemies, it's likely because I'm good. The law can manage only behavior, but Jesus wants to transform our character.

In the last half of Matthew 5, Jesus gave six examples of deeper righteousness. In essence, he said, "The heart of the matter is the heart of the matter." Here are the six and why they matter so much:

1. Murder is against the law, not just the Mosaic law but virtually every code of laws known to humanity. However, murder is merely a symptom. Anger is the actual impetus for murder. So Jesus demanded that we deal with anger (verses 21–26). If we don't, we wind up doing precisely what he predicted: insulting, slandering, accusing, and dividing. While libel may not be a crime, it's more lethal than murder. Far more families are destroyed by gossip than homicide. Far more businesses fail through slander than manslaughter. Jesus was right to address the heart of the issue, not the resulting action.
2. Adultery may be considered wrong, but lust is generally accepted as inevitable. For Jesus, this was a perverse oversight (verses 27–30). Dealing with our lust is so essential that he suggested we amputate offending limbs. Obviously, this is hyperbole and not to be taken literally. Yet that doesn't mean it should be taken lightly, particularly given the pornography available in everyone's pocket. Our sex-saturated society has been fueled by lust. We're experiencing unprecedented levels of sexual dysfunction. Never has Jesus's call to personal purity been more relevant or critical. This isn't an issue of protecting prudish puritanism. It's an issue of family health, mental health, human decency, and even societal stability.

3. Divorce was perfectly legal in Judaism—and for almost any reason. Jesus wanted to put a stop to marital destruction when he said, "I say to you that everyone who divorces his wife, except on the ground of sexual immorality, makes her commit adultery, and whoever marries a divorced woman commits adultery" (verse 32). This saying has unfortunately been used to cause pain when Jesus intended it to reduce pain for divorcées. Remember, Jesus's point is not a stronger law but a deeper morality.

   The Pharisees said that a man could divorce a woman with impunity, but they couldn't commit adultery. Jesus was pointing out that divorce causes the same damage and exploitation as adultery. Clearly the two transgressions of divorce and adultery aren't the same thing, yet they do effect the same consequences. In fact, many women abandoned by a man through divorce may largely be innocent yet suffer identical effects as an adulterous woman. Both lose economic security, both are ostracized as sinners, and both are vulnerable to predatory males. Those Pharisees who justified their divorces as legal would have then had to explain to Jesus how the consequences of their actions were any different from forcing their spouses to commit adultery.
4. Oaths are an attempt to differentiate situations that require honesty from those that do not. In normal situations we can fudge the truth or lie outright. But under oath a magic wand is waved that requires us to be more moral than normal. Jesus pointed out what nonsense that is (verses 33–37). Either we're honest or we aren't. Oaths gave a false impression of trustworthiness. Why? Because some oaths were considered binding and others were not. Specifically, binding oaths were those naming collateral that you were obligated to pay. So according to Matthew 23:16–18, if you swore by the temple, you could never pay that collateral because you couldn't sell the temple, since it belonged to God, not you. So it wasn't a binding oath. If you swore by the altar, this was invalid for

the same reason. However, if you swore by gold in the temple or the gift on the altar, you could actually ransom that. Hence, these were binding oaths. If you didn't have the legal expertise to tell the difference, too bad for you. This hypocrisy is colossal. Here's a better idea: say what you mean and mean what you say. Or, to quote Jesus's brother James, "Let your 'yes' be yes and your 'no' be no" (James 5:12).

5. The law of Moses limited retaliation to equal actions: "An eye for an eye and a tooth for a tooth" (Matthew 5:38; see Exodus 21:24). Jesus mandated a far more effective alternative to retaliation: nonviolent resistance. The idea is simple: don't just submit to your oppressors but overcommit to them; that way you'll expose their true motives and the crowds will see their true colors, causing them to come to your defense.

   His famous illustration is to turn the other cheek. Yet look more carefully: "If anyone slaps you on the *right* cheek, turn to him the other also" (Matthew 5:39). If your attacker (we'll assume he's right handed) gives you a backhanded slap on your right cheek, you expose your left cheek, forcing him to hit you again—only open-handed and with greater force. By this, the observant crowd will see the true aggression and violence motivating the insult. Again, Jesus said, "If anyone would sue you and take your tunic, let him have your cloak as well" (verse 40). For a first-century Jew that meant giving that person your outer garment (cloak) in addition to your inner garment (tunic). By giving your aggressor both garments, you stand there naked and exposed. Such embarrassment drives home the point that your oppressor's real motive is to strip you of everything and leave you exposed. The final illustration is more of the same: "If anyone forces you to go one mile, go with him two miles" (verse 41). The Roman imperial forces had the legal right of conscription. They could force the locals to carry their bags for a mile. By going two, you showed that their true intent was not to get support but to enslave you. This nonviolent resistance is a brilliant strategy proved effective by the likes of Mahatma Gandhi and Martin Luther King Jr.

6. Everyone agrees that you should love your neighbor, your family, and your friends. Jesus said, "Love your enemies and pray for those who persecute you" (verse 44). This is perhaps his most offensive command ever. It's not merely counterintuitive; it's culturally ludicrous. Remember, Jesus said this in the Middle East, where terrorism was prevalent. To love your enemies was not to feel good about them but to support them. It might mean harboring a fugitive, feeding a refugee, or protecting an adversary. This takes us back to the seventh beatitude: "Blessed are the peacemakers, for they shall be called sons of God" (verse 9). To be a son of someone means that you act like that person. You reflect the person's character and actions. In short, "like Father, like son." Jesus explained the reason for his unprecedented command to love our enemies: "so that you may be sons of your Father who is in heaven. For he makes his sun rise on the evil and on the good, and sends rain on the just and on the unjust" (verse 45). God's blessings on this good earth fall on all those who inhabit the planet. Should our behavior be any different if we share our Father's character?

To punctuate the point, Jesus admonished us, "Be perfect, therefore, as your heavenly Father is perfect" (verse 48, NIV). This is not a call to moral perfection. Rather, the word *perfect* indicates "mature" or "holistic." In the current context, Jesus was saying we should love as holistically, maturely, and openly as God does if we want to carry out his agenda in our culture. For Jesus, unconditional love is the heart of morality. Just when we're tempted to protest, we remember Jesus's model of prayer for his enemies with his dying breath: "Father, forgive them, for they know not what they do" (Luke 23:34).

Key Points

- Jesus called us to deeper, not broader, righteousness.
- In each of the six illustrations Jesus gave, we're forced to get to the root of morality, and that is our motive.
- To love our enemies is not only Jesus's most offensive statement and most challenging moral expectation but also the one he devoted his life and death to.

This Week

- ☐ **Day 1:** Read the essay.
- ☐ **Day 2:** Memorize Matthew 5:20.
- ☐ **Day 3:** Read Judges 15–16.
- ☐ **Day 4:** Meditate on Matthew 5:32, 44, 48.
- ☐ **Day 5:** Write a note to yourself, identifying your nearest enemy—whom you need to love as Jesus does.

Overachiever Challenge: Memorize Matthew 5:44.

Bonus Read: Bob Goff, *Love Does: Discover a Secretly Incredible Life in an Ordinary World.*

20

Prayer

Our Father in heaven,
hallowed be your name.
Your kingdom come,
your will be done,
    on earth as it is in heaven.
Give us this day our daily bread,
and forgive us our debts,
    as we also have forgiven our debtors.
And lead us not into temptation,
    but deliver us from evil.

—Matthew 6:9–13

Question: How should I pray?

Communication is the foundation of every relationship. This applies to our relationship with God as well. If we want to have a meaningful relationship with him, we need to learn how to talk to him. That may sound intimidating, but we have an open invitation to pray. Jesus himself said, "Ask, and it will be given to you; seek, and you will find; knock, and it will be opened to you. For everyone who asks receives, and the one who seeks finds, and to the one who knocks it will be opened" (Matthew 7:7–8).

Moreover, God created each of us with an instinct to pray. With minimal coaching and practice, anyone can become proficient in prayer.

The most famous model prayer comes from Jesus in what we now call the Lord's Prayer. This simple prayer gives us five important insights for mastering the practice.

"Father": Leverage Your Connection

Far and away, the most important lesson on prayer is in the first sentence: "Our Father in heaven, hallowed be your name" (Matthew 6:9). It seems simple to address God as Father. However, before Jesus, no one ever did this consistently. Yet Jesus almost always opened his prayers with "Father" or the Aramaic equivalent, "Abba." The only exception was his prayer from the cross, when he quoted Psalm 22:1: "My God, my God, why have you forsaken me?" (Matthew 27:46).

This is a powerful point. When we recognize that our God in heaven is our loving Father, it transforms our conversation. This alone will overcome every deficiency in our prayers. By getting to know God as our doting Father, those who don't pray enough would become effusively chatty, and those who pray only out of duty would drop the formality and speak to the One who loves them. As for those who pray frivolously, one true glimpse of the loving Father would remind them that his capacity and purposes are greater than our petty demands and desires.

Calling God "Father" can be difficult for those who've had a traumatic childhood. Nonetheless, even those without a father (or with a cruel one) have an instinctive longing for a good father. That's God's design. Good fathers on earth model the ideal Father in heaven.

How do we recognize God's divine nature as Father? "Hallowed be your name" (Matthew 6:9). That's a poetic way of saying, "God, we pledge to make your reputation honorable." This kind of pledge is also known as praise. It's probably more common than you think. We use praise all the time with lovers, friends, and coworkers by simply completing one or both of these sentences:

- You are (*name an attribute*).
- You did (*name the action*) with excellence.

If you want to practice praising God, just fill in the blanks with as many attributes and actions of God as you can think of. God will love hearing you praise him as much as you love hearing people praise you.

The Lord's Prayer begins with praise, and so should ours. When we magnify the nature and holiness of God, it changes the tone of prayer from mere petition to praise, from expectation to exaltation. It changes our view of God from genie to the father whose best interests will shape our conversation.

Hezekiah's prayer in a moment of severe crisis (2 Kings 19:15–19; Isaiah 37:16–20) illustrates well how praise on the front side will improve your prayers. Putting the Father on the throne of your heart gives you boldness to speak, especially during life's low tides. As Hebrews 4:16 says, "Let us then approach God's throne of grace with confidence, so that we may receive mercy and find grace to help us in our time of need" (NIV).

"Kingdom": Embrace God's Agenda

Jesus directed us to pray, "Your kingdom come, your will be done, on earth as it is in heaven" (Matthew 6:10). The power of prayer is not primarily in asking God for what you want but in aligning your life with His agenda. When we know God's purpose, we can pray for things, and God will say yes.

God will never answer a prayer that forces him to contradict what he has already said in the Bible. So if we ask him to eliminate war, the answer will be no; the Bible says there will be "wars and rumors of wars" until the end of time (24:6). Jesus said the poor will always be with us (26:11), so save your breath praying to eliminate all poverty.

On the other hand, there are a number of requests to which God promises a yes, if we just ask. These include requests for wisdom (James 1:5), for the Holy Spirit (Luke 11:13), for escape from temptation (Luke 22:40; 1 Corinthians 10:13), and for the ability to promote Jesus (Matthew 9:37–38). To practice this part of the prayer, choose two of those items and pause right now to ask God for them. Use your own language. Don't try to impress God with words; just express simply and honestly what's in your heart.

Only when we get these first two areas of prayer right can we begin to ask God for what we need.

"Give": Acquire Resources

When deciding what requests to make, we must simply answer the question "What do I need to do my job?" When we align ourselves with God's purpose in life, Jesus promised that he would give us everything we need to accomplish everything God wants us to do: "If you ask me anything in my name, I will do it" (John 14:14). God is ready to say yes to your prayers. The greatest mistake in prayer is not asking for too much but asking for too little. Oh sure, some people pray selfishly. But Jesus's brother put it this way: "You do not have, because you do not ask. You ask and do not receive, because you ask wrongly, to spend it on your passions" (James 4:2–3). Most of us pray with too little imagination and boldness.

To practice this aspect of prayer, make a wish list for God. Cross off those items that are selfish and leave on the list those things that would honestly make you a more effective ambassador for Jesus. Now ask boldly. Next to each item, place the date when you first asked and leave room to add the date when God answers. (Caution: this list may last for decades, and each request may have multiple waves of answers.)

Why doesn't God answer all our prayers immediately? Some answers are postponed because it's not yet time or we're not yet ready. But many of our prayers are postponed because we've imposed barriers on God's approval. The last two items of the Lord's Prayer reveal the most common barriers that postpone a yes.

"Forgive": Remove Barriers

Sometimes our prayers are hindered because we haven't forgiven someone who has hurt us. Anger, resentment, and bitterness are barriers between God and us as much as between others and us. It doesn't matter if your hurt was recent or long ago. It doesn't matter if you're justified in your anger or not. That's why Jesus said, "Whenever you stand praying, forgive, if you have anything against anyone, so that your Father also who is in heaven may forgive you your trespasses" (Mark 11:25).

Forgiving others frees us to have an open relationship with God. When we forgive others as God forgave us, our prayers will flow more freely and be answered more readily.

Consider for a moment whether there's a person (dead or alive) whom you're at odds with. Just speak that person's name before God and ask for the strength to forgive. If you can't yet forgive, ask for the desire to forgive. If you can't yet desire, thank God for forgiving you and ask for his Spirit to change your heart. Remember, your Father wants to say yes to this prayer.

Forgiveness is so important that it's the only part of the prayer Jesus commented on: "If you forgive others their trespasses, your heavenly Father will also forgive you, but if you do not forgive others their trespasses, neither will your Father forgive your trespasses" (Matthew 6:14–15).

"Deliver": Follow a Guide

Sin is another barrier to answered prayers. When we're purposefully participating in behaviors that dishonor God and degrade our human dignity, it's hard for us to have open communication with God.

Here's one example of how that happens: "Husbands, live with your wives in an understanding way, showing honor to the woman as the weaker vessel, since they are heirs with you of the grace of life, so that your prayers may not be hindered" (1 Peter 3:7).

To practice this aspect of prayer, simply tell God what he already knows. Confess out loud one or two habits or activities you're not so proud of. Genuinely apologize and ask God to give you strength to resist temptation. This is not a time to beat yourself up. Jesus's death on the cross saved you from this. But if you don't confess, it will weigh you down.

Behold, the LORD's hand is not shortened, that it cannot save,
or his ear dull, that it cannot hear;
but your iniquities have made a separation
between you and your God,
and your sins have hidden his face from you
so that he does not hear. (Isaiah 59:1–2)

God removes sin from our lives when we confess it to him and make restitution wherever possible. The Bible calls this *repentance*, and it comes with a promise of forgiveness: "If we confess our sins, he is faithful and just to forgive us our sins and to cleanse us from all unrighteousness" (1 John 1:9). This takes us full circle to the fatherhood of God. He doesn't want you isolated or separated from him. This gives us confidence to pray even if our behavior has strayed.

Key Points

- The most important lesson on prayer is to recognize God as Father.
- When our prayers are aligned with God's agenda, our requests are approved.
- Our prayers will be hindered by withholding forgiveness from others and by continuing habits of sin.

This Week

- ☐ **Day 1:** Read the essay.
- ☐ **Day 2:** Memorize Matthew 6:9–13.
- ☐ **Day 3:** Read John 17.
- ☐ **Day 4:** Meditate on Numbers 6:24–26; 2 Chronicles 7:14; Matthew 7:7–8.
- ☐ **Day 5:** Use the Lord's Prayer as a template to guide your prayers today.

Overachiever Challenge: Memorize Matthew 7:7–8.

Bonus Read: Timothy Keller, *Prayer: Experiencing Awe and Intimacy with God.*

21

Money

> Do not lay up for yourselves treasures on earth, where moth and rust destroy and where thieves break in and steal, but lay up for yourselves treasures in heaven, where neither moth nor rust destroys and where thieves do not break in and steal. For where your treasure is, there your heart will be also.
>
> —Matthew 6:19–21

Question: Is money spiritual?

Many people are put off by sermons on money. "The church is always asking for money," they say, which is seldom the case. Many churches do one financial series a year, stretching three or four weeks. That's about 7 percent of the annual sermons. Imagine what people would say if preachers spoke about money as much as Jesus did. A full 10 percent of verses in the Gospels are about money, and sixteen of Jesus's thirty-eight parables address money and possessions.

In this, Jesus isn't alone in Scripture. Consider that there are over 2,300 verses in the Bible on money but only five hundred on prayer and even fewer on faith.[1] God knows that money is spiritual. There's a direct correlation between financial management and faith development.

Perhaps the clearest summary of God's view of money is in Matthew 6:19–21. In this passage and Acts 20:35, we find three principles that will help us see our finances through God's eyes.

God Wants Our Hearts, Not Our Money

Jesus said, "Where your treasure is, there your heart will be also" (Matthew 6:21). Many people think our money follows our hearts. The idea is that we invest in things we care about. While that's sometimes true, it's *always* true that our hearts follow our money.

Have you ever dabbled in stocks? How many times a day did you check the market? Our time, attention, energy, and excitement follow our finances. Follow the money trail, and you'll find one's faith.

The way we manage money reveals whether "in God we trust." After all, *God owns everything.* Psalm 24:1 says, "The earth is the LORD's and the fullness thereof, the world and those who dwell therein." Your spouse, children, home, and occupation are all his resources. Your credit card, bank account, and stocks are in the same category as the Milky Way, nuclear energy, and the Amazon—all his. Since God is the creator, he's also the owner.

Where does that leave you? Merely as a manager. Which actually takes a lot of pressure off, even as it piles responsibility on. Our task with "stuff" is to steward, not seize.

From this truth flows another essential financial-spiritual principle. If all our possessions are on loan from God, claiming ownership is actually embezzlement. Taking control of God's resources replaces God's rule with our own. When we remove God from his throne, the objects we possess become idols that possess us.

If money is your master, God cannot be. This is Jesus's idea, not mine: "No one can serve two masters, for either he will hate the one and love the other, or he will be devoted to the one and despise the other. You cannot serve God and money" (Matthew 6:24).

Stewardship Is Spiritual

Money is typically viewed as secular, not sacred. We have church, prayer, and Scripture in one category, and money, bills, and mortgage in another. That's not God's perspective. Whether we recognize it or not, how we manage money affects our spiritual progress. It can hinder or accelerate prayer. It can replace or promote worship. It can drive us toward or away from the church. It can blind us to God's Word or open windows to his wisdom.

From God's perspective, our money is an eternal resource. Though you can't take it with you, you can send it on ahead. Jesus said as much: "Do not lay up for yourselves treasures on earth, where moth and rust destroy and where thieves break in and steal, but lay up for yourselves treasures in heaven, where neither moth nor rust destroys and where thieves do not break in and steal" (Matthew 6:19–20). Because of this, we need to treat our finances as a kingdom-building resource.

One of the most important encounters of Jesus's life was with a rich young ruler (19:16–22). He asked Jesus how to inherit eternal life. What a great question! Jesus's response was simple: "Keep the commandments" (verse 17). He went on to recite a few from the Ten Commandments: "You shall not murder, You shall not commit adultery, You shall not steal, You shall not bear false witness, Honor your father and mother" (verses 18–19). Notice that each of these commands deals with our horizontal relationships. The man was doing all that. What he lacked was a relationship with God (the first four commandments of the Ten Commandments). Jesus's solution: "Sell what you possess . . . and come, follow me" (verse 21). In order to free himself to follow Jesus, he would have to remove the ankle weights of his wealth. Like most of us, this young man could never run with Jesus until he loosed his financial fetters.

It would be unfair to assume that Jesus's command to sell everything would extend to every individual. But if you're reading this, you're rich by worldly standards. Nearly every person you know enjoys the benefits of the modern West and fits the bill of the economic elite. We're in danger of making money an idol.

If that seems like too strong a statement, listen to Paul's words in Colossians

3:5: "Put to death therefore what is earthly in you: sexual immorality, impurity, passion, evil desire, and *covetousness, which is idolatry.*" Our lust for possessions and security is the single greatest hindrance to fully following Jesus. Whatever we own ultimately owns us.

Not only does our ownership affect our relationship with God; it also determines our effectiveness in making Jesus famous. Our iron grip on possessions and resources keeps us from fulfilling God's purpose for our lives.

Paul is a great example to follow. There were times in his travels when he was well funded and enjoyed comfortable accommodations. At other times he had to work a second job just to make ends meet. Here's his own assessment of his ministry: "I can do all things through him who strengthens me" (Philippians 4:13). Many take this as a mystical dependence on supernatural power. It is not. It's a financial statement. This verse is evidence of Paul's financial freedom throughout his missionary travels. It's not about supernatural spiritual strength but about money management. The context is clear: whether Paul had adequate or inadequate financial support, he successfully fulfilled God's calling. In other words, he used money to accomplish ministry, not letting it be a hindrance to ministry (like the rich young ruler). Paul used his resources to invest in the kingdom of God rather than in his own comfort. To this extent, stewardship is always spiritual.

Generosity Brings Blessing

Typically, we focus on generosity as a blessing to those who receive it. God focuses on the blessing that generosity offers to those who provide it.

We have Paul to thank for a quote from Jesus in Acts 20:35 (which is the only saying of Jesus that wasn't recorded in the Gospels): "It is more blessed to give than to receive." We all know this is true. Even around the tree on Christmas morning, our greatest joy comes when others are unwrapping gifts we gave them.

Not only does giving bless you, but it also opens the floodgates of God's blessing on your life. It's as if God gives us wealth for redistribution and eagerly awaits our emptied hands to pour out more. The more we reallocate God's resources to build God's kingdom, the more he funnels our direction. As wise King Solomon said, "Honor the LORD with your wealth and with the firstfruits of all your produce; then your barns will be filled with plenty, and your vats will be bursting with wine" (Proverbs 3:9–10). Jesus paraphrased the principle with this famous quote: "Give, and it will be given to you. Good measure, pressed down, shaken together, running over, will be put into your lap. For with the measure you use it will be measured back to you" (Luke 6:38). Hence the oft-cited saying "You cannot outgive God."

The Bible summarizes this kind of redistribution under two concepts: tithes and offerings.

The tithe is the first 10 percent of all our earnings. When we give that to God, it affirms his ownership of the other 90 percent. Don't make the mistake of giving your last 10 percent. That's merely a tip that says, "Thank you." A tithe is the first 10 percent given to God that says, "I submit to you as owner of it all." As we read in Leviticus 27:30, "Every tithe of the land, whether of the seed of the land or of the fruit of the trees, is the LORD's; it is holy to the LORD."

Let's be clear: We don't *give* a tithe. We *return* a tithe. It belongs to God in the first place, so we can only return it. How? Or perhaps more accurately, Where?

According to Malachi 3:10, tithes should be returned to the storehouse in the temple. The closest comparable institution in our cultural context is the local church. This is important. Though it's good to give to godly organizations, the tithe belongs to the church. Why? The church alone is the hope of the world. All other Christian organizations are to support and augment the core community of God's people.

Beyond the tithes are offerings given at your own discretion. These could be handouts to the helpless, contributions to Christian or charitable organizations, or personal gifts to bless individuals you care about. Generosity is an offering that exceeds the tithe. This is where the full joy of generosity lives and breathes. Paul said, "God loves a cheerful giver" (2 Corinthians 9:7). In truth, cheerfulness tends to be the result of giving, not its cause. How do we know? Jesus said, "It is more blessed to give than to receive" (Acts 20:35).

Key Points

- God wants your heart, not your money.
- Stewardship is spiritual.
- Generosity blesses the generous.

This Week

- ☐ **Day 1:** Read the essay.
- ☐ **Day 2:** Memorize Matthew 6:19–21.
- ☐ **Day 3:** Read Joshua 5:13–7:26.
- ☐ **Day 4:** Meditate on Matthew 19:16–30; Acts 20:35; Philippians 4:13.
- ☐ **Day 5:** Talk with a financial coach this week to strategize either how to begin tithing or how to move beyond the tithe to generosity.

Overachiever Challenge: Memorize Philippians 4:13.

Bonus Read: Robert Morris, *The Blessed Life: Unlocking the Rewards of Generous Living.*

22

The Golden Rule

Whatever you wish that others would do to you, do also to them, for this is the Law and the Prophets.

—Matthew 7:12

Question: What is true religion?

Hundreds of years before Jesus, Confucius supposedly said, "Do not do to others what you would not wish done to yourself." Later, between the time of Malachi and Matthew, the book of Tobit 4:15 said, "What you hate, do not do to anyone."[1] Later still, a man dared the great rabbi Hillel to explain the entirety of Jewish law while the man stood on one foot. Hillel replied, "What is hateful to you, do not to your neighbour: that is the whole Torah, while the rest is the commentary."[2] So it appears that several sages had declared what we might call the "Silver Rule" prior to Jesus's ministry.

Others had said, "*Don't* do to others." Jesus said, "*Do* to others." There's a sliver of a difference between the Silver Rule and the Golden Rule—from negative to positive. This subtle change transformed not only the rule but also all of religion.

As you read these words, sitting quietly, you're perfectly practicing the demands of the Silver Rule. You're doing nothing to others that they would consider repugnant. At the same time, you're doing nothing that would satisfy the demands of the Golden Rule. The Golden Rule demands relentless action. Such is the difference between the rules of religion and Jesus's call to sacrificial service. Jesus's call to right religion has a simplicity that fits in a tweet yet encompasses our entire existence. The power and purity of the Golden Rule inspire our best efforts to emulate Jesus.

Pure and Undefiled Religion

James weighed in on the Golden Rule. In many ways his little letter is a practical commentary on Jesus's Sermon on the Mount. This is only natural. James grew up with Jesus, his older half-brother, and was influenced by him throughout his childhood. In his twenties, however, he had some serious disagreements with Jesus. He rejected Jesus's claims to be Messiah (John 7:5). It wasn't until after the Resurrection, when James met the risen Christ face to face (1 Corinthians 15:7), that he became a believer. By that time he'd missed the bulk of Jesus's public ministry and teaching. So we can assume the book of James reflects the teachings of Jesus before his public preaching. James was privy to that. When we read the book of James, we're actually hearing the earliest influences of Jesus.

That brings the most clarity to James 1:27. We're hearing the heart of Jesus come through his brother's commentary on the Golden Rule. Let's read the verse and then establish the connection: "Religion that is pure and undefiled before God the Father is this: to visit orphans and widows in their affliction, and to keep oneself unstained from the world."

The purpose of religion is *not* merely to keep oneself unstained by the world. The purpose of pure religion is first to serve the community, particularly its most vulnerable members. Anyone familiar with the Old Testament prophets will recognize the theme of caring for orphans and widows as a primary obligation of Judaism (Isaiah 1:17; Ezekiel 22:25; Zechariah 7:10; Malachi 3:5). Does this mean that personal morality is unimportant? Of course not. However, as a matter of practicality, personal morality is less a cause of service than a result of it. Why?

When personal morality is our motivation, we tend to be isolationists. Isolationists avoid bars so they won't drink. They avoid neighbors who swear. They avoid inner cities where crime and drugs are rampant. The means of morality is avoiding "sinners" who become stumbling blocks. However, when service is our motivation and our mechanism for expressing our love for God, avoidance gives way to engagement. We purposely enter the places and relationships where God's love is most needed. The truly religious become God's ambassadors.

What does that do to our personal morality? Rather than endangering it, we're more often motivated to live to a higher standard because other people are spiritually dependent on us. This is always true: responsibility breeds more personal growth than self-control does. Personal morality (or living "unstained from the world," to use James's phrase) is far more likely through engagement than avoidance.

So let's be clear: neither Jesus nor James is replacing ethics with social service. The biblical word *righteousness* implies both. The question is how best to achieve both. Many assume that going to church, reading the Bible, and praying will lead to a life that honors God. Too often those practices lead only to arrogance, isolationism, and judgment. The Bible's clear: serving others is the most effective mechanism for self-improvement.

Now that both Jesus and James have given their stance, let's look at the genesis of this idea.

What Does the Lord Require of You?

"He has told you, O man, what is good; and what does the LORD require of you but to do justice, and to love kindness, and to walk humbly with your God?" (Micah 6:8). This is one of the more famous statements in the Old Testament. It's one of those rare jewels that reduce religion to its barest essentials. It has massive implications that form the foundation of Jesus's Golden Rule.

The ten northern tribes of Israel were conquered in 722 BC, right in the middle of Micah's prophetic career. That devastating defeat marked Micah's ministry, shaping his words and warnings. During this same period the Greeks launched the first Olympic games (776 BC) and the Romans founded their nation (753 BC). Assyria was the local superpower, but two other major players were on the rise at the very time that Israel's borders were shrinking.

Therefore, Micah's message is a warning that if Israel didn't repent, history would repeat itself. Their nation would fall as others had before them.

Does this sound at all familiar? We stand at a similar point in history—a great nation whose moral failure may be its own undoing. Which raises this critical question: How are we to repent?

The answer might surprise you. It's not by going to the temple, praying, or making sacrifices. The people in Micah's day were doing all that. In Micah's words, "Shall I come before him with burnt offerings, with calves a year old? Will the Lord be pleased with thousands of rams, with ten thousands of rivers of oil?" (6:6–7). This is a foundational principle throughout Scripture: *the right actions with the wrong heart are offensive to God.* Why? Because when we go to church, say our prayers, and perform our religious duties without the right heart, our sacrifice becomes a bribe to God, not a blessing to his people.

We see this principle when the prophet Samuel said to King Saul, "To obey is better than sacrifice" (1 Samuel 15:22). King David sang a song about it: "In sacrifice and offering you have not delighted. . . . Burnt offering and sin offering you have not required" (Psalm 40:6). This very psalm is quoted again in Hebrews 10:5–6. It was that big of a deal.

David's son Solomon said, "To do righteousness and justice is more acceptable to the Lord than sacrifice" (Proverbs 21:3). But probably the most similar passage is from Micah's contemporary, the prophet Isaiah, who opened his book with this devastating critique from God:

> What to me is the multitude of your sacrifices?
>   says the Lord;

I have had enough of burnt offerings of rams
  and the fat of well-fed beasts;
I do not delight in the blood of bulls,
  or of lambs, or of goats.

When you come to appear before me,
  who has required of you
  this trampling of my courts?
Bring no more vain offerings;
  incense is an abomination to me. . . .
  Remove the evil of your deeds from before my eyes;
cease to do evil,
  learn to do good;
seek justice,
  correct oppression;
bring justice to the fatherless,
  plead the widow's cause. (1:11–13, 16–17)

That brings us right back to Micah 6:8. What does the Lord require of us?

1. *Do justice.* The phrase literally means "to make justice." This is not an internal attitude but a social structure. We use our influence and resources to reshape our communities so the poor and oppressed have a fighting chance.
2. *Love kindness.* This word *kindness* is one of the weightier words in the Old Testament. It implies the *covenant loyalty* of God. We would use it today in relation to marriage, adoption, or even a last will and testament. It's more than the behavior of that "nice guy" in the next cubicle or the friendly checker at the store. It's a covenant loyalty.
3. *Walk humbly with your God.* Why does this take humility? A quick look at one last passage will make it apparent.

> In Matthew 23, during the last week of Jesus's life, he criticized the religious leaders in the very temple of God. Here's his charge: "Woe to you, scribes and Pharisees, hypocrites! For you tithe mint and dill and cumin, and have neglected the weightier matters of the law: justice and mercy and faithfulness. These you ought to have done, without neglecting the others" (verse 23). Notice that his concern is the same as Isaiah's, the same as Micah's. People did their duties with the wrong motives, and their religious acts became bribes rather than sacrifices.
>
> Pride can blind us to the motives God sees. We think we're very religious because of our behaviors, but God judges our motives.

How does God view our religious activities? Are they sacrifices or bribes? The quickest way to tell is whether our religious deeds improve the plight of the poor in our communities. If our church doesn't care for the community God cares for, history will inevitably repeat itself.

Key Points

- Jesus's Golden Rule tweaked the Silver Rule, thus massively transforming religion.
- When James spoke of religion as care for widows and orphans, he showed how his perspective matched that of his older brother, Jesus.
- James, like the Old Testament prophets, called us to justice, kindness, and humility as true religious expression.

This Week

☐ **Day 1:** Read the essay.

☐ **Day 2:** Memorize Matthew 7:12.

☐ **Day 3:** Read Luke 10:25–37.

☐ **Day 4:** Meditate on Isaiah 1:11–17; Micah 6:8; James 1:27.

☐ **Day 5:** Schedule one hour today to live in total alignment with the Golden Rule.

Overachiever Challenge: Memorize James 1:27.

Bonus Read: Dale Carnegie, *How to Win Friends and Influence People*.

23

The Cross

Jesus told his disciples, "If anyone would come after me, let him deny himself and take up his cross and follow me. For whoever would save his life will lose it, but whoever loses his life for my sake will find it."

—MATTHEW 16:24–25

Question: Who do you say Jesus is?

Past the halfway mark of his three-year ministry, Jesus peeled off with his apostles for a watershed moment. They hiked to the northernmost border of Israel in the area of Caesarea Philippi, where Jesus asked a simple question: "Who do people say that the Son of Man is?" (Matthew 16:13). Public opinion varied: John the Baptist, Jeremiah, Elijah—all prophets and all dead.

Jesus then got personal: "Who do *you* say that I am?" (verse 15).

The Confession

Peter answered for the whole group and vastly improved on public opinion: Jesus is the Messiah—"the Christ, the Son of the living God" (verse 16). Peter was spot on. Jesus quickly let him know that God had revealed this truth to him. (Clearly, Peter on his own wasn't *that* good!)

This long-awaited confession was anticipated in the opening chapters of all four gospels (Matthew 1:1; 2:4; Mark 1:1; Luke 1:31–35; 2:11; John 1:17, 49). At long last, the apostles confessed what you may already know—Jesus is the Christ. Therefore, it's at this crucial moment that Jesus not only affirmed Peter's confession but also clarified it (Mark 8:31–32). They expected a king who would conquer their enemies. What they got was a Savior who would die for their sins. Jesus would not kill his enemies but die for them—which was entirely surprising.

The Objection

When Jesus pointed out his divine destiny in death, Peter reacted sharply: "Far be it from you, Lord! This shall never happen to you" (Matthew 16:22). The original Greek wording is stronger than the English translation—something like "When Gehenna freezes over!" (which you might expect from a fisherman like Peter). Jesus retorted with arguably his harshest word ever: "Get behind me, Satan!" (Mark 8:33). He equated his right-hand man with the devil.

Oddly, the ignorant crowds were closer in their confession than Peter. While the populace damned Jesus with faint praise, Peter's protest could have derailed Jesus's mission. Jesus's rebuke placed Peter in the same category as the demons Jesus had earlier silenced when they confessed his identity (Mark 3:11–12; 5:7). Jesus was harsh but not unfair. Satan's confrontation with Jesus during the temptation ran precisely this same track. The devil tried to derail Jesus from his mission by tempting him to use his power and prestige to short-circuit the cross. Rather than the gruesome call to sacrifice, Satan (and Peter) urged Jesus to assert his divine prerogatives to avoid the human experience of pain and suffering.

This temptation is hardly new. It goes all the way back to the division of the kingdom of Israel (in 930 BC). If you track this historical review, it will put into clearer perspective Jesus's political agenda.

After Solomon's death, his son Rehoboam took the crown. His citizens assembled to plead for reduced taxes because Solomon had built his kingdom on the backs of the commoners. They wanted relief from the oppressive burden. Before giving his answer, Rehoboam sought counsel. His aggressive young staff told him to show strength (not an uncommon political policy in the Middle East). Rehoboam heeded their advice, quoting it to the crowds: "My father made your yoke heavy, but I will add to your yoke" (1 Kings 12:14). In short, their burden was about to get heavier, not lighter.

Because of that insolent answer, the people of the ten northern tribes crowned another man, Jeroboam, as their king. Jeroboam set up golden calves at both Bethel and Dan for the people to worship (verses 26–29). This led the northern tribes into catastrophic idolatry. It was Jeroboam's attempt to keep his people in his borders and away from worship in Jerusalem. It was political savvy and religious heresy.

Fast-forward to Jesus. He and his disciples at that very moment stood in the shadow of Jeroboam's now-defunct altar at Dan. This is precisely why Jesus had led the disciples north to the border. Jesus's apostles would have understood where they were and what had happened there more than nine hundred years earlier: Israel had been derailed. Jesus returned to where the king of Israel took the wrong advice.

Now return with me to Rehoboam and the older men whose advice he scorned. This was their wisdom: "If you will be a servant to this people today and serve them, and speak good words to them when you answer them, then they will be your servants forever" (1 Kings 12:7). Though Rehoboam scorned that advice, Jesus intended to follow it—as we can see from his reply to Peter. Jesus intended to take Israel back to that pivotal moment and reunify the tribes under a very different kind of leadership.

The Call

Jesus followed Peter's rebuke with what would become his most frequently cited saying in the Gospels: "If anyone would come after me, let him deny himself and take up his cross and follow me. For whoever would save his life will lose it, but whoever loses his life for my sake will find it" (Matthew 16:24–25).

Now, this is curious indeed. Jesus was talking no longer about his own impending death but about that of his disciples. The core requirement of a Christian is crucifixion. We don't typically think that way. We remember Jesus's death in communion. We wear *his* cross as jewelry. We follow his steps on the Via Dolorosa (the path Jesus took to where he would be crucified). We too are called to take up a cross.

Yet before Jesus was crucified, he commanded his followers to take up their own crosses. Long after Jesus's crucifixion, Paul identified discipleship as cross-bearing. For example, "I have been crucified with Christ. It is no longer I who live, but Christ who lives in me. And the life I now live in the flesh I live by faith in the Son of God, who loved me and gave himself for me" (Galatians 2:20). The cross isn't merely what Jesus *did* for us. It's what he *modeled* for us. Being a disciple is not just receiving what Jesus did; it's imitating how he lived.

The gruesome reality of the Crucifixion is not an easy conversation. In fact, we know surprisingly little about this ancient mode of execution precisely because it was so shameful. It was not to be discussed in polite company. Perhaps that's why the clearest description of the practice outside the Gospels comes from Psalm 22, which Jesus quoted on the cross: "My God, my God, why have you forsaken me?" (Matthew 27:46; quoting Psalm 22:1). Though it was composed a thousand years before Jesus's execution (and five hundred years prior to the Persians inventing the practice), this poem contains graphic details: piercing of hands and feet, heart melting like wax, bones out of joint, enemies surrounding him, public mockery, naked exposure, gambling for his garments, and extreme thirst. The prophecy is extraordinarily precise, even if the graphic description is uncomfortable.

Equally uncomfortable is our own execution. Perhaps it's not something we want to talk about, but we need to. Jesus said if we don't take up a cross, we're unable to follow him (Matthew 10:38). We must live as the walking dead. Only then will we be able to conquer our sinful passions.

That's a truth we sense in our breast. Yet there's something more, both more important and more impressive: Jesus's death saved our souls. We sing this at church and we hear this from pulpits. We thank God for his grace in sending his Son to save us for eternity. Clear enough. So what's the purpose of *our* crosses?

It's not simply self-denial to build self-control. It's not to make a better version of us. Like Jesus's death, our suffering and sacrifice have saving power, not for the individual soul but for society as a whole. As Jesus died to atone for our personal sins, so we die to reverse the effects of sin in society, families, and communities.

As we in the church sacrifice ourselves, we have the actual capacity to eliminate the foster-care system. If the church were to focus our medical attention on malaria, we could effectively eliminate one of the single greatest causes of loss of life in human history. Only in the church is there a realistic hope of eradicating racism. Only in Christ have Jew and Greek, slave and free, male and female been united in fellowship and purpose (Galatians 3:28). The list could go on, and it's long.

We know this is true because we have a track record that's impressive. Beginning with the first-century church, the greatest social strides in culture, art, medicine, compassion, education, poverty relief, and the protection of women, children, and the marginalized have come primarily from those who follow Jesus with crosses strapped to their backs.

This circles back to our original question: Who do you say Jesus is? If he's merely a prophet from the past, a hero of our faith, we likely have missed the purpose of the Messiah. Suffering and sacrifice are his greatest achievements. As his disciple, they will be yours as well.

If we confess him as Lord, we're obligated to follow his example. We cannot celebrate a Lord we won't imitate.

Key Points

- Jesus being the Messiah includes his suffering and death.
- Jesus's leadership reunifies Israel (and the whole world) through sacrifice and suffering.
- Jesus's leadership is an example for us to follow in serving and sacrificing for the society and community around us—by taking up our own crosses.

This Week

- ☐ **Day 1:** Read the essay.
- ☐ **Day 2:** Memorize Matthew 16:24–25.
- ☐ **Day 3:** Read Mark 15.
- ☐ **Day 4:** Meditate on 1 Kings 12:7; Psalm 22; Galatians 2:20.
- ☐ **Day 5:** Identify one area of your life that you've not yet submitted to the lordship of Jesus. Then identify the first step to release this area to God's control.

Overachiever Challenge: Memorize Galatians 2:20.

Bonus Read: Brennan Manning, *The Signature of Jesus.*

24

Election and Predestination

Many are called, but few are chosen.

—Matthew 22:14

Question: For what did God choose me?

Jesus's stories were fiction that mirrored spiritual realities. Here's one that's told in Matthew 22:2–13, and it relates to all of us.

The Parable

Once upon a time, a king threw a banquet celebrating his son's wedding. All who were invited refused to come, and some of them shamelessly abused and even murdered the very messengers inviting them.

The king, of course, was furious. In a vengeful rage, he destroyed the murderers and leveled their city. Yet the wedding hall was still empty. So he sent other servants to invite all and sundry. One would never suspect these folks could attend such a grand feast. But they came in droves, and most were delighted.

But there was one in attendance who didn't bother to dress for the occasion. This was an affront to his majesty. That callous guest was thrown out and severely punished.

Here, then, is the story's summary: "Many are called, but few are chosen" (verse 14).

This word *chosen* (which could also be translated "elected") is pregnant with theological meaning. Because of that, people often import complicated theological explanations into the parable. Before we run too far afield, let's start with the simple context. Jesus's parable explains the basic process of election: they were invited, and they came. It's that simple. Many prominent people were invited but refused to come. They were *not* elected. Others never deserved an invitation but received one and came gladly. They *were* elected. One guy came for the wrong reason and without the dress of respect. He was rejected.

In a nutshell, that's the meaning of election. Let's tease that out with a few other notable statements about election.

The Principle

At the risk of oversimplification, there are two basic views of election: (1) God alone chooses who goes to heaven and who does not, and (2) God has determined the parameters of salvation, and we get to choose whether or not to enter.

Very smart (and godly) people differ on the definition of election and with good reason. With all due respect to other views, we'll start with Jesus's own definition of election as drawn from the above parable: God's invitation *and* our acceptance. God determines the time, place, and parameters of the party. We choose whether to accept the invitation.

Let's clarify a few important points.

- *Everyone is invited.* The rich and poor of the parable all got an invite. Some in Jesus's audience had inherited religious clout. Others were farmers, day laborers, or outcasts whose daily means of survival might render them unclean. From the top of society to the bottom, all were invited.

  After Jesus's day, the church spread across geographic and cultural boundaries. The message went from Jews to Gentiles. The early church was stunned by the breadth of the invitation: it included

Gentiles, slaves, and women. All got an invite. Isn't this, after all, the implication of John 3:16? It's spelled out in 2 Peter 3:9: "The Lord is not slow to fulfill his promise as some count slowness, but is patient toward you, not wishing that any should perish, but that all should reach repentance." According to Scripture, God "desires all people to be saved" (1 Timothy 2:4).

That's not new with the gospel. As far back as Ezekiel 18:32, God showed his cards: "I have no pleasure in the death of anyone, declares the Lord God; so turn, and live."

- *Not everyone gets the same invitation.* God is all inclusive, but he is not egalitarian. According to the parable, the invite starts with the elite. In historical terms, that means the Jews had greater access to God through the Torah and temple. In theological terms, that means God elected the Jewish people to bear the promise and then the Christian church to extend it to the world. In sociological terms, it means that all economic groups, all tribes, all tongues, and all political affinities have open access to election but not necessarily *equal* access. The reality is that those born in the modern West have more opportunity to hear the gospel and respond freely than those born in the Middle East or those born in other eras. Does that mean God isn't fair? Yes, that's exactly what it means. God isn't fair; he is gracious *to all.* For reasons above and beyond our comprehension, God chose a man, Abraham, to father a nation. He chose that nation to build the temple and preserve the law. From that nation arose a Messiah who would eventually be proclaimed Lord across all continents. This foreordained plan of God was immensely gracious but not nearly egalitarian.
- *You must respond to the invitation.* Election is not just the invitation. It's a particular response to the invitation. God alone invites. Humans, however, under God's sovereignty, are obligated to respond.

That's why the Bible consistently encourages those invited to

RSVP. Jesus himself exhorted us, "Strive to enter through the narrow door" (Luke 13:24). The writer of Hebrews implored, "Let us draw near" (Hebrews 10:22; see also 4:16; 7:25; 11:6).

Clearly the chief weight of responsibility is God's. But his invitation is not complete without our response.

Again, this is nothing new. After Joshua led the chosen people into the promised land, he gave them this famous challenge: "Choose this day whom you will serve, whether the gods your fathers served in the region beyond the River, or the gods of the Amorites in whose land you dwell. But as for me and my house, we will serve the Lord" (Joshua 24:15).

- *God knows who will respond.* God doesn't force your hand, but he does see it under the table. In other words, he knows what you'll do before you ever do it.

This may sound mysterious, but every parent has had a similar experience. You can see your kid and *know* that she is about to jump, touch, cry, or succeed. It's the same with God, except that he sees further out.

The New Testament calls this *foreknowledge.* The Greek word literally means "knowing beforehand." Peter addressed his first letter "to those who are *elect* exiles . . . according to the *foreknowledge* of God the Father" (1 Peter 1:1–2). The elect who respond to God's invitation are seen by God long before they ever come to him, long before they are even born. That's where the word *predestine* comes into play. It's a rare Greek word (*proorizō*), used only six times in the New Testament. It means "to determine beforehand." The root is where we get *horizon.* It basically means "to set boundaries." God determines the boundaries of salvation. He sees who will respond and who will not. His call is to all; his election is for those he sees will step into his predetermined boundaries of salvation.

Paul summarized it this way:

> Those whom he *foreknew* he also *predestined* to be conformed to the image of his Son, in order that he might be the firstborn among many brothers. And those whom he *predestined* he also *called*, and those whom he called he also justified, and those whom he justified he also glorified. (Romans 8:29–30)

The Purpose

All this makes sense except for one thing. If God's predestination sets boundaries of salvation, then his election should be corporate, not individual. In other words, God declares beforehand the *kind* of people who would be saved. If, however, God starts *naming* those who are saved, it looks as if he's playing favorites. Those he likes go to heaven; those he doesn't take the down elevator.

To be fair, God is God. He gets to do that if he likes. But he isn't like that—not according to the Bible. His love is perfect and universal (Matthew 5:48; John 3:16). To use the common parlance of the Bible, "God shows no partiality" (Acts 10:34; Romans 2:11; see also Deuteronomy 10:17; 2 Chronicles 19:7; Job 34:19; Ephesians 6:9; 1 Peter 1:17).

So what do we do with individual predestination? Both the Old and New Testament highlight names of individuals whom God elected and predestined. The list is long:

- Abraham (Nehemiah 9:7)
- Jacob (Genesis 25:19–34; 27:1–41; Malachi 1:2–3; Romans 9:10–13)
- Pharaoh (Exodus 9:16; Romans 9:17)
- David (1 Samuel 16:1–13)
- Josiah (1 Kings 13:1–3)
- Cyrus (Isaiah 41:25; 44:28; 45:1–13; 2 Chronicles 36:22–23)
- Jeremiah (Jeremiah 1:5)
- John the Baptist (Isaiah 40:3; Malachi 4:5–6; Luke 1:17)
- Jesus (Isaiah 42:1; Matthew 12:18; Luke 9:35; Acts 2:23; 4:28)

- Judas Iscariot (Psalm 41:9; 69:25; 109:8; Mark 14:10; Acts 1:20)
- The twelve apostles (Luke 6:13; John 6:70; 15:16)
- Paul (Acts 9:15; 13:2; Romans 1:1; Galatians 1:15–16; Ephesians 3:7)
- Rufus (Romans 16:13)

We should notice first in this that God ordains individuals to a *task,* not a destiny (with the possible exception of Judas Iscariot). Abraham was called to found a nation, and Pharaoh to release that nation. David was chosen to lead a kingdom, and Cyrus was to restore that kingdom after captivity. John was destined to prepare for Jesus's coming, and Jesus, to die on a cross. Judas Iscariot was fated to betray Jesus, and the other apostles, to testify to his resurrection. Paul and Jeremiah were elected from birth to preach a message for which they would suffer.

If God calls *you* to a task, you *will* perform that task—either his way or yours. Nonetheless, you *will* do what God calls you to do.

Second, we should notice that not everyone gets the same invitation, but all are invited. Not everyone gets the same call, but all are called. God has a practical purpose for your life. This is not to say God has just one specific thing you're to do in your lifetime. Rather, in every season of your life, God wants to meet you at the intersection of your gifts, passions, and experiences to use the unique you to glorify him. There's something right here, right now that only you can do for God's honor. Discover that, and you'll find your voice, your passion, and your purpose.

Key Points

- According to Jesus, election is God's invitation plus a person's response.
- Predestination is God setting the boundary of salvation and seeing beforehand who would enter in.
- Individuals are predestined to a task, not a destiny.

This Week

- ☐ **Day 1:** Read the essay.
- ☐ **Day 2:** Memorize Matthew 22:14.
- ☐ **Day 3:** Read Acts 9:1–31.
- ☐ **Day 4:** Meditate on Joshua 24:15; Romans 8:29–30; 2 Peter 3:9.
- ☐ **Day 5:** Identify what you alone are qualified to do for God. Share this with a friend or mentor who can help you determine action steps to carry it out.

Overachiever Challenge: Memorize Joshua 24:15.

Bonus Read: Robert Shank, *Elect in the Son: A Study of the Doctrine of Election.*

25

The Supernatural

He will say to those on his left, "Depart from me, you cursed, into the eternal fire prepared for the devil and his angels."

—Matthew 25:41

Question: Is there really a spiritual world active around me?

Heaven and hell, demons and angels—these are fuel for science fiction and horror flicks. But that makes them no less real. On the authority of Jesus alone, we can affirm them all. In fact, this verse encompasses all facets of the supernatural world.

This essay is a simple survey with a single point—to raise our awareness that we're not alone in this world. There's an unseen reality raging all around us.

Fast Facts on Heaven

Most people believe the cartoon version of heaven—you know, the one with naked cherubs covering their private parts with harps. They float on clouds and sing delicate chants resembling medieval monks. If that's the real heaven, it's little wonder pagans are not repulsed by hell.

That version of heaven is unappealing and untenable. According to the Scriptures, heaven isn't a place that's monochromatic or "fluffy." The robust description in Revelation 21–22 includes resurrected bodies, a resplendent city fourteen hundred miles *square,* gigantic gates of single pearls, pavement of pure gold—and, of course, the tangible presence of God, harking back to the beauty of Eden. In addition to music, there appears to be food, pleasure, rest, learning, celebration, and creativity. The real shock for most people is that our true eternal destination is actually the new *earth,* where we'll live eternally in physical bodies unstained by sin.

There's a lot we don't yet know about heaven, like the nature of our new bodies or whether we'll retain painful memories from this life. But what we do know is compelling. There'll be no police, soldiers, physicians, lawyers, or preachers. There will be no need for Kleenex, clocks, locks, coffins, or courts. No longer will there be the IRS, ICE, CIA, FBI, AARP, or CDC. Furthermore (and this is most extraordinary), without Satan, corrupt culture, time constraints, or arrogance, we will actually experience sinlessness. Let that sink in. We'll have the realistic capacity to completely eliminate sin in our new bodies.

No one currently inhabits the new earth. All who have died in Christ await the resurrection, just as we do. Several passages in the New Testament give us information about this temporary place of comfort and peace. According to Jesus's story of the rich man and Lazarus, the righteous are at "Abraham's side" (Luke 16:22). Paul simply said death would bring him into the immediate presence of Jesus (Philippians 1:21–24). Finally, in Revelation 6:9–11, the martyred saints wear white robes and wait before God's throne. In short, those who die in Christ, though comforted, still long for new bodies and the ultimate justice of final judgment.

Fast Facts on Hell

Hell is a buzzkill. Who wants to talk about it? For many, it's so offensive they say with an air of superiority, "I can't believe in a God who would send someone to hell." Really? I can't believe in a God who wouldn't! For all our cultural discourse about social justice, how could we ignore eternal justice? How could a

God remotely good ignore the pain and evil of this world? For this reason, the Bible's description of hell emphasizes justice and righteousness.

According to Scripture, hell is a real place of torment, described with the metaphors of flames, sulfur, worms, darkness, and gnashing of teeth (Isaiah 66:24; Matthew 22:13; 25:41, 46; Mark 9:48; 2 Thessalonians 1:8–9; Revelation 14:11; 20:10). Because these passages describe future and spiritual realities, it's difficult to know how literally to take those details.

It's surprising to most people that our most common images of hell come more from a fourteenth-century poetic masterpiece—Dante's *Inferno*—than from the pages of Scripture. Dante's imaginative description was more literarily creative than theologically accurate. So let's set some of the record straight.

Technically speaking, hell (or "Hades," to use the Greeks' term) is only a temporary holding cell, whereas the ultimate prison, not yet inhabited, is the lake of fire mentioned in Revelation 20:10. This lake of fire is the eternal place of punishment for our sins on earth. This may seem excessive, but perhaps that's because we fail to see sin from God's perspective: as mutiny against perfect holiness.

Another truth that often eludes us is that a person's damnation is not God's desire but that person's own decision. Technically, God doesn't throw people into hell. Individuals reject God's presence; where else are they to go but to a place inhabited by those who refuse God's rule? Let's be frank: people who reject God on this earth have made their own hell here. Perhaps the descriptions in the Bible have less to do with God's design than the environment unbelievers inevitably create for themselves, apart from the control of the Holy Spirit.

Fast Facts on Demons

Demons are real, and they're no joke. They know who Jesus is (Mark 1:24, 34) and believe in God (James 2:19), yet they choose to follow Satan, who is himself a fallen angel (Revelation 12:7–9). They seek to inhabit human beings (Matthew 12:43). Yet they're innately destructive, causing blindness (Matthew 12:22), deafness and muteness (Mark 9:25), deformity (Luke 13:11), seizures (Matthew 17:14–18), mental illness (Matthew 11:18; Luke 7:33; John 7:20; 8:48, 52; 10:20, 21), and suicidal impulses (Matthew 17:15; Mark 5:5). They tend to be loud (Mark 1:26) and are organized into a global force (Revelation 16:14). While they wield considerable influence (Mark 8:33), they'll ultimately be destroyed (Revelation 20:1–10). Though they can perform some miracles (Revelation 16:14), their power is limited by God (Romans 8:38–39; Revelation 9:20).

Demons tend to get a foothold in a human soul through four conduits: cultic activities (such as séances) and the classic triad of sex, drugs, and any musical style that honors the dark spiritual world. Participation in these is not a guarantee that a demon will gain access. They are, however, the most common conduits.

The actual biblical term for demonic control of a person is not *demon possession* but *demonization.* There are multiple levels or gradations of demonic influence:

1. Temptation—external situations that increase your access to sin.
2. Oppression—physical or emotional harm caused by an external attack (an accident, sickness, death, etc.).
3. Influence—mental influence toward anger, depression, violence, or self-harm.
4. Possession—the physical body is controlled, in whole or in part (hands, voice, eyes, supernatural muscular strength, etc.).

The deeper the level of influence or control, the more aggressive the response must be. If someone is at level 3 or 4, an experienced exorcist may be required to intervene. It's complicated and messy. (A helpful resource is Neil Anderson's *The Bondage Breaker.*)

For the vast majority of us, there are three quick steps to minimize demonic influence: Scripture (reading or quoting aloud), worship music, and praying aloud in Jesus's name. These three activities drive demons crazy. You can actually irritate them away, not completely or permanently, but it will offer a reprieve. The more entrenched the foothold of a demon, the more radical will be the measures needed to repel it.

This takes us to Ephesians 6:12: "We do not wrestle against flesh and blood, but against the rulers, against the authorities, against the cosmic powers over this present darkness, against the spiritual forces of evil in the heavenly places." Paul went on to list the specific armament we have as Christians (verses 13–18). The only offensive weapon Paul mentioned is "the sword of the Spirit, which is the word of God" (verse 17). Interestingly, this word for "word" signifies not the printed text of the Bible but rather the spoken word. It's not enough to merely know theology; we have to verbalize the promises of God. As we open our mouths to testify to Jesus, especially in evangelism, demons are put to flight—or at least put on notice that their tactics won't end well.

The other offensive weapon in the passage (not part of the armor itself) is prayer (verse 18). Believers who speak the truth of God, sing the praise of God, and petition the living God are far more likely to come out less scathed in the spiritual battles they wage. Don't play defense with demons; play offense!

Fast Facts on Angels

Angels pop up all over the Bible. The New Testament has more than 170 mentions of angels. The word *angel* is used sixty-seven times in Revelation alone.

Angels have three primary functions. First and foremost, they're messengers. That's actually the meaning of the Greek word *aggelos*. Notice how angels hover around the coming of Jesus—whether it's his first coming or his final coming.

Second, angels minister to Jesus (Mark 1:13) and to his people (Psalm 91:11–12). They comforted Jesus in Gethsemane (Luke 22:43), carried Lazarus to Abraham's side (16:22), and released the apostles from prison (Acts 5:19; 12:7–11). An angel led Philip to the Ethiopian eunuch (8:26); another assassinated Herod Agrippa (12:23); still another predicted Paul's safe arrival in Rome (27:23–24). In fact, Hebrews 1:14 says, "Are not all angels ministering spirits sent to serve those who will inherit salvation?" (NIV).

Third, angels validate God's men by mere association. In other words, you stand an angel next to a guy, and he suddenly wears a white hat. This was true for Moses (Acts 7:35) and Cornelius, who was the first Gentile convert (10:3–4). Being in company with an angel marks a person as God's. Thus, angels rejoice in heaven whenever a sinner repents (Luke 15:10).

Key Points

- Heaven and hell are real places described in the Bible with the best metaphors available.
- Demons gain greater access through the occult, sex, drugs, and dark music. Conversely, they're hindered through Scripture, praise, and prayer.
- Angels announce Jesus whenever he comes, assist believers in carrying out their call, and affirm those God approves.

This Week

- ☐ **Day 1:** Read the essay.
- ☐ **Day 2:** Memorize Matthew 25:41.
- ☐ **Day 3:** Read Revelation 12–13.
- ☐ **Day 4:** Meditate on Ephesians 6:12; Hebrews 1:14; Revelation 20:10.
- ☐ **Day 5:** Ask three Christian friends whether they've ever encountered an angel or a demon. Try to learn from them how their experience aligns with biblical descriptions.

Overachiever Challenge: Memorize Ephesians 6:12.

Bonus Read: Neil T. Anderson, *The Bondage Breaker.*

26

Our Co-Mission

All authority in heaven and on earth has been given to me. Go therefore and make disciples of all nations, baptizing them in the name of the Father and of the Son and of the Holy Spirit, teaching them to observe all that I have commanded you. And behold, I am with you always, to the end of the age.

—Matthew 28:18–20

Question: What's the mission of the church?

Global evangelism is not *our* mission; it's *God's* mission. It's merely our *co*-mission. Hence, we call it the Great Commission. We're not trying to evangelize the world on our own; we're merely trying to partner with God in what he's already doing in our midst to rescue the world he loves.

This is a crucial concept for Christians. The world is not our responsibility but God's. Ours is merely to be available to go where God needs us to go and to be who we already are, influencing those whom we already have a relationship with. That's the implication of the Greek word for "go." It could literally be rendered "as you are going." In other words, "As you go about your business, remember to make Jesus famous." We don't need marketing skills, sales tactics, or intellectual answers to people's questions. We simply need to follow Jesus and help others walk along with us.

The Great Commission is simple: walk with people as you walk with Jesus. Before long, they'll meet each other.

The Great Commission isn't complicated. It is, however, a big deal. In fact, all four Evangelists have their own version of the commission, as does the apostle Paul:

> [Jesus] said to them, "Go into all the world and proclaim the gospel to the whole creation. Whoever believes and is baptized will be saved, but whoever does not believe will be condemned." (Mark 16:15–16)

> Repentance for the forgiveness of sins should be proclaimed in his name to all nations, beginning from Jerusalem. You are witnesses of these things. (Luke 24:47–48)

> "As the Father has sent me, even so I am sending you." And when he had said this, he breathed on them and said to them, "Receive the Holy Spirit. If you forgive the sins of any, they are forgiven them; if you withhold forgiveness from any, it is withheld." (John 20:21–23)

> You will receive power when the Holy Spirit has come upon you, and you will be my witnesses in Jerusalem and in all Judea and Samaria, and to the end of the earth. (Acts 1:8)

> We are ambassadors for Christ, God making his appeal through us. We implore you on behalf of Christ, be reconciled to God. (2 Corinthians 5:20)

All of the Call

Clearly the Great Commission calls for "all hands on deck." Every Christian in every vocation at all times is a participant in expanding God's global enterprise. How?

It feels intimidating to share our faith. What if someone asks us a question we can't answer? What if my life falls short of the good example to back up my words? What if my friends reject me because of my witness or I lose my job? These are all valid questions that Jesus dealt with in the commission.

"*All authority* in heaven and on earth has been given to me" (Matthew 28:18). Because of Jesus's impeccable life, sacrificial death, and victorious resurrection, God made him ruler and judge of the world. When we enter his service, we carry his authority. As his ambassadors, our words carry his weight. Paul made that clear in 2 Corinthians 5:20: it's all about "God making his appeal through us." Consequently, we have the authority to actually offer forgiveness of sins on Jesus's behalf.

Obviously, we can do that only by his authorized channel of grace through faith. In other words, we cannot offer forgiveness to anyone who hasn't pledged allegiance to Jesus. But let's not miss the magnitude of this authority. We offer God's grace through Jesus's blood. This is not a job reserved for a priest or bishop but the right and responsibility of every Christ follower.

In political terms, we're Christ's ambassadors (2 Corinthians 5:20). Our declarations are not empty pageantry. Ambassadors bear the weight of the government that authorizes them. As an ambassador of Christ, you can declare a person a friend of God or his enemy based on that person's response to Jesus.

So if someone asks you a question you can't answer, that does little to affect the declaration you're able to make. But what if it's an essential question that needs an answer?

Imagine you're an ambassador sitting at a conference table with foreign leaders. They ask about a process of peace. You don't know the answer. Your president is listening in on a conference call. Don't you suppose he would send you an email or shoot you a text with the proper response? Of course.

This is precisely the promise Jesus made: "When they deliver you over, do not be anxious how you are to speak or what you are to say, for what you are to say will be given to you in that hour. For it is not you who speak, but the Spirit of your Father speaking through you" (Matthew 10:19–20). If our fear of not having answers keeps us from sharing our story, it's because we lack faith in Jesus to keep his word. There's no way God is going to abandon you if you open your mouth. Why? Because this is *his* mission and *your* commission. He's more committed to the process than we will ever be.

"Make disciples of *all nations*" (Matthew 28:19). One of the most extraordinary things about Jesus is his global aspirations. You probably couldn't have predicted that during his three-year ministry. After all, he focused on Israel, not foreigners. Prior to his death, he never ordered his disciples onto foreign soil. He never traveled outside the traditional boundaries of Israel. So why all of a sudden would he aim at global conquest?

The fact of the matter is that Jesus always had that in mind. He started with his own people and culture because the nation of Israel was the hope of the world. Even at the earliest stages, however, Jesus's ministry was always outward focused. His healings, preaching, and commands always push us further and further away from the center.

This is in stark contrast to virtually every other religious tradition that drives its adherents further inward. Through deeper devotion, more demanding rituals, or higher knowledge, the disciple of Islam or Judaism or Buddhism or whatever religion will seek a higher position in the religious hierarchy. But for Christians, it's our outward focus through evangelism and social service that fulfills our deepest obligations in Christ Jesus.

"Teaching them to observe *all that I have commanded you*" (verse 20). This is, at first, overwhelming. Who can possibly remember, let alone obey, all the commands of Jesus?

Well, they're not that hard to remember, since Jesus reduced all the commands of the Old Testament to two simple instructions: love God and love people (Matthew 22:37–40). While that's easy to memorize, it's impossible to perfect. That's why it requires teaching. The role of every Christian is to help apply these commands. It's the role of the mother with her children, the husband with his wife, the employer with his workers, the coach with her players. Wherever God places you, your purpose is clear: to help at least one person take at least one step toward God and others.

Lest we think this is too much to ask, Jesus added to the commission a promise: "Behold, *I am with you always,* to the end of the age" (Matthew 28:20). Because this is God's mission and our co-mission, he's fully prepared to be fully present. Jesus himself will continue to be with us through the Holy Spirit, who will guide, chide, and provide the wisdom, power, and opportunities.

The completion of this command will usher in the new age of eternity. When our full obedience fulfills his commission, his presence will become tangible, and our troubles will meet the end of time.

Make Disciples

Matthew 28:18–20 packs a powerful punch. The commission is a single sentence with only one verb, which happens to be an imperative. It isn't "baptizing." That's not our command. Nor is it "go." We may or may not be sent to far-flung places. The singular command of this commission is to "make disciples."

That command comes with considerable freight, to be sure. There are shelves of books on discipleship. All kinds of authors argue for all kinds of methods. Most of these can be helpful. Many of the books are insightful. Nonetheless, right here, right now, let's keep this simple. In a single sentence, *a disciple is a learner*—a student, so to speak.

However, the particular type of learning in Jewish culture had less to do with information and more to do with transformation. It was more about behavior than about books. It's what we would call mentoring or life coaching. A learner would observe and imitate the practices a mentor would model. That's the core of the commission, and it's the obligation of every Christ follower.

Though all of us are at different levels of maturity, all of us have someone who looks up to us. For some it's a child; for others, an athlete; for others, a newbie at work. We can each leverage those relationships to help someone else walk a bit closer to Christ.

Before Jesus left this earth, he gave us one last command. The "all of the call" requires that "each one reach one." From the moment we drip dry in the baptistery until we cross the threshold of eternity, our commission—our partnership with God—is to make Jesus famous.

Key Points

- The Great Commission is God's mission, not ours.
- This command is universal: reach *all* people in *all* places at *all* times.
- Our prime directive is to make disciples by mentoring others to loyalty to Jesus.

This Week

☐ **Day 1:** Read the essay.

☐ **Day 2:** Memorize Matthew 28:18–20.

☐ **Day 3:** Read Acts 10–11.

☐ **Day 4:** Meditate on Mark 16:15–16; John 20:21–23; 2 Corinthians 5:20.

☐ **Day 5:** Identify by name one person whom you could bring at least one step closer to Jesus.

Overachiever Challenge: Memorize 2 Corinthians 5:20.

Bonus Read: Bill Bright, *How You Can Help Fulfill the Great Commission.*

27

The Gospel

The beginning of the gospel of Jesus Christ, the Son of God.

—Mark 1:1

Question: What is the gospel?

The word *gospel* literally means "good news." In one sense, the gospel is the summary of the Christian message. That is, the gospel is the content of what we preach. Paul used it this way in Romans 1:16: "I am not ashamed of the gospel, for it is the power of God for salvation to everyone who believes, to the Jew first and also to the Greek." In a broader sense, the gospel is a biography. Specifically, it's the story of Jesus's life and death.

The New Testament opens with four gospels, individual narratives of Jesus's ministry. So *gospel* can be a message, or it can be the narrative of Jesus's life, death, and resurrection. Both are Christian. However, *gospel* wasn't originally a religious word. It originated as a political term.

The Gospel and Politics

In every major city across the Roman world, there were couriers bringing good news from the capital. The crowds gave their attention because they knew it was an important announcement. The good news of the Roman heralds was usually something about the highest leader of the land. When the emperor got married, for example, the good news was relayed by official ambassadors to all parts of the empire. They wanted the citizens to know that the emperor would be able to pass on his heritage to the next generation. Likewise, when the ruler had a child, the message was proclaimed far and wide.[1]

Aside from emperors, generals also generated good news after a military victory.[2] Couriers carried the official script to cities and suburbs: "Good news: we won the war."

Military success, marriage, and procreation were the common core of these political gospels. Their contents were inscribed on parchment, stones, and pillars so the people could celebrate and rally around their ruler. That's an important sentence. Read that last clause again: *so the people could celebrate and rally around their ruler!*

One example from 9 BC was found in the city of Priene. An inscription about Octavian reads,

> Because providence has ordered our life in a divine way . . . and since the Emperor through his epiphany has exceeded the hopes of former good news [*euaggelia,* the Greek word for "gospel"], surpassing not only the benefactors who came before him, but also leaving no hope that anyone in the future will surpass him, and since the birthday of the god was for the world the beginning of his good news [may it therefore be decreed that] . . .[3]

Set aside for a moment the obvious blasphemy and political propaganda. This inscription clarifies the purpose of any gospel. The good news was to unify the people around a political figure who could promote and protect them.

Christians adopted this term for exactly the same reason. They wanted to exalt their emperor, Jesus, who could promote and protect their spiritual prosperity. Christians made this claim in direct opposition to the Roman emperor's claim to be the ruler of the world. By the very use of the term, they were asserting a counternarrative to imperial Rome's. They were suggesting that the emperor had been trumped by Messiah. As near as we can tell, this claim was first made by young John Mark as he wrote his gospel under Peter's influence in the capital city of Rome.

The Gospel and the Gospels

Mark wasted no time confronting the imperial powers. He opened his book with these words: "The beginning of the gospel of Jesus Christ, the Son of God" (1:1). This set the tone for the rest of the book. He offered two political titles for Jesus in this opening: "Messiah" and "Son of God." The first is Jewish; the second, Roman; both mean essentially the same thing.

Every Jew would know the basic meaning of *messiah*. The word literally means "anointed one." It referred primarily to the regal son of David (Israel's most famous king). He was to restore the Jewish kingdom to its glory days under David. He would conquer Israel's enemies, sit on a royal throne, and restore the order and purity of the temple. He would be king, liberator, and national hero. *Messiah* may mean more, but it cannot mean less.

Mark's Roman readers knew little about Jewish messianic hopes or the history of ancient Israel. What they would understand, however, is the term *Son of God*. That's a title commonly used to refer to the emperor. This world ruler had divine rights. The emperor's predecessor attained divine status. During the time Mark penned his gospel, emperors were being worshipped as gods. That's why Mark's introduction could have landed him in prison. He was asserting a new world ruler.

Why would John Mark talk like that? The following historical reconstruction offers a plausible explanation. According to tradition, he was a teenager when Jesus ate the Last Supper upstairs in his home. As the apostles gathered for the Last Supper, Mark's parents provided an upper room. Undoubtedly, young Mark strained to hear Jesus's farewell speech. Later he would listen as the apostles left and headed to the garden. So when the soldiers showed up to arrest Jesus, Mark raced to the garden to warn him. Try as he might to outrun the troops, he arrived too late to warn Jesus of his impending arrest. Mark had left home so quickly he was wearing only his inner garment. When a soldier caught him by the collar, he wriggled loose and ran for his life. Mark 14:51–52 records this odd event of a secret streaker. Who else could it be but John Mark? Though his actions may have been ill advised, they were nonetheless courageous. Jesus was his national hero and one worth rescuing.

If John Mark risked his life in the garden to protect Jesus, is it any wonder that in Rome he proclaimed Jesus as a political ruler? This young man accompanied Paul and Barnabas on Paul's first missionary journey (Acts 13–14). Again he failed to finish what he started. For that reason, Paul refused to allow him to reengage on his second itinerant tour (Acts 15:36–38). So Barnabas and Paul separated, and Barnabas took John Mark with him (verse 39). Eventually John Mark made his way to Rome as an assistant for Peter, the other "pillar" apostle. Like so many of us, John Mark had a history of failure but a heart to keep promoting Jesus. This time he got it right. His gospel begins where Jesus's own life ended, by confronting one of the most challenging questions for an individual and a society: Who gets to be the boss?

The Gospel and the Church

The Gospels use some form of the word *Gospel* ("good news") twenty-three times. The rest of the New Testament has more than a hundred uses after Jesus's resurrection. The gospel is not merely the story of Jesus *for* the church but the proclamation of salvation *through* the church. Simply put, the purpose of the church is to announce Jesus as the emperor, King of kings, ruler of heaven and earth. The gospel is the good news that each of us can have our sins forgiven. Yet it's more than good news for an individual. It's the good news of a new nation.

We call this nation the kingdom of God because it's a global *and* eternal enterprise. Jesus is our emperor and we're his envoys. This isn't merely our message; it's our responsibility. Paul put it this way: "If I preach the gospel, that gives me no ground for boasting. For necessity is laid upon me. Woe to me if I do not preach the gospel!" (1 Corinthians 9:16).

Because this announcement is of utmost importance, Satan will work overtime to make sure it doesn't receive a full hearing. From the time the Gospels were written until our own day, there has been a concerted satanic and cultural attack against the message of Jesus's reign. We're to be vigilant not only in proclaiming the gospel but also in keeping it pure. Listen to Paul's criticism of the Galatians who'd polluted his preaching:

> I am astonished that you are so quickly deserting him who called you in the grace of Christ and are turning to a different gospel—not that there is another one, but there are some who trouble you and want to distort the gospel of Christ. But even if we or an angel from heaven should preach to you a gospel contrary to the one we preached to you, let him be accursed. As we have said before, so now I say again: If anyone is preaching to you a gospel contrary to the one you received, let him be accursed. (Galatians 1:6–9)

There's only one true gospel of Jesus. Hence, we're to do everything in our power to put him on his throne. This isn't merely a metaphor. Through his church, Jesus *reigns* in this world. It's our responsibility and privilege to be his couriers, announcing to far-flung places this singular truth that we have a king named Jesus who sits on the throne in God's heaven to bring healing to God's earth.

This message is so badly needed. This good news feels so desperately overdue. Let the declaration of the apostle Paul become your own: "I do not account my life of any value nor as precious to myself, if only I may finish my course and the ministry that I received from the Lord Jesus, to testify to the gospel of the grace of God" (Acts 20:24).

Key Points

- The word *gospel* literally means "good news" and was originally a political term.
- Mark was the first Christian writer to use the term; he did so in direct opposition to the emperor's claims to be the ruler of the world.
- Even more than the description of Jesus's life, the gospel is the announcement of the church. Our prime directive is to proclaim Jesus as the one true king of the world.

This Week

- ☐ **Day 1:** Read the essay.
- ☐ **Day 2:** Memorize Mark 1:1.
- ☐ **Day 3:** Read John 2.
- ☐ **Day 4:** Meditate on Acts 20:24; Romans 1:16; Galatians 1:6–9.
- ☐ **Day 5:** Ask yourself two questions: (1) If you claimed Romans 1:16 for your life, would your friends and family have enough evidence to defend your claim? (2) What practical steps can you take to make Acts 20:24 a reality in your schedule this week?

Overachiever Challenge: Memorize Romans 1:16.

Bonus Read: Scot McKnight, *The King Jesus Gospel: The Original Good News Revisited.*

28

Faith

> The time is fulfilled, and the kingdom of God is at hand; repent and believe in the gospel.
>
> —MARK 1:15

Question: What is faith?

It seems odd that we would even need to ask the question. Isn't it obvious? Actually, no. To many and for far too long, faith has been reduced to belief. A rational recognition that Jesus died and rose from the dead doesn't always translate into a life transformed. After all, even the demons believe that (James 2:19).

Now, to be clear, there's nothing wrong with belief; there's just not enough right with it.

Rationalism equates faith to right thinking. Existentialists equate it to personal experience. Neither reaches the depth of biblical faith.

So let's begin with the Bible's own definition of *faith:* "Faith is the assurance of things hoped for, the conviction of things not seen" (Hebrews 11:1). This is important because just a few verses later we read, "Without faith it is impossible to please him, for whoever would draw near to God must believe that he exists and that he rewards those who seek him" (verse 6).

Faith as Fidelity

There's no reason to allow either rationalists or existentialists to hijack faith. We can eavesdrop on a first-century Jewish conversation to sharpen our focus on faith. Flavius Josephus was a Jewish aristocrat roughly contemporaneous with the apostle Paul. He became a general during a Jewish revolt against the Romans. He fought against Vespasian (who later became the emperor). Josephus was badly beaten by Vespasian—who, rather than killing Josephus, used him for political propaganda.

Over the course of the next few decades, Josephus penned two books that are the most reliable historical sources about the Jews and their homeland during this period. His first, *The Wars of the Jews,* was a deliberate attempt to persuade his countrymen of the invincibility of Rome and the futility of revolt. His second book, *The Antiquities of the Jews,* was propaganda aimed in the opposite direction. Here he tried to present Judaism favorably to his Roman audience. His writing, though somewhat prejudiced, is among the best eyewitness accounts of the critical events surrounding Jerusalem's demise.

In his autobiography, Josephus recorded a story that uses almost identical verbiage to Mark 1:15. The year was AD 67. The rebellion had begun, and a number of factions were vying for power. Josephus had been appointed general and was sent from Jerusalem to Galilee to speak with rebel leaders. Those opposing Josephus's leadership hired a man—who (confusingly) was named Jesus—to attack Josephus. Josephus learned of the plot and thwarted it. Rather than destroying his would-be attacker, he attempted to turn him. Here is Josephus in his own words:

> I then called Jesus to me by himself, and told him, that "I was not a stranger to that treacherous design he had against me, nor was I ignorant by whom he was sent for; that, however, I would forgive him what he had done already, if he would *repent* of it, and *be faithful* to me hereafter."[1]

Josephus offered the man a chance to alter his destiny by transferring his loyalties. That's an excellent summary of biblical faith.

The words *repent* and *be faithful* in Josephus's account are the very Greek words found in Mark 1:15. Josephus wasn't telling his enemy to feel sorry about what he'd done. He wasn't calling him to a higher moral path. On the contrary, Josephus was challenging him to a new allegiance. From that starting point, we can understand with greater clarity Jesus's own call.

First, his call to repentance was not about feeling sorry. It was a long-term commitment to shift allegiance to a new master. Second, Jesus wasn't inviting us to lay down our abilities or passions. Rather, he was inviting us to bring those, along with all the aspirations they represent, and offer them to the service of God. Third, faith is not what Jesus called us to believe. It is a pledge of allegiance he was asking us to make.

Faith is fidelity—loyalty and commitment. Anything less is shallow and ineffective. Just as Josephus called his adversary to show him loyalty, Jesus Christ calls us to pledge our allegiance to him. He *is* the good news. He's the new emperor and king. He's the Savior and sovereign Lord.

Every soldier, husband, and frat brother knows the weight of a pledge. This is the loyalty Jesus Christ demands from us.

Fidelity as Obedience

When we start talking about adding obedience to faith, this is where so many theologians get nervous. It feels as if we're claiming to be saved by works, not faith alone.

That concern is duly noted. After all, the single greatest difference between Christianity and all other religions is the fact that *God* saved us; we didn't have to work to save ourselves. Correctly understood, however, obedience is not added to faith. It's the natural response of fidelity.

Again, let's be clear. We're not saying that obedience saves us. We're not even saying that obedience validates our faith, as if it confirms the adequate intensity of our belief. Rather, we're asserting that faith in essence is loyalty. *Obedience is the expression of loyalty, not the proof of it.* Our "works" are the natural and inevitable expression of the fidelity we pledge to our king.

Nowhere is this more clearly stated than in the letter from Jesus's own brother James: "Faith by itself, if it does not have works, is dead. But someone will say, 'You have faith and I have works.' Show me your faith apart from your works, and I will show you my faith by my works" (2:17–18). He went on to give two examples of people who lived lives of loyalty. First, Abraham, the father of faith, demonstrated by his obedience that he truly believed God: "Was not Abraham our father justified by works when he offered up his son Isaac on the altar? You see that faith was active along with his works, and faith was completed by his works" (verses 21–22). Second, Rahab, a prostitute, demonstrated her faith when she shifted loyalty from her comrades in Jericho to the invading Israelites: "In the same way was not also Rahab the prostitute justified by works when she received the messengers and sent them out by another way?" (verse 25).

In no way does this mean that Abraham earned his salvation by keeping the law. In fact, Abraham is the very example Paul used to prove we're *not* saved by the rules we keep: "If Abraham was justified by works, he has something to boast about, but not before God. For what does the Scripture say? 'Abraham believed God, and it was counted to him as righteousness'" (Romans 4:2–3). Likewise, Paul said this in Galatians 2:16:

> We know that a person is not justified by works of the law but through faith in Jesus Christ, so we also have believed in Christ Jesus, in order to be justified by faith in Christ and not by works of the law, because by works of the law no one will be justified.

Neither James nor Paul discounted works. Both insisted that works be put in their right place. As an attempt to earn God's grace, works fail. Yet when good works are "in Christ," they demonstrate faith in God's free gift of salvation. Paul said we were "created in Christ Jesus for good works" (Ephesians 2:10). Good works in Christ are an inevitable expression of our faith. Furthermore, when we obey God, our lives get better. In this sense, obedience is more God's favor to us than our offering to him. This is ancient wisdom: "Trust in the LORD with all your heart, and do not lean on your own understanding. In all your ways acknowledge him, and he will make straight your paths" (Proverbs 3:5–6).

We see this clearly every time the final judgment is described in the New Testament. Our works are what is judged, since they're the tangible and visible expression of our fidelity. Jesus said it first: "Do not marvel at this, for an hour is coming when all who are in the tombs will hear his voice and come out, those who have done good to the resurrection of life, and those who have done evil to the resurrection of judgment" (John 5:28–29). Paul confirmed what Jesus said:

> He will render to each one according to his works: to those who by patience in well-doing seek for glory and honor and immortality, he will give eternal life; but for those who are self-seeking and do not obey the truth, but obey unrighteousness, there will be wrath and fury. (Romans 2:6–8)

Peter, the other great apostle, concurred: "If you call on him as Father who judges impartially according to each one's deeds, conduct yourselves with fear throughout the time of your exile" (1 Peter 1:17). John concluded Revelation with the same affirmation: "I saw the dead, great and small, standing before the throne, and books were opened. Then another book was opened, which is the book of life. And the dead were judged by what was written in the books, according to what they had done" (20:12).

In conclusion, here's a simple litmus test you can use to measure your faith. Those who are trying to earn salvation through works ask, "Is this all I have to do?" Those who are living their allegiance to God ask a different question: "What else can I do?"

Simply put, faith *works*.

Key Points

- *Faith* (the same Greek word as "belief") should be read as "fidelity" or "loyalty."
- We're saved "by grace . . . through faith . . . for good works" (Ephesians 2:8–10).
- Obedience (or "good works") is not a means of earning salvation but an inevitable expression of allegiance by those who've been saved.

This Week

☐ **Day 1:** Read the essay.

☐ **Day 2:** Memorize Mark 1:15.

☐ **Day 3:** Read Genesis 6:9–9:17.

☐ **Day 4:** Meditate on Proverbs 3:5–6; Hebrews 11:1; James 2:17–18.

☐ **Day 5:** Watch a patriotic film such as *The Patriot, A Few Good Men,* or *Captain America: The First Avenger,* and ask how *faith* would be defined through that movie.

Overachiever Challenge: Memorize James 2:17–18.

Bonus Read: Dietrich Bonhoeffer, *The Cost of Discipleship.*

29

Rest

> The Sabbath was made for man, not man for the Sabbath. So the Son of Man is lord even of the Sabbath.
>
> —Mark 2:27–28

Question: How can I find rest?

In a world as frenzied as ours, rest is rare. Worker bees race to the office for a barrage of meetings and tasks. Then they fight their way home through rush hour just in time to sit on the sidelines of a kid's event, before collapsing in a recliner until it's time to repeat the cycle.

We desperately need a way off the treadmill.

Sabbath Is the Only Eden We Have Left

You can change your schedule all you want, but until you change your master, you'll never find rest for your soul.

As a culture, we're in crisis. We have no time for the things that matter most. From the very beginning, God knew our need for rest and modeled a radical practice to ensure we would enjoy it. It's called the Sabbath, and we need it now more than ever.

To many, the Sabbath seems archaic and irrelevant. But the Sabbath isn't just one of the Ten Commandments. It's a rhythm originating in Eden:

> On the seventh day God finished his work that he had done, and he rested on the seventh day from all his work that he had done. So God blessed the seventh day and made it holy, because on it God rested from all his work that he had done in creation. (Genesis 2:2–3)

God didn't rest because he was tuckered out. He rested in celebration of creation, and he embedded the Sabbath principle in the physical earth. Land is to lie fallow every seventh year (Leviticus 25:3–4). Animals sleep as part of their daily cycle. Humans are to cease from work one day a week (Exodus 23:12).

The principle is simple: creation's greatest productivity is within a cycle that includes rest. For humans, that means we'll get more done in six days of work than seven. Our minds, emotions, and bodies need time to marinate, clear the clutter, dream, and reorganize. Without rest, our work is impeded because our creativity is stifled. Research shows that after fifty hours of work in a week, our productivity drops precipitously.[1]

In the Ten Commandments, the two prohibitions against idolatry and Sabbath work make up a mere 20 percent of the commandments (Exodus 20:3–17). Yet those commands and the commentary God offered on them make up more than 60 percent of the text. In other words, God had more to say about these two commands than all the others combined. Why? Because he knows that the idolatry of materialism and our refusal to rest from work go hand in hand. He also knows the devastating effects these have on our families, our bodies, and our churches. Typically, the commands regarding the Sabbath and idolatry are violated in tandem.

When we recognize God's ownership of our time and treasure—our two most valuable commodities—we live longer, we're more productive, and we're more generous.

As a consequence of Adam and Eve's sin, humans were expelled from the garden. We were alienated from God. Our use of the earth became more difficult, even cursed. Our marriages got strained (irreparably for many). Our bodies aged and died. The only part of Eden we still have full access to is the Sabbath. If we'll return to the rest we had in Eden, the remainder of our lives will be freer from the curse of Adam's sin.

Jesus Is Lord of the Sabbath

Jesus got sideways with the religious leaders for a number of reasons. He ate with sinners, he didn't perform all the ritual washings, he claimed to be God's son, etc. Yet his most frequent fight was over Sabbath regulations. The Jewish establishment took the simple command "Don't work on the Sabbath" and turned it into a small encyclopedia of prohibitions.

For example, one regulation stated that if you could latch your sandals with one hand, that didn't constitute work. If it took two hands, that was prohibited as "work." A person could carry two acorns of weight; that was okay. If, however, you had three acorns, you had to eat one first before moving on. Women were prohibited from looking in a mirror on the Sabbath lest they see a gray hair and lack the self-control not to pluck it out.

These are pretty petty regulations, but none was so arbitrary as this one: an egg laid on the Sabbath was off limits. Now, you could hatch that egg and eat the chicken. Or you could eat the eggs laid by a chicken hatched from the egg that was laid on the Sabbath. But you couldn't eat that egg laid on the Sabbath.

Is it any wonder Jesus rejected those rules that turned the blessing of rest into a fretful list of regulations requiring us to walk on eggshells?

Jesus consistently rejected the traditional Sabbath regulations. On the Sabbath, he healed a man with a shriveled hand (Mark 3:1–6), a woman bent over (Luke 13:10–17), a man with dropsy (Luke 14:1–6), a lame man at Bethesda (John 5:1–9), and a man born blind (John 9:1–7, 14). Taken as a whole, the point of each of these events could be simply summarized: *humanity should be served by the Sabbath, not burdened by it.* Or to use Jesus's memorable phrase: "The Sabbath was made for man, not man for the Sabbath. So the Son of Man is lord even of the Sabbath" (Mark 2:27–28). Jesus was reclaiming the Sabbath from religion and giving it back to humanity.

Now, any prophet might have said, "The Sabbath should be a blessing, not a burden." The second sentence, however, crossed the boundary of blasphemy: "The Son of Man is lord even of the Sabbath." To be clear, Jesus wasn't claiming control of some esoteric ritual. The Sabbath, along with circumcision and dietary regulations, marked the social boundaries between Israel and the pagan world. In other words, the Sabbath was a key element of being Jewish. Anyone who altered a Mosaic command would have to claim to be on par with Moses. However, to claim to control the Sabbath itself was a claim to stand on par with God. That's the point!

Jesus pressed his lordship with the issue of the Sabbath. He took on squarely one of the central practices of Israel, and he claimed control over it. At the same time, he used that very authority to practice compassion, particularly through healing. This is precisely what we've come to expect from the King of kings, who said, "The Son of Man came not to be served but to serve" (Mark 10:45).

A Critical Warning About Sabbath Keeping

In the Judaism of Jesus's day, God's gift of the Sabbath was turned into law through human regulations. These meticulous rules became a burden rather than a blessing because the principle of rest became a ruler to measure righteousness. The Sabbath is not another rule to be added to your spiritual disciplines. Rather, it's a creational principle to be celebrated as a gift. The Christian life is not a contest to see who can follow the most rules.

Paul gave this important warning about legal regulations, which we should apply here to Sabbath keeping (among other religious rules): "If with Christ you died to the elemental spirits of the world, why, as if you were still alive in the world, do you submit to regulations—'Do not handle, Do not taste, Do not touch'?" (Colossians 2:20–21). Paul's shrewd insight in that passage uncovers the empty arrogance of legalism. What we avoid doesn't make us righteous. Nor do the religious practices we observe. What makes us righteous is the blood of

Jesus. Religious activities are valuable only inasmuch as they train us for serving others. And the prohibited things we avoid are not feathers in our caps. The old rules of religion were crutches we used to help get us through the week, but they're no longer needed, since we're empowered by the Spirit of Christ.

So let's be clear. Our religious acts—attending worship, praying, Bible reading, and keeping the Sabbath—are God's gift to us, not our gift to him. And our choice to avoid certain things is not because outsiders are icky and we are awesome. What we avoid are old habits, no longer relevant since they've been replaced by things far better, deeper, and longer lasting.

The Sabbath is a pause in our week to remember this. Consequently, our practice of Sabbath is a gift we receive, resting from work to refresh our souls, worship God with other believers, and reconnect with family and friends so we can invest in our communities. When the rhythm of rest punctuates our work, we'll experience more productivity at work and more connectivity at home. This is the life God wants for you as much as you do.

Key Points

- Sabbath rest was instituted in Eden as part of the order of creation.
- Jesus claimed authority over the Sabbath to restore its true purpose.
- Legalism makes the Sabbath a burden, not a blessing.

This Week

- ☐ **Day 1:** Read the essay.
- ☐ **Day 2:** Memorize Mark 2:27–28.
- ☐ **Day 3:** Read Mark 2–3.
- ☐ **Day 4:** Meditate on Genesis 2:2; Matthew 11:28–30; Colossians 2:20–21.
- ☐ **Day 5:** Friends and family can read us better than we can read ourselves. Ask them where in your life you need to rest. Inform them of your intention to practice Sabbath in a practical way, and let them hold you accountable.

Overachiever Challenge: Memorize Colossians 2:20–21.

Bonus Read: Richard Swenson, *Margin: Restoring Emotional, Physical, Financial, and Time Reserves to Overloaded Lives.*

30

Leadership

Even the Son of Man came not to be served but to serve, and to give his life as a ransom for many.

—Mark 10:45

Question: How can I achieve greatness?

The disciples expected Jesus to reign as a literal king over Jerusalem. They anticipated serving in his cabinet. After all, Jesus already promised they would sit on twelve thrones (Matthew 19:28). Their hopes fanned into flame an already-smoldering competition among them. Each of them coveted a special appointment.

The Request of James and John

As they were traveling to Jerusalem, James and John approached Jesus. They had their sights on the chief seats at Jesus's right and left. They had the audacity to ask Jesus to grant whatever they asked (Mark 10:35). King Herod earlier used these same words to make an offer to his pubescent stepdaughter: "Ask me for whatever you wish, and I will give it to you" (Mark 6:22). As you might recall, that foolish offer cost Herod dearly, resulting in the beheading of a prophet he respected. Jesus is a different kind of king from Herod and would never submit to such an ill-advised request.

In an honor-shame culture, the positions of power that James and John sought were coveted because of the enormous advantages they could offer to one's friends and family. That's precisely why Salome, their mother, assisted her sons in seeking these seats (Matthew 20:20–21). Because Jesus had already given James and John special privileges, it was not unreasonable to hope he just might grant their request. They had to act quickly, however, lest Peter weasel his way ahead of James. Peter was, after all, a member of the inner circle of three—Jesus's primary assistants. Even Judas Iscariot might make a power play as the group's CFO.

The entire political history known to the disciples would encourage such seeking of rank. From Alexander to Augustus, from David's "mighty men" to the Maccabees, this was the way of political power.

Jesus didn't grant their request. He left that up to God. Instead, Jesus asked whether they were willing to suffer. The synonymous metaphors of "cup" and "baptism" foreshadow suffering. The "cup" was usually a metaphor for God's judgment (Jeremiah 25:15–29; Zechariah 12:2). Likewise, baptism was a metaphor for being drowned in sorrow or suffering: "I have a baptism to be baptized with, and how great is my distress until it is accomplished!" (Luke 12:50).

They thought Jesus was talking about "paying the cost to be the boss." Many regime changes require great sacrifice, even loss of life. They claimed they were up to the challenge. What followed, however, clarified that Jesus had something different in mind. Suffering isn't the price one pays on the way to achieving positions of power. Rather, suffering—particularly through service—is the vocation of all leaders in the kingdom of God.

Greatness in the Kingdom

The request of James and John infuriated the other apostles (Mark 10:41)—not because it was inappropriate but because the others were envious. All of them wanted those seats. Jesus was also scandalized by their request but for a different reason. His reply is telling. Our translations suggest that rulers are recognized as such by those they rule: "those who are regarded as rulers" (verse 42, NIV). The original Greek seems to suggest a different meaning: "those who give the impression [or have the reputation] of ruling." Those who give that impression are the rulers, not the ruled. Thus, Jesus's phrase implies that those in power promoted *themselves* as rulers and sought popular support to substantiate their claim. Doesn't that sound more realistic? Rulers try to jockey for position and popular acclaim. They try to look "presidential" or impress people with their power. These self-promoting leaders give the impression that they're ruling, even though Jesus taught that God alone is the true ruler. Jesus, of course, has been described as a ruler in Mark. Yet here's what's important (and a clear model for any of us who claim to be Christian rulers): each time Jesus exercised his authority—by teaching the crowds, healing people, or casting out demons (Mark 1:22, 27; 2:10–12; 3:15)—he did so for the benefit of the lowly.

Jesus identified worldly leaders as "rulers of the Gentiles" (10:42). In Mark's book there are two who fit this profile—Herod and Pilate. Mark labeled Herod a king, when in fact he was not. Herod did pursue that title at the instigation of his wife, Herodias. However, instead of being given a crown, he was exiled by the emperor in AD 39 because of his ambitions. In Mark's gospel, Herod beheaded John the Baptist through the scheming of his wife and the snare of his teenage stepdaughter (6:21–28). Herod was ruled by a couple of "powerless" women in his own household. They forced him to do what he never would have willingly done had he not been addicted to the perception of power.

As for Pilate, he crucified Jesus against his better judgment (15:12–15). He capitulated to the crowds when they threatened him with blackmail. They suggested he would be no friend of Caesar if he didn't kill Jesus (John 19:12).

Neither Herod nor Pilate had control, even though they had power. They both caved to their subordinates for fear they would lose their title or influence. Here's the universal rule of rulers: *those who present themselves as rulers are ruled by their desire to be seen as rulers.*

What proved true within Mark's gospel was just as true in the larger world of Roman politics, all the way up to the emperor. One coin showed the head of Emperor Tiberius with this inscription: "He who deserves adoration." While Tiberius was an especially terrible example of a self-promoting leader, no emperor from Julius to Hadrian was much different.

There's hardly a fraction of difference between Tiberius and the political rulers in our own day. Technology has changed, but political psychology hasn't budged an inch. Those who desire to be seen as rulers are ruled by their desires. Rulers are slaves to the populace.

Jesus is so different from every other politician. He taught that "whoever would be great among you must be your servant, and whoever would be first among you must be slave of all" (Mark 10:43–44). If we want greatness in Jesus's realm, it will be by serving more, not acquiring higher status in seats of honor.

Jesus's Ultimate Advice on Leadership

"Even the Son of Man came not to be served but to serve, and to give his life as a ransom for many" (verse 45)—this is perhaps the most important thing Jesus ever said. It's certainly the most important leadership lesson he ever gave. Mark 10:45 is a summary of Jesus's biography. He's the Lord who died for the sins of the world. However, if we see only Jesus in this verse, we'll miss two critical leadership lessons.

First, sacrificial suffering is not merely what Jesus did for us but what he modeled for us. Thus, the cross of Jesus is not only a gift to be received; it's also a vocation to be accepted.

Second and more importantly, divorcing Mark 10:45 from its context makes Jesus's statement a religious principle rather than a political practice. In short, Jesus's death is often viewed as only paying the spiritual price for our personal sins rather than being a national ransom for Israel. This is not to deny the unique substitutionary and atoning nature of Jesus's death. It's to affirm, however, that the cross of Jesus is central to his political agenda—the (re)establishment of God's kingdom. It's also to affirm our own role in imitating his practice, not just believing his teaching. Jesus saw his death as the means by which Israel would be liberated from the consequences of her sins in order to establish God's kingdom. Our role is to do the same thing in our own culture: to bring the salvation of Jesus to people in our spheres of influence.

Perhaps nowhere is this seen more clearly or misunderstood more woefully than in Ephesians 5:21, where Paul spoke of "submitting to one another out of reverence for Christ." Paul was as clear as he could be that those who imitate Jesus live in submission to those they serve. All of us are to submit to one another as servants. The next sentence, however, states that wives are to be in submission to their husbands (verse 22). That verse has triggered an avalanche of politically correct misrepresentations of Christianity, as if women are somehow placed in brutal bondage by the expectation of submission. Yet how is that expectation different for any of us? If we follow Jesus, leadership means self-abnegation. This is not humiliation but exaltation in imitation of our Lord Jesus Christ.

This whole theology of humility was nothing new for Jesus. Earlier he told an unlikely parable, recorded in Luke 12, about a master who went away to fetch his bride; when the master returned, his servants were to be ready and waiting. But the story didn't end the way anyone expected. Here are Jesus's own words: "Blessed are those servants whom the master finds awake when he comes. Truly, I say to you, he will dress himself for service and have them recline at table, and *he will come and serve them*" (verse 37). Never had such a thing actually happened. No king, no governor, no leader ever served his servants, especially not at his own wedding—until Jesus. The night before he died, Jesus actually washed his disciples' feet (John 13:1–17). Immediately afterward, he spoke these famous words: "If I then, your Lord and Teacher, have washed your feet, you also ought to wash one another's feet" (verse 14). If Jesus washed feet, there's no task below any of us. Servant leadership historically began with Jesus. Any of us who dare call ourselves leaders had better be proficient with a basin and a towel.

Key Points

- Those who present themselves as rules are ruled by their desire to be seen as rulers.
- The cross isn't merely what Jesus did for us; it's an example of how we should live for others.
- Submission in service to others is a universal expectation that Jesus modeled by washing his disciples' feet.

This Week

- [ ] **Day 1:** Read the essay.
- [ ] **Day 2:** Memorize Mark 10:45.
- [ ] **Day 3:** Read John 12:1–8; 13:1–14.
- [ ] **Day 4:** Meditate on Luke 12:37; John 13:14; Ephesians 5:21.
- [ ] **Day 5:** Go out of your way this week to serve someone in a way that person could never expect or demand.

Overachiever Challenge: Memorize Ephesians 5:21.

Bonus Read: John Howard Yoder, *The Politics of Jesus.*

31

The Greatest Command

Jesus answered, "The most important is, 'Hear, O Israel: The Lord our God, the Lord is one. And you shall love the Lord your God with all your heart and with all your soul and with all your mind and with all your strength.' The second is this: 'You shall love your neighbor as yourself.' There is no other commandment greater than these."

—MARK 12:29–31

Question: What moral issue is most important to God?

This was the last question Jesus answered from his enemies before he died: "One of the scribes came up and heard them disputing with one another, and seeing that [Jesus] answered them well, asked him, 'Which commandment is the most important of all?' " (Mark 12:28). On the surface that might seem to be a difficult question. After all, the Jewish Bible had 613 recorded commands. However, one command towered above the rest. It comes from Deuteronomy 6:4–5. This command was so famous that it has been—and continues to be—featured in every synagogue service. It was a prayer recited daily by Jews and printed, then rolled into little scrolls and tucked into phylacteries on the rabbis' heads and into mezuzahs hung on Jewish doors.

Jesus had been asked a similar question a year earlier. A lawyer approached him—not a lawyer as we think of but a professional in the Mosaic legislation. He asked a question designed to trip up Jesus: "Teacher, what shall I do to inherit eternal life?" (Luke 10:25). Jesus's response was brilliant. He let the lawyer answer his own question, knowing that most lawyers would rather talk than listen. Jesus replied, "What is written in the Law? How do you read it?" (verse 26). The lawyer answered, "You shall love the Lord your God with all your heart and with all your soul and with all your strength and with all your mind, and your neighbor as yourself" (verse 27).

Notice that the lawyer's answer in Luke 10 is identical to Jesus's own answer in Mark 12. Both answers identify two commands: to love God and to love our neighbor. The reason the second command is always connected to the first is simple. One cannot love God without loving one's neighbor. After all, you can't really climb a stairway to heaven to give God a hug or offer him a care package. *Our love of God can be enacted only through our care for our neighbor.*

How Does One Love God?

Let's look at the original command in Deuteronomy 6:4–5: "Hear, O Israel: The Lord our God, the Lord is one. You shall love the Lord your God with all your heart and with all your soul and with all your might." In the original Mosaic command, we were to love God with three parts of our being: our heart, our soul, and our might. This core command is echoed throughout the book of Deuteronomy (10:12; 11:13; 13:3; 30:6), though it's shortened to loving God with our heart and soul. Obviously, this doesn't mean that we no longer have to love God with our might. It's simply an abbreviated way of saying you must love God with all you've got! In fact, whatever combination we use—heart, soul, mind, strength, etc.—the implication is the same: total commitment to God. Anything less lacks the devotion God's dignity demands.

In an interesting addition, Mark's rendition has Jesus saying we're to love God with four parts of our being, not three: "You shall love the Lord your God with all your heart and with all your soul and with all your mind and with all your strength" (12:30). Mark added "with all your mind." Why? Well, Mark wrote his book in Rome to Greek-thinking people, not his native Hebrew neighbors. The Greeks separated the soul into separate parts—the breathing part and the thinking part. Remember, the main idea—whether it's two parts, three, or four—is to love the Lord with your "everything."

So let's look briefly at these parts, one at a time. The *heart* is the center of feelings. It's more than mere emotion; it's the desires that drive our actions. The *soul* represents our energy. It's the life force that jolts us into action. It's the twinkle in our eyes, the bounce in our step, and the giddy in our giddyap. Our *mind* represents the will, even more than our intellectual capacity. Anyone who has raised a two-year-old understands children have a mind of their own—a nearly impenetrable resolve. It's not that kids are so sophisticated as much as they're stubborn. Our *strength* represents our resources, not just our muscles. It's the total force of our money, time, influence, and social connections.

Let's pause a moment and ask a question: Are you loving God with all the resources at your disposal? For example, if you have an emotional passion for God but this doesn't translate into energy utilized for his purpose on this earth—isn't there a deficiency in your affection? Or if you're studying the Bible, thinking you're loving God with your mind, but you're not allowing God's Word to direct the decisions of your day—aren't you failing to loyally love your God? Or perhaps you find yourself attending church, even singing songs of praise, but you're not wielding your influence at work or leveraging your finances to promote the kingdom of God. Isn't this also a truncated love of God?

Let's examine one more passage, then draw some conclusions. In the modern Western world, we assume that love is an emotion rather than an action. It's therefore easy for us to feel as if we're loving God well because we have passion. However, passion without putting it into practice can never honor God as he deserves or demands.

This was especially true in ancient Israel. Love was an action (not emotion) that can be adequately expressed only through loyal obedience. Deuteronomy 10:12 makes this perfectly clear: "Now, Israel, what does the Lord your God require of you, but to *fear* the Lord your God, to *walk* in all his ways, to *love* him, to *serve* the Lord your God with all your heart and with all your soul."

So what's the difference between fearing the Lord, walking in his ways, loving him, and serving him? Answer: nothing! It isn't possible to fear the Lord without serving the Lord. It isn't possible to love him and not walk in his ways. You might think that fearing the Lord and loving him are contrary. They're not. As a father of my own two children, I never distinguished between their loving me and their fearing me; it's both that caused them to obey me. And because of their fear of me, their love for me brought them peace, knowing I was capable of protecting them.

What conclusions can we draw? First, love is an action, not an emotion. I suspect that those who are married understand this well. Saying words without actions to back them up leads to a shaky, even self-destructive relationship. A husband who says "I love you" but doesn't pay the bills, come home after work, or help with the children is engaged in a manipulative farce. If we say we love God, we should show it by living lives that honor him and demonstrate respect for his commands.

The second conclusion builds on the first. We can't love God with only part of who we are and claim that it's actual love for God. If we're moved at church, we must move into our communities. We can't read the Bible eagerly and not change our habits, our hearts, and our schedules. It makes no sense to trust God with our eternity but not with our finances. Nor can we trust God to forgive us our sins and not turn around and forgive those who've sinned against us. It's senseless to thank God for the job we have but not rest on the Sabbath when he promised it would increase our productivity. We could go on, but this sufficiently makes the case.

The third conclusion has to do with the second command—to love our neighbor as ourselves. By now, this should be apparent: the most tangible way of expressing our love for God is in caring for our neighbors. Jesus couldn't have been clearer than he was in Luke 10. The lawyer who asked him about the greatest command tried to justify his neglect of his neighbor by asking, "Who is my neighbor?" (verse 29). Without getting distracted with the linguistic details, you should know that the lawyer used the narrower definition of *neighbor*. He asked not who his fellow citizens were but rather who were those in close enough proximity to merit his love. Jesus answered with a memorable story. We call it the parable of the good Samaritan.

This legal guru was asking Jesus, "Who lives close enough to me that I'm obligated to care for them?" Notice that Jesus changed the question by the end of the story. It's no longer "Who is my neighbor?" but "Who is neighborly?" With that, Jesus also redefined *neighbor*. It's not someone who lives near us but anyone to whom we draw near. We tend to love those who are near geographically, economically, culturally, or ethnically. Jesus's command is not that we like those who are like us but that we serve those who surround us. When we become the tangible hands and feet of Jesus, it becomes clear where our loyalties lie. By this we demonstrate that we love God with all we are.

Key Points

- The greatest command is to love God with all we are and with all we possess.
- Loving God, fearing God, honoring God, and obeying God are all synonymous.
- Practically speaking, the only real way to love God is to care for the people we come in contact with.

This Week

- ☐ **Day 1:** Read the essay.
- ☐ **Day 2:** Memorize Mark 12:29–31.
- ☐ **Day 3:** Read Exodus 20.
- ☐ **Day 4:** Meditate on Deuteronomy 6:4–5; 10:12; Luke 10:26–27.
- ☐ **Day 5:** Identify a random act of kindness you could do in each of these spheres: at work (or school), at home, and in the community.

Overachiever Challenge: Memorize Deuteronomy 6:4–5.

Bonus Read: Jay Pathak and Dave Runyon, *The Art of Neighboring: Building Genuine Relationships Right Outside Your Door.*

32

The Incarnation

> The Word became flesh and dwelt among us, and we have seen his glory, glory as of the only Son from the Father, full of grace and truth.
>
> —John 1:14

Question: Is God Jesus?

John 1:14 is one of the most extraordinary claims ever made. The idea it expresses is what theologians have called the Incarnation. It's the claim that the God of the universe wrapped himself in the frailty of human flesh. In short, God became a man.

If you were raised in the church, you heard over and over again that Jesus is God. To those not raised with this presupposition, it really is an outrageous claim. In fact, this has been the greatest point of contention between Christianity and virtually every other religion. If you think about it, you can understand why. How can the eternal God squeeze into such a small package? Of course, those who really believe in God recognize the impossibility of limiting God from limiting himself. But for many, it's unthinkable that God would reduce himself to a human being.

For the last two thousand years, Christians have been debating skeptics over the mystery of the Incarnation. Typically this question is asked: Is Jesus really

God? It's an important question, and I believe Christians have offered some substantive answers. However, for the sake of our discussion here, I'd like to turn the question around. Rather than asking, "Is Jesus God?" I'd like to ask, "Is God Jesus?" This is perhaps a perplexing turn of phrase. So for clarity I'm simply asking whether Jesus is a better representation of God than anything our own imaginations could produce.

I'm asking this question because of John 1:18: "No one has ever seen God, but the one and only Son, who is himself God and is in closest relationship with the Father, has made him known" (NIV). What John wrote is right. *Our best chance of knowing God is through the life Jesus lived.*

What I want to suggest is simple. If you believe Jesus is God, then the God you believe in is different from any religious deity. The Christian view of God differs in three particular ways. These three beliefs don't just alter our view of God; they transform our lives and how we treat other people.

The Incarnate God Is Near

The first thing the Incarnation implies is that *God is near.* He isn't disengaged in some distant galaxy. We know God and experience God because God came to us. He revealed himself to us through the life and love of Jesus Christ. No other religion teaches this. There are indeed some religions that teach that the divine is near. For example, animistic religions believe that the divine force is found in the world, all around: rocks, rivers, animals, and trees. However, those religions don't promote a personal relationship with God; he's like the Force in *Star Wars*—all around us, but not clear to us.

On the other hand, there are religions with a robust view of God's identity, even naming him—Yahweh (Judaism) or Allah (Islam). However, when God is personalized, he's always distanced. For example, in Judaism, only the high priest could go directly into God's presence—and then only once a year in a very specific room in the temple. In Islam, Allah is too powerful to be personal or present in our realm of the mundane.

The concept of Christianity is decidedly different. We're taught that God came to us in the person of Jesus so we could know God through our experience with Jesus. In fact, we're encouraged to pray directly to God using the most personal title, *Abba,* which means "Father" (Romans 8:15).

At one point, a man named Philip, one of Jesus's apostles, asked Jesus to show them the Father (John 14:8). Listen to Jesus's response: "Have I been with you so long, and you still do not know me, Philip? Whoever has seen me has seen the Father. How can you say, 'Show us the Father'?" (verse 9). *Because of Jesus, God is near*—personally available to every individual.

Again, only Jesus can grant us access to the heavenly Father. Hence, it was perfectly reasonable for Jesus to say three verses earlier, "I am the way, and the truth, and the life. No one comes to the Father except through me" (verse 6).

Peter would later put it another way: "There is salvation in no one else, for there is no other name under heaven given among men by which we must be saved" (Acts 4:12).

The Incarnate God Is Love

A second idea from the Incarnation is that *God loves us.* Now, clearly there are religions that portray God as loving his own people—though they're fewer than you might imagine. In most world religions, deity is indifferent to humanity. Certainly there are gods who protected their people. For example, Yahweh rescued the Jews, and Allah rewards jihadists. Christianity teaches something entirely different: God loves his enemies. "God shows his love for us in that while we were still sinners, Christ died for us" (Romans 5:8).

The death of Jesus is a prerequisite for any theology of God loving his enemies. The first words of Jesus on the cross reflect this: "Father, forgive them, for they know not what they do" (Luke 23:34). That gives Jesus the moral authority to command us to love our enemies (Matthew 5:44). Jesus showed us how.

But I'm getting ahead of myself. We'll talk about the implications of this in a moment.

The Incarnate God Suffered

A third idea from the Incarnation is that *God can suffer.* Going back to Greek mythology and dozens of religions, it's pretty clear that this is a foreign concept. The gods are supposedly beyond our human experience of cold, hunger, loss, or emotional turmoil. They're "above and beyond." But that's not the picture of God as painted through the life of Jesus. He suffered on the cross for the sins of the world.

There's precious little in the Old Testament that would help us predict God's suffering, but two passages stand out: Isaiah 53 and Zechariah 12:10. They're so out of step with Jewish theology that the rabbis found interpreting them to be challenging. Because Christians believe that Jesus fulfilled these texts, they have a clear explanation of these ancient prophecies. This is not to be critical of other religious leaders. Nonetheless, if you don't have the model of the Incarnation, you'll be confused by the concept of God suffering.

So there you have it: three ideas about our God that are possible only because of the incarnation of Jesus. Furthermore, these are the most important ideas we believe about God. These aren't just interesting ideas in the history of religion. The Incarnation isn't just what happened in the life of Jesus. It's a model of how to live as God intended. If you want the best possible life, live incarnationally.

Let's revisit each attribute of God and ask what it means to live like that.

Why Does This Matter?

God is near—he has made himself available. If we could live like that, we would improve every relationship we have.

Husbands and wives often keep secrets and distance to protect their hearts. Parents are often present but not available because of the barriers of technology, fatigue, or secret sin. Friendships are fractured because of our pride or laziness.

Now, becoming more available and near doesn't mean gushing emotions on strangers at the grocery store or revealing our secret insecurities on a first date. However, it does mean that we're to be present where we are—which is easier said than done. But few things would improve productivity at work or relationships at home more than this.

Be present. When a husband comes home, spending five minutes in conversation with his wife can alter the evening. Five minutes of prayer in the morning with your family can change the trajectory of the day. Being honest with a roommate, confessing sins to a friend, or simply listening deliberately to a child has a huge impact on how strong and satisfying our relationships are.

God came near in Jesus to model how we can make ourselves available to others. This simple action would radically alter our relationships with the people we care about the most.

Second, *God loved sacrificially*—not just his friends but those who were opposed to him. Jesus put it this way when he unpacked his life's purpose: "The Son of Man came not to be served but to serve, and to give his life as a ransom for many" (Matthew 20:28). Again, that's not merely what he did for us; it's a model he expects us to follow. In practical terms, that means listening more than talking, tithing rather than hoarding, volunteering rather than self-indulging, bragging about others rather than self-promoting. Oddly, in the end, sacrifice turns into gain.

Finally, *God suffered.* We avoid suffering at all costs, and that's understandable. Pain is not fun. However, our greatest growth comes from our suffering, not from our success. It's the pain, loss, and inconvenience we endure that build the character we crave. We want shortcuts and comfort at the risk of losing our souls.

The person we want to become is worth the sacrifice it takes to get there. In a real sense, we're to trade success for significance and pleasure for purpose. God himself modeled the way: not to achieve but to *become.* Our suffering for others in the name of Jesus offers more than creature comforts and personal satisfaction can. It offers life. Incarnational living turns out to be the most successful, satisfying, and purposeful path in life.

John 1:14 is a powerful theological window; we see God most clearly in

Jesus. But it's more than a window. It's a door through which we pass to enter the kind of life God designed for our greatest good *and* the salvation of the world. Imagine a world where God's people imitated his best attributes by following the incarnational life of Jesus.

Key Points

- Incarnation means Jesus is God in human form. It also means that only those who know Jesus will truly know God.
- Nearness, love, and suffering are attributes of God seen best in the Incarnation.
- The incarnation of Jesus is not merely a theological truth but a practical model of successful relationships.

This Week

- ☐ **Day 1:** Read the essay.
- ☐ **Day 2:** Memorize John 1:14.
- ☐ **Day 3:** Read Matthew 2; Luke 2.
- ☐ **Day 4:** Meditate on John 1:18; 14:6; Acts 4:12.
- ☐ **Day 5:** Share these three attributes of Jesus and God with someone you live with (spouse, roommate, coworker, friend), and ask that person which of the three you should develop in your life.

Overachiever Challenge: Memorize John 1:18; 14:6; Acts 4:12. (Yes, all three!)

Bonus Read: Timothy Keller, *Hidden Christmas: The Surprising Truth Behind the Birth of Christ.*

33

Love

God so loved the world, that he gave his only Son, that whoever believes in him should not perish but have eternal life.

—John 3:16

Question: How can I love and be loved?

If Christianity were reduced to a single word, it would be *love.* That sounds cliché. After all, doesn't everyone talk about the importance of love? Isn't that the message of every religion?

In a word, *no.* Love is a common conversation, even in pop culture, movies, and music. However, love is romanticized, even sexualized, so we must clarify what we mean by love to see just how unique and rare the biblical definition of true love is.

Two observations help us recognize God's love. First, the English language has some confused notions about love because we lump all kinds of emotions under one word. The Greek language was far more specific. It used four words for love. *Philia* was the most common, which referred to what we call friendship. *Storgē* encompassed familial affection—love between parents and children, siblings, etc. *Eros,* from which we get the word *erotic,* described all forms of sexual desire and lust. Finally, there was the unique word *agapē.* It's the Greek word used in every verse cited in this essay. *Agapē* denotes unconditional and unmerited love. It's the love that causes people to sacrifice their lives for others. It's the love offered freely, regardless of the recipient's value, merit, or ability to repay.

However, this Greek word didn't have that definition until after John used it in his gospel to describe God's sacrificial love by giving his son, Jesus Christ. The nature of love as undeserved, unmerited, unchangeable, and sacrificial comes from the description of the gospel message of Jesus Christ. In this sense, Christianity created *agapē*.

A second crucial observation is that love in our language commonly describes a feeling. In Christianity, however, it's first and foremost an action. Love is not how we feel. Love is what we do. Furthermore, the command to love is based on what God did for us in Christ rather than what we initially do to earn or achieve God's love. This is an extraordinary difference between the Christian message and all other religions.

God Loves Us

The most famous verse in the Bible is our core verse, John 3:16. It's the core of Christianity. But why does God love us? It's certainly not because we're so lovable.

God loves us because he cannot help himself: "Anyone who does not love does not know God, because God is love" (1 John 4:8). Fish swim, birds fly, little girls giggle—they just can't help themselves. For this same reason, God loves. It's not just what he does; it's who he is.

This extraordinary truth inflamed the apostle Paul to pen one of the most heartening passages ever written:

> I am sure that neither death nor life, nor angels nor rulers, nor things present nor things to come, nor powers, nor height nor depth, nor anything else in all creation, will be able to separate us from the love of God in Christ Jesus our Lord. (Romans 8:38–39)

According to John 3:16, God's love is well beyond raw emotion. It's an act of extraordinary self-sacrifice. God gave his own son as a sacrifice for the sins of the world. How such substitutionary atonement works is a divine mystery. The consequence, however, is clear enough. Because God loved us so sacrificially, those who call themselves children of God are obligated to behave similarly toward all those around them (1 John 4:11).

The Bible calls that "love your neighbor" (Matthew 19:19). To that end, the clearest commentary on John 3:16 is 1 John 3:16–17: "By this we know love, that he laid down his life for us, and we ought to lay down our lives for the brothers. But if anyone has the world's goods and sees his brother in need, yet closes his heart against him, how does God's love abide in him?" This agapē is not how you feel but how you help with the physical and financial needs of a fellow human being.

It simply won't pass muster to claim to love God without sacrificially serving our fellow human beings. John's teaching originated with Jesus in the upper room the night before he sacrificed his life: "Greater love has no one than this, that someone lay down his life for his friends" (15:13). For Jesus, love has no limits.

We Love God

Jesus reduced the entire Old Testament law to two commands in Mark 12:29–31:

> The most important is, "Hear, O Israel: The Lord our God, the Lord is one. And you shall love the Lord your God with all your heart and with all your soul and with all your mind and with all your strength" [quoting Deuteronomy 6:4–5]. The second is this: "You shall love your neighbor as yourself" [quoting Leviticus 19:18]. There is no other commandment greater than these.

Jesus is right, of course. These are not two separate commands. You cannot love God except by loving your neighbor. If love were a feeling, you could. One could worship at church, pray and praise in private, or any number of other expressions of adoration, and call it a complete love for God. However, Christian love is an outward orientation of action, not an internal emotion of affection. So how could one treat God with sacrificial love? God doesn't need anything from us. You can hardly feed him, clothe him, or provide medical assistance. How can we express our love for God practically? Every parent knows the answer: love his children. When we treat someone's children with kindness, it's the highest expression of love for the parent.

To that end—loving God's children—we're to love three broad categories of people.

We love neighbors. The single most powerful description of love is 1 Corinthians 13. The whole chapter is worth a read, but this snippet will suffice:

> Love is patient and kind; love does not envy or boast; it is not arrogant or rude. It does not insist on its own way; it is not irritable or resentful; it does not rejoice at wrongdoing, but rejoices with the truth. Love bears all things, believes all things, hopes all things, endures all things. (verses 4–7)

Most of us have heard that passage read at weddings, where it's completely unnecessary. It's easy to feel love at the altar; it's far more difficult to enact love in a divorce court. This passage was written not to newlyweds but to a robust body of believers in Corinth whose diverse ethnic, economic, and cultural backgrounds made potluck dinners tense. Loving neighbors requires grit, humility, and patience. That's why Paul added the following virtues to make love possible: "Walk in a manner worthy of the calling to which you have been called, with all humility and gentleness, with patience, bearing with one another in love" (Ephesians 4:1–2).

We love family. Every family relationship is God's training ground for loving him and loving neighbors. Yes, marriage is for our enjoyment and protection. But marriage is far more. It's a theological laboratory where we learn how to behave as we believe. Paul commanded, "Husbands, love your wives, as Christ loved the church and gave himself up for her" (Ephesians 5:25). That's John 3:16 enacted at the kitchen table and in the bedroom. Similar advice is given throughout Scripture to children, siblings, and aging parents. If we're to love God and love our neighbors, that begins at home, emanates out to our local communities, and ultimately extends to the ends of the earth.

We love enemies. Probably the most offensive thing Jesus ever said was "Love your enemies" (Matthew 5:44). When Jesus said this, it was a novel idea. Two years later, he would exemplify that love on the cross. Remember the first thing Jesus said from the cross: "Father, forgive them, for they know not what they do" (Luke 23:34). One who forgives his enemies in the middle of a crucifixion has the moral authority to ask us to do the same. As difficult as that was for Jesus, it paled in comparison to the sacrifice of the Father in offering his own son to the disobedient and rebellious. That's *all* of us—not just the Jewish leaders and Roman soldiers at Golgotha. We're all undeserving recipients of God's love.

Paul reminded us, "God shows his love for us in that while we were still sinners, Christ died for us" (Romans 5:8). While we were enemies, God loved us enough to send his own son. Because of that love, we found hope and help. Because of that love, we've been transformed from sinners to saints. Surely that's part of the mystery in 1 Peter 4:8: "Above all, keep loving one another earnestly, since *love covers a multitude of sins.*" God's love for his enemies birthed Christianity. Our love for our enemies expands the boundaries of his kingdom.

Love birthed the church. Love will inaugurate eternity. Come Judgment Day, because of God's love for us and our love for others, we'll stand boldly, head high, chest out.

> There is no fear in love, but perfect love casts out fear. For fear has to do with punishment, and whoever fears has not been perfected in love. We love because he first loved us. (1 John 4:18–19)

Key Points

- Sacrificial love is the core of Christianity and was actually "invented" by Christianity.
- Sacrificial love is what we do, not what we feel. And it originated with God.
- God's example of love in Jesus empowers us to love our neighbors, family, and enemies.

This Week

- ☐ **Day 1:** Read the essay.
- ☐ **Day 2:** Memorize John 3:16.
- ☐ **Day 3:** Read 1 Corinthians 13.
- ☐ **Day 4:** Meditate on Romans 5:8; 8:38–39; 1 John 3:16–17.
- ☐ **Day 5:** Clean out a closet, garage, or storage unit, and find a place to donate those items.

Overachiever Challenge: Memorize Romans 5:8.

Bonus Read: Francis Chan, *Crazy Love: Overwhelmed by a Relentless God.*

34

Worship

> God is spirit, and those who worship him
> must worship in spirit and truth.
>
> —John 4:24

Question: What does it really look like to worship God?

In John 4 Jesus met a woman at the local well. She was a Samaritan, from a people group despised by the Jews. She was all alone, as was he. This made their conversation a bit awkward, especially when Jesus told her to go fetch her husband. She didn't have one. Her current live-in lover followed a string of five divorces. She was undoubtedly the subject of a lot of raging rumors in that small town. She simply replied, "I have no husband" (verse 17). Jesus already knew that. When he revealed the details of her sordid past, she was obviously eager to change the subject. So she asked him to settle a bitter debate between their peoples: Where is the proper place of worship? Was it Jerusalem or Mount Gerizim? The fact that they were standing in the shadow of Mount Gerizim added tension to the question.

This launched one of the most significant discussions on worship in all the New Testament. Jesus's response is worth repeating:

> Woman, believe me, the hour is coming when neither on this mountain nor in Jerusalem will you worship the Father. You worship what you do

> not know; we worship what we know, for salvation is from the Jews. But the hour is coming, and is now here, when the true worshipers will worship the Father *in spirit and truth,* for the Father is seeking such people to worship him. God is spirit, and those who worship him must worship *in spirit and truth.* (verses 21–24)

What does real worship look like? Jesus repeated it so we wouldn't miss it. Real worship is in *spirit* and *truth.*

Churches often debate the proper form of worship. Should a priest preside? What style of music? Does the building matter? What elements should worship include? These are all practical questions, but they don't get at the heart of the issue.

For Jesus, the real question is not about the style of worship but about the heart of the worshipper. Valid worship arises from the Spirit and Truth—both words deliberately capitalized. In the gospel of John, Spirit and Truth are more persons than virtues. Jesus is identified as the embodiment of Truth (1:14, 17; 5:33; 7:18; 8:32, 40, 45–46; 14:6; 18:37), and the Holy Spirit is described as the "Spirit of truth" (14:17; 15:26; 16:13). The strikingly new nature of Christian worship honors the Father, as experienced through Jesus, by the indwelling of the Spirit.

Judaism focused only on God. Without Jesus, however, we don't have a clear view of God. Without the Holy Spirit, we don't have the true heart of Jesus. Hence, when we worship in Jesus by the power of the Holy Spirit, it opens access to God himself.

True Worship Honors God in Our Hearts

The word John used for "worship" is *proskyneō* (John 4:24). It's actually a combination of two words that together mean "to kiss toward." It's easy to imagine an adoring crowd throwing kisses toward a king passing through their village. Or when people entered the king's throne room, they would kneel before the king and kiss his ring. Hence, this word *proskyneō,* used sixty times in the New

Testament, implies bowing no less than twenty times. This is actually more important than it first appears. You see, many people equate true worship with love or peace or joy. While those emotions can be by-products of true worship, the New Testament equates worship with a different emotion: *fear*. This isn't the kind of emotion felt toward a terrifying enemy. It's the kind of fear felt toward a kind ruler or a good father. It is reverence.

Bottom line: *true worship is recognizing God's position.* He's our king, our sovereign, our Lord. He's not to be trifled with or taken for granted. Hence, the posture in the Bible most commonly associated with worship is not hands lifted high but heads bowed low. In fact, the most common response to close contact with God is falling prostrate on the ground.

Fear is a better barometer of worship than peace or joy. Why? Because fear places God on his throne. From that position he can truly reign in our lives.

True Worship Praises God with Our Lips

There are several Greek words hovering around the idea of verbal praise. *Eulogeō* (from which we get *eulogy*) means "to bless." A second word is *doxazō* (related to our word *doxology*), meaning "to glorify." Strictly speaking, we don't give God glory; we simply recognize his glory. This glory already belongs to God alone (Romans 1:21, 23). That's why it's so striking that throughout the Gospels, Jesus shares God's glory (Matthew 16:27; 19:28; 25:31; Mark 10:37; Luke 9:26; John 1:14; 12:28, 41; 13:31–32; 17:1–5). This explains why people praise God when they see a Christian live well (2 Corinthians 9:13; Galatians 1:24; 1 Peter 2:12). Our actions cause others to compliment God.

A third word is *aineō,* simply translated "to praise." Specifically, this praise recognizes what God has done historically. It often follows miracles (Luke 18:43; Acts 3:8–9) or momentous events (Luke 2:20; 19:37; Acts 2:47).

These three words, taken together, demonstrate an important truth about worship. Our verbal praise of God runs on two parallel tracks. First, we recognize who God is—his character. Second, we recount what God has done—his actions. This kind of worship permeates the entire book of Revelation (4:8–11;

5:9–14; 11:16–18; 19:1–8). Moreover, as with the use of *glory* in the Gospels, praise in Revelation is directed to both God and Jesus as if they stand on equal divine footing. This is striking in comparison with Judaism.

This kind of praise can be offered through a variety of mechanisms, including prayer, singing, or bodily posture. Yet these are merely vehicles to express worship. They must never substitute for worship itself. Worship is not the movement of our bodies but the expression of our spirits. Watchman Nee, in his book *The Release of the Spirit,* observed that we're made up of three parts: body, soul, and spirit. The body (our external shell) is animated by the life-giving force of the soul (our emotions, thoughts, and will). The soul is driven by something deeper—the spirit (the most interior part of our being). It's through the spirit that we truly connect with God.[1]

True worship is therefore spiritual. It emanates from the deepest part of us. Some people just go through the physical motions of worship—stand, sit, sing, kneel. All this involves the body, but it may involve nothing more. Others worship with great emotion (in singing) or intellectual concentration (through preaching). Both of these are functions of the soul. Neither may penetrate further.

Physical, emotional, and intellectual worship may reach only our bodies and souls. Spiritual worship, however, passes through all three. What starts in the spirit inevitably touches our emotions and minds and is ultimately expressed through our physical bodies.

Looking from the outside, it's impossible to know how deep another's worship goes. Two people standing side by side in church may both pray, sing, weep, and shout yet have very different experiences with God in their spirits.

This is why Jesus's statement to the Samaritan woman is so critical. True worship is in the Spirit and in Truth. This is why most people's prayers never reach the depth of worship. They tend to start with petitions (requests) and end with thanksgiving. Every parent knows how important these two are. We should feel comfortable asking our heavenly Father for what we need. Moreover, we should be a grateful people expressing our thanks fully and freely. Nonetheless, requests and thanksgiving fail to reach the level of praise because they both focus on us. Proper praise focuses on God. If we start with true worship—what God has done and who he is—our requests and thanksgiving will grow to have more depth and maturity.

True Worship Serves Other People

There are two words for "worship" that are most important for Christians: *latreuō* and *leitourgeō* (from which we get *liturgy*). Both words describe the vocational duties of priests in the Old Testament (Hebrews 10:11). They offered sacrifices. They cleaned up blood. They lit fires and locked doors. Under the new covenant, this word describes what all Christians do in the new temple—the church. It's not about buildings but about people. When we in the church feed, protect, counsel, and coach others, we *leitourgeō.* That's why connecting with the church is essential for personal worship. As Scripture commands, "Let us consider how to stir up one another to love and good works, not neglecting to meet together, as is the habit of some, but encouraging one another, and all the more as you see the Day drawing near" (verses 24–25).

In fact, the very first missionary journey grew out of worship: "While they were worshiping the Lord and fasting, the Holy Spirit said, 'Set apart for me Barnabas and Saul for the work to which I have called them'" (Acts 13:2). This is New Testament worship in its highest form. Our words and songs are meaningful only when our lives are sacrificial.

Hear Paul's words on this: "I appeal to you therefore, brothers, by the mercies of God, to present your bodies as a living sacrifice, holy and acceptable to God, which is your *spiritual worship*" (Romans 12:1). What ups the ante is that this "spiritual worship" is the only thing we'll take to heaven (Revelation 7:15; 22:3). Worship is our eternal occupation.

There's one final word for "worship" in the New Testament. *Sebō* often refers to piety, which is classic religion. Nothing wrong with that, but it's *not* the core of Christianity. We do many things that look like other religions. The framework of our worship services has involved "religious" kinds of activities ever since the early church: "They devoted themselves to the apostles' teaching and the fellowship, to the breaking of bread and the prayers" (Acts 2:42). What differentiates Christian worship from other religious activities is the Spirit. The Spirit leads us to the Truth embodied in Jesus, who escorts us directly to the Father. That's what true worship looks like.

Key Points

- True worship recognizes God's position, which leads us to experience appropriate fear.
- Praise is recognizing who God is and what he has done.
- Serving the body of Jesus is the highest form of worship.

This Week

- ☐ **Day 1:** Read the essay.
- ☐ **Day 2:** Memorize John 4:24.
- ☐ **Day 3:** Read Exodus 40.
- ☐ **Day 4:** Meditate on Acts 2:42; Romans 12:1–2; Hebrews 10:24–25.
- ☐ **Day 5:** Find a way to volunteer weekly with your local church.

Overachiever Challenge: Memorize Acts 2:42.

Bonus Read: Watchman Nee, *The Breaking of the Outward Man for the Release of the Spirit.*

35

Communion

Jesus said to them, "Truly, truly, I say to you, unless you eat the flesh of the Son of Man and drink his blood, you have no life in you."

—John 6:53

Question: Why is communion so central to the church?

Communion has been practiced in some way by every church in history. It has also caused more fights than any other issue. In fact, more Christians have been killed by other Christians over a different practice of communion than any other issue.

Some use juice; others insist on wine. Some take it weekly; others practice sporadically. Some insist it's a sacrament; others teach it's a mere metaphor. We can't even agree on what to call it: communion, the Lord's Supper, or the Eucharist (from the Greek word meaning "to give thanks"). So it deserves a conversation about what it means and how it should be celebrated.

Jesus instituted the Lord's Supper the night before he died (Luke 22:17–20). It was during a Passover meal surrounded by his closest disciples. The church, since that time, has memorialized Jesus's sacrifice in a simple miniature Passover with bread and wine. Some twenty years later, the apostle Paul recounted the original moment in detail: "When [Jesus] had given thanks, he broke it, and said, 'This is my body, which is for you. Do this in remembrance of me.' In the same way also he took the cup, after supper, saying, 'This cup is the new covenant in my blood. Do this, as often as you drink it, in remembrance of me' " (1 Corinthians 11:24–25). Paul then wrote a brief commentary about the meaning of this memorial (verse 26). Even today, his words offer unparalleled clarity on communion.

Communion Looks Backward

Communion has roots in an ancient practice that actually predates the church. It goes all the way back to the founding of Israel. In fact, Jesus's word *remembrance* could be translated as "memorial."

This observance isn't merely thinking about what Jesus did. It's more like reenacting. Every year since the Exodus (fifteen centuries earlier), Jews had gathered in family groups around a table with a very specific script and props. The unleavened bread represented the haste with which they left Egypt. For Jesus, the wine represented the blood of the covenant. The Passover lamb retold the story of their escape from Egypt (Exodus 12). The bitter herbs—dipped in the special sauce, haroseth—represented their bitter bondage. The table itself was the storyboard of Israel's founding as a nation.

Because Jesus fulfilled all Jewish history and hopes, this meal became his own prophetic script the night before he died. He identified the historical elements on the table with his own impending execution. This interpretation is nothing short of astounding, since nothing was more patriotic for Jews than Passover. Jesus therefore had to be either a crazed megalomaniac who hijacked this sacred ceremony—or the true son of God, the one this national memorial prefigured.

This astounding reinterpretation of Passover as his own personal biography was something Jesus had pondered for years. His preparation for that night goes back at least a year, when he miraculously fed the five thousand. He scandalized the crowd by saying, "Truly, truly, I say to you, unless you eat the flesh of the

Son of Man and drink his blood, you have no life in you" (John 6:53). Clearly, he knew his destiny. He knew that this miniature meal would encapsulate all Jewish history.

However, communion doesn't just look to the past; it points to the future.

Communion Looks Forward

Paul said, "As often as you eat this bread and drink the cup, you proclaim the Lord's death *until he comes*" (1 Corinthians 11:26). This weekly memorial was a reminder in the early church that Jesus was, in fact, returning. When he comes, there'll be a spectacular banquet. "Blessed are those who are invited to the marriage supper of the Lamb" (Revelation 19:9).

We're not there yet. Yet Jesus predicted that it's coming, even as he instituted the Eucharist. In his own words, "I have earnestly desired to eat this Passover with you before I suffer. For I tell you I will not eat it until it is fulfilled in the kingdom of God" (Luke 22:15–16).

What followed this statement that night is curious. Jesus passed around a cup of wine, then the bread, and then another cup of wine (verses 17–20). Why two cups? Actually, there are four cups in Jewish tradition. According to one interpretation, the four cups are a toast to each of the four lines of Exodus 6:6–7.

- With the first cup: "Say therefore to the people of Israel, 'I am the Lord, and I will bring you out from under the burdens of the Egyptians'" (verse 6). This cup was blessed by the head of the family and signaled the official beginning of the meal.
- With the second cup: "I will deliver you from slavery to them" (verse 6). This was likely the first cup Jesus gave to his disciples (Luke 22:17–18).[1] It pointed to Jesus's death that would deliver us from the slavery of sin.
- With the third: "I will redeem you with an outstretched arm and with great acts of judgment" (Exodus 6:6). This was the cup following the bread. Jesus identified this cup as "my blood of the covenant, which is poured out for many for the forgiveness of sins"

(Matthew 26:28). Redemption is the price paid for our sins. Hence, it is Jesus's shed blood that redeems us.

- With the fourth: "I will take you to be my people, and I will be your God, and you shall know that I am the LORD your God, who has brought you out from under the burdens of the Egyptians" (Exodus 6:7). This cup is the one Jesus said would have to wait until his return (Matthew 26:29). This makes perfect sense, since the fulfillment of this verse won't come until Revelation 21:3: "Behold, the dwelling place of God is with man. He will dwell with them, and they will be his people, and God himself will be with them as their God." By applying this promise to himself, Jesus was claiming to be equivalent to Yahweh—the very one who would welcome us into our eternal home in heaven.

Because of the rich historical symbolism in this meal, we don't just reenact Passover; we also proclaim the story of Jesus woven throughout Jewish history. Everyone who partakes of the Lord's Supper preaches the entire gospel message. It's an enacted sermon, just as baptism is. Communion is a corporate sermon without the preacher ever saying a word. And here's some really good news about this sermon: we cannot proclaim it incorrectly because the elements themselves tell the story.

The Passover inaugurated Jewish history; the Eucharist will be its culmination at the marriage supper of the Lamb (Revelation 19:9) when Jesus will be our God with us (Immanuel) and we will be his people.

Communion Looks Inward

The Lord's Supper is the most introspective element of our worship services. It's appropriate, even obligatory, that we reflect on our relationship with God. It's not that we measure our worthiness to partake; Jesus's sacrifice alone is what makes us worthy. Rather, we ready our minds and hearts for the sacredness of the celebration. It's no small thing to drink the blood of Jesus or to eat his body through this symbolic meal.

Paul offered this warning:

> Whoever, therefore, eats the bread or drinks the cup of the Lord in an unworthy manner will be guilty concerning the body and blood of the Lord. Let a person examine himself, then, and so eat of the bread and drink of the cup. For anyone who eats and drinks without discerning the body eats and drinks judgment on himself. That is why many of you are weak and ill, and some have died. (1 Corinthians 11:27–30)

The fact that Christians fell ill or even died by partaking in communion without being prepared indicates that this memorial is more than a symbol. It's a sacrament. Something spiritual, mystical, and powerful takes place.

Be forewarned: the cosmic Christ is present in the elements.

Communion Looks Outward

Communion isn't just about communing with Jesus. It is a communal meal with other Christians.

Originally this was a full meal in someone's home where worship services were held (before separate buildings were built for the church to gather). Consequently, the meal followed the preaching. The banquet hall was cleared and tables set up. The problem was that you could fit far fewer people in the banquet hall after you set up tables. So the majority of the congregation ate in the courtyard, which was more spacious. Who got to stay in the banquet hall? Not surprisingly, it was the wealthy believers who'd acquired their seats of honor before ever being baptized.

Old habits die hard. Hence, the shocking news that the poorer Christians went home hungry and the wealthier Christians went home hammered: "In eating, each one goes ahead with his own meal. One goes hungry, another gets drunk" (1 Corinthians 11:21). This explains why the full meal was soon replaced by the more moderate miniatures we have today. Paul explained, "My brothers, when you come together to eat, wait for one another—if anyone is hungry, let him eat at home—so that when you come together it will not be for judgment" (verses 33–34).

There's good reason not to have a full meal in our modern context. However, something essential has been lost. We barely recognize the communal nature of communion. It has become the most individualistic time of the service. Somehow we need to recover the "we" over "me" of this meal. Just as the original meal commemorated the birth of a nation, so this continued celebration is the mark of a Christian community. And that's why communion is the only celebration shared by every church throughout history.

Key Points

- Communion is a Christian extension of the annual Jewish Passover meal.
- Communion is a reminder of Jesus's past sacrifice and future return.
- Though communion is a time for personal reflection, the name reminds us that it's a communal event binding the body together in Christ.

This Week

- ☐ **Day 1:** Read the essay.
- ☐ **Day 2:** Memorize John 6:53.
- ☐ **Day 3:** Read Exodus 12–13.
- ☐ **Day 4:** Meditate on Matthew 26:26–28; Luke 22:14–20; 1 Corinthians 11:24–25.
- ☐ **Day 5:** Have a communion celebration in your home around a full meal.

Overachiever Challenge: Memorize 1 Corinthians 11:24–25.

Bonus Read: Rose Publishing, *The Lord's Supper: Holy Communion Explained.*

36

Eternal Security

I give them eternal life, and they will never perish, and no one will snatch them out of my hand.

—John 10:28

Question: Can Christians lose their salvation?

Many Christians wrestle with questions related to eternal security, especially when Scripture appears to offer contradictory conclusions. Let's commit to wrestle with the text, not with one another. And let's be sure to embrace both promises and warnings of God's word.

The Tension of Eternal Security

We're saved by the grace of Jesus Christ. End of story. It's not by our effort or intellect nor by our works or worthiness. Jesus himself assured us of our security: "All that the Father gives me will come to me, and whoever comes to me I will never cast out" (John 6:37). And again in John 10:28, our core verse, he spoke not to Christians but to the Pharisees, who were in fact attempting to intimidate his disciples into abandoning him. In other words, Jesus fights for us! Paul echoed this sentiment of security in the poetic crescendo of Romans 8:38–39, where he declared that nothing can separate us from the love of Christ. The guarantee of our security is none other than the Holy Spirit himself (2 Corinthians 5:5).

All this to say, our security in Jesus is certain.

There is, however, a whole constellation of passages that warn Christians not to let go of Jesus. The most obvious is Hebrews 6:4–6:

> It is impossible, in the case of those who have once been enlightened, who have tasted the heavenly gift, and have shared in the Holy Spirit, and have tasted the goodness of the word of God and the powers of the age to come, and then have fallen away, to restore them again to repentance, since they are crucifying once again the Son of God to their own harm and holding him up to contempt.

Jesus himself said, "If anyone does not abide in me he is thrown away like a branch and withers; and the branches are gathered, thrown into the fire, and burned" (John 15:6). With a similar agricultural metaphor, Paul said, "[The Jewish branches] were broken off because of their unbelief, but you stand fast through faith. So do not become proud, but fear. For if God did not spare the natural branches, neither will he spare you" (Romans 11:20–21). Additional scriptures could be added, but these suffice to make the point.

So there we have it: two constellations of Scripture that appear to be in conflict. The first cluster assures us that we're secure in Jesus. The second suggests that we can in fact abandon Jesus. How are we to manage that tension?

Notice that this isn't Jesus versus Paul. Rather, it's Jesus versus Jesus and Paul versus Paul. Unless we suggest that they contradicted themselves, we should assume there's a way of understanding both emphases.

Most preachers lean in to one set of Scriptures and explain away the other, often with creative mental gymnastics. Their arguments make sense for any single passage. But at some point, when the "face value" of multiple texts has been dismissed, one suspects that the Bible is being explained away rather than simply explained.

Can we hold in tension these two seemingly contrary positions? I believe we can. Christians *are* eternally secure in Jesus, while also somehow having some responsibility for their own destiny. To be clear, we'll never answer all the theological questions people have. What we can do (and must do) is understand and apply the practical principles behind these biblical truths.

Practical Principles for Understanding Eternal Security

Knowing what Jesus and Paul said is helpful for comprehension; knowing *why* they said it is critical for transformation. Here are some principles that will help.

1. *Pastors need to promote both sides to maximize ministry in real-life settings.* The warnings against falling away are helpful for believers experiencing either suffering or success. Suffering can tempt us to let go of Jesus. Success can seduce us to ignore our loyalty to Jesus. Most of us have friends or family who walked away from Jesus because of either suffering or success.

   On the other hand, promises of our security can bring great comfort to beleaguered souls walking the painful path of suffering.

   As a pastor, I would hate to lose emphasis on either constellation. Our people would be poorer for it.

2. *Our perseverance in Jesus depends more on him than on us.* Spiritual security isn't solely or even primarily dependent on our own efforts. The Good Shepherd of our souls takes seriously his obligation to protect and keep his own flock. He's responsible for bringing us into the flock (John 6:44), and he's resolved to sustain us in the flock (10:27–30).

   The fact is, whether we recognize it or not, God pursued us long before we pursued him. God made us, marked us, and wooed us long before we pledged our allegiance to him. And long after we've wandered away or rejected him, he'll continue to pursue us.

   Anyone who has a child understands the heart of God for us. If your child walked away, what would you do? Wouldn't you fight for your kid? We would be resilient, resolute, inflexible, unflappable stalkers as long as possible. So it is with God.

Is it possible to apostatize (walk away from the faith)? Well, the Bible describes specific individuals who "shipwrecked" their faith and were handed over to Satan (1 Timothy 1:19–20). It is called *apostasy* (1 Timothy 4:1). Nonetheless, it's next to impossible. The hound of heaven never lightly loosens his grip on his children.

Mark this well: God's powerful hand holds his own so that no foreign force can wrest us from his grasp. Nor can we walk away without a prolonged struggle with the One who laid down his life for us. It cost him everything to save us. He'll stop at nothing to keep us.

3. *This whole debate is a moot point.* Some theologians argue that a person can fall away. Others strongly disagree. Yet all of us know someone who used to claim to be a Christian but no longer does. The eternal-security folks argue that this "ex-Christian" was never really saved in the first place, while the fall-away folks say that this person apostatized. Neither side, however, doubts the state of people like Judas Iscariot (John 17:12), Simon Magus (Acts 8:18–23), and Hymenaeus and Alexander (1 Timothy 1:19–20). They're lost.

   So what should we do? The answer is clear: help folks find faith. Which folks? All of them. We can't know where people have been in their journeys with Jesus, so we can't predict the outcome of our evangelism. So whenever and however, we'll love people by proclaiming the saving grace of the Lord Jesus.

   The old eternal-security-versus-falling-away debate is not about what we should do but about what we believe about another person's salvation. Doesn't that make this debate frivolous and potentially dangerous—since we're judging another's faith journey that we can't really know?

4. *Both camps can be justly criticized for misguided messaging.* The doctrine of eternal security can be in danger of promoting disloyalty

to Jesus. That's never the intention, of course. But some people have heard a preacher say, "You are saved no matter what you do," and they misinterpret the message to mean they can sin with impunity. We have to admit that's the wrong message from the pulpit.

On the other side, those who deny eternal security have often inadvertently preached eternal *in*security. By overemphasizing our free will to abandon the faith, we've caused some people to live with fear and uncertainty. Clearly that's not a helpful or productive message.

If the Bible seems to promote both sides, it might be wise for church leaders to follow suit. Sure, this goes against the grain of systematic theology. We like to pretend not only that we have it all figured out but also that we've packaged it so neatly that any reasonable person will have to agree with us. Our aversion to paradox is peculiar to the Western world. That doesn't make it evil, but it may make it an expectation foreign to the authors of the New Testament. Life, logic, and biblical doctrine don't always fit into neat categories.

Perhaps we should let each text stand on its own, even if we have difficulty blending or combining two seemingly paradoxical statements. There are wonderful promises about the faithfulness of God in protecting his people (John 10:28; Romans 8:35–39); God expends more effort on sustaining our faith than we generally give him credit for. This should give us immense comfort and confidence. Likewise, there are some clear warnings about abandoning our faith (Romans 11:20–22; Galatians 5:1–4; 1 Timothy 1:18–20; Hebrews 6:4–8). We must communicate those warnings unapologetically.

5. *Love necessitates freedom of choice.* We know this innately, because all of us want to be chosen by friends, family, and lovers. Love, more than anything else, makes life worth living and this world worth saving. Could God have forced us to love him? Technically, yes. He

could have created us without choice. However, that would cease to be love as we know it and as God desires it.

One final note. Freedom to love is the essential core of every covenant, whether human or divine. Can there be a marriage without the choice to love? Wouldn't that make it human trafficking? Can there be a business partnership without the choice to align? Wouldn't that make it slavery?

God could have made a different world—but not if he wanted love. Hence, we were given the choice to be faithful to God's covenant or to abandon it. That was true of the covenant with Abraham, with Moses, with David, and with Christians. Throughout biblical history, God has expected his people to be loyal to the covenant in order to experience the blessings it offers.

Simply put, covenant necessitates fidelity. When an individual refuses to show loyalty to Jesus, that ends the relationship God fought to establish and preserve. This should be a sobering reminder of God's nature, our dignity in his eyes, and our obligation to live loyally and worship relentlessly. God keeps us eternally secure in Christ, offering us the dignity of choosing to be faithful to Jesus.

Key Points

- Plenty of passages support the reality of both eternal security and apostasy.
- Both messages are helpful, even necessary, to pastoral ministry in the local church.
- Paradox isn't a bad thing theologically if it can be justified biblically.

This Week

☐ **Day 1:** Read the essay.

☐ **Day 2:** Memorize John 10:28.

☐ **Day 3:** Read 1 Samuel 17.

☐ **Day 4:** Meditate on John 6:37; Romans 11:20–21; Hebrews 6:4–6.

☐ **Day 5:** Identify three or four ways God pursued you before you ever pledged loyalty to him. In prayer, express your loyalty and gratitude for his pursuit.

Overachiever Challenge: Memorize Hebrews 6:4–6.

Bonus Read: Robert Shank, *Life in the Son: A Study of the Doctrine of Perseverance.*

37

The Holy Spirit

> You will receive power when the Holy Spirit has come upon you, and you will be my witnesses in Jerusalem and in all Judea and Samaria, and to the end of the earth.
>
> —Acts 1:8

Question: What does the Holy Spirit do for us?

The Holy Spirit seems mystifying to most Christians. Yet the Bible teaches that God is even more accessible to us through the Holy Spirit than through Jesus. Jesus is in heaven with the Father; the Holy Spirit is inside us. Jesus himself said as much:

> I will ask the Father, and he will give you another Helper, to be with you forever, even the Spirit of truth, whom the world cannot receive, because it neither sees him nor knows him. You know him, for he dwells with you and will be in you. (John 14:16–17)

The Holy Spirit came in power on the Day of Pentecost in a striking display of tongues of fire (Acts 2:1–4). That was a watershed moment in history. Prior to Pentecost, the Holy Spirit came on people with only temporary power. After

Pentecost, the Spirit took up residence in Jesus's followers permanently. This gives us constant access to God as we carry out his kingdom agenda.

We most often think about the Holy Spirit working in us for transformation. That's certainly the main emphasis of the apostle Paul. According to his letters, the Spirit seals, saves, and rewires us from the inside out. John and Luke, on the other hand, emphasize the Holy Spirit working *through us* to make Jesus famous. His power is for the purpose of evangelism. This is summarized well by Luke in Acts 1:8, our core verse.

Without the Holy Spirit we couldn't be who we were created to be or accomplish what we were made to do. His benefits for believers are many. For the sake of simplicity, we'll summarize them under two broad categories.

Transformation: The Holy Spirit *in* Us

1. *Creation.* The Spirit of God played an integral role in creation (Genesis 1:2), hovering over the waters and forging order from chaos. He was responsible for the very breath that enlivened the human species, breathing into the nostrils of Adam (2:7). In fact, the Spirit of God is responsible for the breath of every living creature (Psalm 104:29–30).

   Thus, it just makes sense that once Jesus removed the curse of our sin, the Spirit could renew our access to the Father. Just as in Genesis 1:2, the Spirit still hovers over the chaos of our lives, seeking to bring about a new creation (or perhaps more accurately, a renewed creation). It's what the Bible calls being "born of water and the Spirit" (John 3:5).
2. *Conversion.* The most significant thing the Spirit does is invisible to the human eye. He seals us: "In him you also, when you heard the word of truth, the gospel of your salvation, and believed in him, were sealed with the promised Holy Spirit" (Ephesians 1:13). This idea comes from the ancient practice of sealing documents with a

signet ring. The inverted image pressed into soft wax or clay marked the item as the permanent possession of the king or dignitary. When we pledge our loyalty to Jesus by faith, there's a permanent change in our ownership. We may never see it, but angels, demons, and the divine most certainly do. This seal provides us with protection, limiting satanic attacks. It determines our eternal destiny. It offers access to God's power and presence.

Sealing, in short, is the capstone of conversion (Titus 3:5). It can be described as nothing less than new life (John 6:63; 7:38–39; Romans 8:11).

3. *Sanctification.* Because we now belong to God, we're set apart for his pleasure and purpose. The Bible calls this process "sanctification" (2 Thessalonians 2:13; see also Romans 15:16). In the instant the Spirit seals us, we become new creatures (1 Corinthians 6:11). Nonetheless, sanctification is also an ongoing work of God to align our actions in the future with Christ's actions in the past. As Paul said, "Now may the God of peace himself sanctify you completely, and may your whole spirit and soul and body be kept blameless at the coming of our Lord Jesus Christ" (1 Thessalonians 5:23). This is a lifelong process driven by the Spirit and protected by the armor the Spirit provides (Ephesians 6:13–18).

Empowerment: The Holy Spirit *Through* Us

1. *Coaching.* The primary work of the Spirit in both the Old and the New Testaments is communication. He's a talker! He seems to have no shortage of strategies to speak into our lives. The Spirit is probably clearest through the Scriptures, of which he's the ultimate author (2 Peter 1:21). If need be, however, he can communicate directly with individuals in their hearts or minds (John 15:26;

Acts 8:29; 10:19–20). He can also communicate through a third party, including but not limited to parents, preachers, counselors, colleagues, and children.

His purpose is more transformation than information. He hopes to teach us truth that enables us to live wisely (John 14:26). To that end he will lead or hinder (Acts 16:6–7), search and reveal (1 Corinthians 2:10), strengthen and comfort (John 14:26), command (Acts 8:29; 13:2), and convict of sin (John 16:8–11). And when he's done talking to us about God, he talks to God about us, interceding on our behalf (Romans 8:26).

2. *Skills.* The Spirit provides the tools we need to accomplish everything God calls us to do. Sometimes this power comes in the form of phenomenal miraculous interventions (Romans 15:19; Galatians 3:5). These could include healings (Acts 5:16), exorcisms (Matthew 12:28), and prophecy and speaking in tongues (Acts 2:4). These power tools are focused mostly on an individual who does something dynamic to expand the kingdom of God.

However, the Spirit's favorite mode of empowerment seems to be corporate rather than individual. The Bible teaches that he indwells our bodies (1 Corinthians 3:16; 6:19; Ephesians 2:22; 1 Peter 4:14; 1 John 3:24; 4:13). So we get the impression the Holy Spirit is inside us individually. That's most certainly true. Each of us has a dynamic internal connection to the Spirit of God. However, the fullness of the Spirit could never exist in a single individual. Rather, the Spirit indwells the body of Christ—the church. The church exhibits the fullness of spiritual gifts.

The Spirit distributes his power throughout the body (Romans 12:6–8; 1 Corinthians 12:4, 7–12; Ephesians 4:11–13). This mutual dependence and service create unity as a dynamic force for good in this world (Ephesians 4:3–4). Because we need one another to accomplish the mission, we stick together.

3. *Character.* Likewise, he develops in us the fruit of the Spirit: "The fruit of the Spirit is love, joy, peace, patience, kindness, goodness, faithfulness, gentleness, self-control; against such things there is no law" (Galatians 5:22–23). Notice that the fruit of the Spirit isn't primarily for our sanctification. There's no fruit of the Spirit that doesn't have its ultimate goal in service to the community. Through these virtues, we carry out the commands of Christ to reach our neighbors with the message of salvation. Without the Spirit's character in us, we could never build God's kingdom in the midst of a hostile world.
4. *Support.* The Spirit has a knack for moving the right people into the right place at the right time. This happens more often than we suspect, primarily in the process of evangelism (Luke 2:27; Acts 8:29, 39; 10:19–20; 11:12; 16:6–7; 20:22). However, his guidance is usually spiritual rather than physical. Sometimes he gives specific instruction for a specific time (Acts 13:2–4; 15:28), even giving us the right words to say (Luke 12:12).

   Most of the time, the Spirit uses general wisdom to guide us on how to live (Ephesians 1:17). This is why the Spirit is called a counselor or coach (John 14:16–17, 26; 15:26). He provides encouragement to the church (Acts 9:31), strength to individuals (Ephesians 3:16), and help for the hurting (Philippians 1:19; 2 Timothy 1:14).

   The Spirit also supports us by ferociously defending us. When others doubt you, the Holy Spirit validates you. He did this for Jesus at his baptism (Matthew 3:16; Mark 1:10; Luke 3:22; John 1:32–33) as well as during his ministry (Matthew 12:18; Luke 4:18; Acts 10:38) but especially in his resurrection and ascension (Acts 2:33; Romans 1:4; 1 Timothy 3:16).

   This courtesy extends from Jesus to all people (Acts 15:8). Rest assured, all who put feet to their faith will have the wind of the Spirit at their backs.

Privately and personally, the Spirit confirms that we're God's children (Romans 8:16–17; Galatians 4:6), and he thus grants us access to God (Ephesians 2:18). Through the Spirit we accept God's love and are filled with it (Romans 5:5; 15:30). Even more, the Spirit intercedes for us before God with groaning too deep for words (Romans 8:26–27).

Surprisingly, one of the most effective ways to hear the Spirit's guidance and encouragement is through corporate singing (Ephesians 5:18–19). Perhaps that's why the presence of God's Spirit is felt most acutely in the presence of God's people. He tends to show up when and where we do.

Sometimes life is tough. In those moments the Spirit sustains us. He'll never leave us alone. He'll be closest to us when we're closest to the heartbeat of the mission—announcing the good news of Jesus Christ.

Key Points

- We have even greater access to God through the Spirit than through Jesus.
- The Spirit works in us through transformation: creation, conversion, and sanctification.
- The Spirit works through us in empowerment: coaching, skills, character, and support.

This Week

☐ **Day 1:** Read the essay.

☐ **Day 2:** Memorize Acts 1:8.

☐ **Day 3:** Read Acts 2.

☐ **Day 4:** Meditate on John 16:13–14; Galatians 5:22–23; Ephesians 1:13.

☐ **Day 5:** Identify one of the benefits the Holy Spirit provides for you that you need most right now. Look up every passage referenced under that benefit.

Overachiever Challenge: Memorize Galatians 5:22–23.

Bonus Read: Francis Chan, *Forgotten God: Reversing Our Tragic Neglect of the Holy Spirit.*

38

The Ascension

When he had said these things, as they were looking on,
he was lifted up, and a cloud took him out of their sight.

—Acts 1:9

Question: Why did Jesus leave?

It was exactly forty days after the Resurrection. From the top of the Mount of Olives overlooking Jerusalem, Jesus gave his disciples one final commission. While he was talking with them, he began to rise from the earth. He defied the laws of gravity, as he'd done before when walking on the water (Matthew 14:22–25).

This miracle marked Jesus's exit from earth. In the background of the story were two men dressed in white. Clearly they were angels sent from God to coach these early disciples what to do next. Luke used a verb tense that indicates the angels were "in the present state of having stood there." In other words, the angels appeared—and went unnoticed. That had to be a bit disheartening for the angels. After all, angels everywhere else in the Bible are impressive figures. When they make an appearance, they strike terror in human hearts. The first thing angels typically say is "Don't be afraid." This time, however, the disciples didn't even notice them. The disciples were gazing toward heaven—but rather than gawking at the sky, they should have been going into all the world.

The angels eventually broke the silence: "Men of Galilee, why do you stand looking into heaven? This Jesus, who was taken up from you into heaven, will come in the same way as you saw him go into heaven" (Acts 1:11). These peasants from Galilee were commissioned to go global: every tongue, tribe, and nation need to hear the redeeming message of Jesus.

For these disciples, the Ascension must have felt like abandonment. It wasn't. In fact, it was exactly what they needed to fulfill their commission. Let's talk through that by answering two critical questions.

Did the Ascension Actually Happen?

Okay, so let's be honest. The story of Jesus being transported from earth to heaven sounds like something from a science-fiction novel. Or worse, it sounds like one of the old superstitions of world religions. After all, one can catalog a list of ascended heroes: Hercules, Buddha, Muhammad.

Another challenge is that Luke, who was not an eyewitness, is the only one to chronicle this event. Can we really trust his account?

We have several reasons to believe the Ascension really happened.

1. Luke was a careful investigator of his eyewitnesses and primary sources (Luke 1:1–4).
2. The presence of living eyewitnesses bolsters his believability.
3. He recorded the event as history, not with the fantastical details common in nonbiblical accounts of ascension.
4. For Jesus, this was the return trip. In the case of Hercules, Muhammad, and any others, their translation to heaven was a one-way ticket. But Jesus came from heaven in the first place. For him to return there just makes sense.

   Psalm 68:18 records this prophecy: "You ascended on high, leading a host of captives in your train and receiving gifts among men, even among the rebellious, that the Lord God may dwell there." The apostle Paul used this verse to clarify that Jesus was only returning to where he started: "In saying, 'He ascended,' what does it mean but that he had also descended into the lower regions, the earth? He who descended is the one who also ascended far above all the heavens, that he might fill all things" (Ephesians 4:9–10).

5. The Ascension was prophesied. We see this not only in Psalm 68:18 (which we just read) but also in Psalm 110:1: "The Lord says to my Lord: 'Sit at my right hand, until I make your enemies your footstool.' "

   Jesus himself also predicted his ascension: "No one has ascended into heaven except he who descended from heaven, the Son of Man" (John 3:13; see also John 6:62; 20:17). "From now on the Son of Man shall be seated at the right hand of the power of God" (Luke 22:69). If Jesus was right when he predicted his death and resurrection, why should we doubt his prediction of the Ascension?

6. Christ's ascension is affirmed throughout the rest of the New Testament. Paul said that God "raised [Christ] from the dead and seated him at his right hand in the heavenly places" (Ephesians 1:20). Paul also told us to "seek the things that are above, where Christ is, seated at the right hand of God" (Colossians 3:1).

   The author of Hebrews, in his book's introduction, declared this about God's son: "After making purification for sins, he sat down at the right hand of the Majesty on high" (Hebrews 1:3). Peter wrote that Jesus "has gone into heaven and is at the right hand of God, with angels, authorities, and powers having been subjected to him" (1 Peter 3:22).

   Other passages could be added, but these are enough to prove that Luke's account of the Ascension is no isolated reference. It was a truth affirmed by every New Testament author except James and Jude. This near-universal assent to the Ascension gives us confidence in the Ascension's reality.

7. Nothing else explains why Christ's resurrection appearances ceased. If you think about it, the Ascension isn't something the church

would have invented. After all, continued claims to see Jesus would have bolstered their authority.

But if Jesus did in fact rise from the dead—if the Resurrection really happened—shouldn't we expect Jesus to return to heaven? If God can raise Jesus from the dead, then his further raising him from the earth should not be impossible or even difficult.

All told, the evidence weighs in on the side of Luke's trustworthiness.

How Does Jesus's Ascension Help Us Fulfill Our Commission?

1. *Jesus finished his work of redemption.* Listen to Jesus's prayer to his Father: "I glorified you on earth, having accomplished the work that you gave me to do. And now, Father, glorify me in your own presence with the glory that I had with you before the world existed" (John 17:4–5). Jesus came to earth from heaven. He laid down his divine rights to dwell with humanity (Philippians 2:6–8). When he returned to heaven, it showed the depths to which he had descended as well as the heights to which he can take us. From that point of view, the Ascension is critical to raising Jesus to his proper position.
2. *Jesus is preparing a place for us.* On the night of his arrest, Jesus promised his followers that he would go and prepare a place for them: "In my Father's house are many rooms. If it were not so, would I have told you that I go to prepare a place for you?" (John 14:2). On earth, Jesus died for our sins to make a way for us to get to God. Now he's preparing a place for us in eternity, not as a construction worker building a heavenly mansion but as a defense attorney defending us before God (Romans 8:34).
3. *Jesus intercedes for us while seated at the right hand of his Father.* He's not sitting down on the job. Rather, he's seated as a judge, pleading our case.

We can imagine it as something like this. Whenever we sin on earth, Jesus leans to his left, points to the scars on his hands, and says to his Father, "See these scars? These paid for that sin. Let's call it even." Paul painted the picture like this: "Who is to condemn? Christ Jesus is the one who died—more than that, who was raised—who is at the right hand of God, who indeed is interceding for us" (Romans 8:34).

4. *Jesus sent us his Holy Spirit.* We aren't suggesting that Jesus had to leave so the Spirit could come. There's no divine rule that says at least two members of the Trinity have to reside in heaven at any given time. Rather, the point is that Jesus returned to heaven to complete his work of interceding. In doing so, he opened the door for the Spirit's work of conviction, guidance, and support for the growing movement of God on earth.

   The Holy Spirit is no cheap substitute for Jesus. He is not the second string of the Trinity. Rather, he has the same heartbeat as Jesus and the same mission as the Father. Yet he offers us one advantage that the resurrected Jesus couldn't. Because of his nature, the Spirit can be equally present with every Christian at the same time.

   Jesus recognized that: "It is to your advantage that I go away, for if I do not go away, the Helper will not come to you. But if I go, I will send him to you" (John 16:7). This provides a strategic advantage both to the church at large and to individual Christians as they carry out Jesus's mission to tell the whole world about him (Matthew 28:19–20).

5. *Jesus is preparing for his return.* "Behold, he is coming with the clouds, and every eye will see him, even those who pierced him, and all tribes of the earth will wail on account of him. Even so. Amen" (Revelation 1:7). When Jesus returns, he'll bring to fulfillment God's ultimate plan. He'll bring human history to

completion, usher in the Day of Judgment, and restore Eden in the new earth.

Key Points

- There are strong historical reasons to believe in the literal ascension of Jesus.
- Jesus is now in heaven, interceding for us.
- Because of the Ascension, the Holy Spirit was sent to continue Jesus's work (John 16:7).

This Week

- ☐ **Day 1:** Read the essay.
- ☐ **Day 2:** Memorize Acts 1:9.
- ☐ **Day 3:** Read Acts 1.
- ☐ **Day 4:** Meditate on John 16:7; Ephesians 4:8–10; Revelation 1:7.
- ☐ **Day 5:** Take a moment to imagine Jesus enthroned next to the Father. How could that image alter your actions today?

Overachiever Challenge: Memorize Revelation 1:7.

Bonus Read: Tim Perry and Aaron Perry, *He Ascended into Heaven: Learn to Live an Ascension-Shaped Life.*

39

Baptism

> Repent and be baptized every one of you in the name of Jesus Christ for the forgiveness of your sins, and you will receive the gift of the Holy Spirit.
>
> —Acts 2:38

Question: Why should I be baptized?

Baptism is a big deal. Every church throughout Christian history has practiced it in some form. Yet churches practice it in different ways and with differing emphases. So there is clearly some confusion about what it means and how we should do it.

Many traditions baptize infants; others baptize only adults. Some use sprinkling; some, pouring; others, full immersion. Nonetheless, like the Lord's Supper, it's a core Christian practice—what some call a sacrament. That means it's not merely a symbol representing something else on earth but rather a sacred reenactment on earth that accomplishes (or reflects) something happening in heaven. That makes it of utmost importance.

In fact, baptism was crucial enough that Jesus himself began his ministry by being immersed (Matthew 3:16–17). This marked a pivotal point in his career.

Baptism can do the same for you. It's both an amazing gift and a core command. So the purpose of this essay is to answer some of the common questions about baptism, removing any barriers someone might have. Let's start with a tactical question.

Should We Immerse Rather Than Sprinkle?

For the first several centuries of the church, immersion was the normative form of baptism. It makes sense, since the Greek word for baptism (*baptizō*) means "to immerse" or "to dip." John the Baptist baptized where "water was plentiful" (John 3:23). Philip and the Ethiopian eunuch "went down into the water" (Acts 8:38).

Perhaps more importantly, immersion paints a powerful picture of Jesus's death, burial, and resurrection (Romans 6:4–5). No other form of baptism is as clear a portrait as immersion. This is not to cast aspersions on those who are sprinkled. It's merely to affirm immersion as the original biblical model of baptism. This is important, since baptism for many may be the only time family and friends will gather to see this reenactment of Jesus's death and resurrection.

Many who have been sprinkled as infants are concerned that adult baptism may insult their parents. That should never be the case. You're not saying to your mom and dad, "You were wrong." Rather, you're saying, "Thank you! I now confirm with my own confession that you completely accomplished your role to instill faith in my life." Your parents should feel affirmed that what they started in you has come to full fruition through the Spirit.

Is Baptism Essential?

Let's be clear: we're saved when the Holy Spirit marks us. God determines when, where, and how we're saved. But the Bible does teach that baptism culminates the process of conversion.

Different people are at different stages of their faith. Various Bible passages describe different steps in the process of conversion: hearing the gospel, responding in faith, repenting of our past, and confessing our sins. Each is a critical step as a person transfers allegiance to Jesus. Immersion is the end of the beginning—the culmination of conversion.

Throughout the book of Acts, people's public confession of faith was in the act of immersion (2:41; 8:12; 10:48; 16:33). Hence, baptism is compared to new birth (John 3:5; Titus 3:5), to clothing oneself with Christ (Galatians 3:27), and to the Jewish entry rite of circumcision (Colossians 2:11–12).

Baptism in no way earns your salvation. The very thought of gaining heaven by getting wet is preposterous. Baptism is, however, the appropriate expression of faith in God. We're aware that "faith apart from works is dead" (James 2:26). So the question is not "*Should* we respond to God's gracious gift of Christ?" but "*How* should we respond to God's gracious gift of Christ?"

When the Jews, convicted of their need for salvation, first asked the question "What shall we do?" the apostle Peter gave this answer: "Repent and be baptized every one of you in the name of Jesus Christ for the forgiveness of your sins, and you will receive the gift of the Holy Spirit" (Acts 2:37–38).

Can Someone Be Saved Who Hasn't Been Baptized?

Of course. God can grant salvation in his time and in his way. However, the New Testament assumes that every believer will accept this beautiful gift from God.

Yes, a person who believes in Jesus and who bears spiritual fruit but who never submits to baptism can be saved. It's much like a cesarean-section birth. A child can be brought into the world without passing through the mother's birth canal. This is not the first choice for either a woman or her physician. But if the life of the mother or child is at risk, it is the best choice. If humans are clever enough to figure out a C-section, don't you suppose that God, the giver of life, is too? God loves life, and he'll make a way.

But God's design (and command) is for every repentant believer to be baptized. It's a really great design.

What Are the Benefits of Baptism?

1. *Baptism makes us disciples.* The last command of Jesus was to go and make disciples by baptizing them:

    > Go therefore and make disciples of all nations, baptizing them in the name of the Father and of the Son and of the Holy Spirit, teaching them to observe all that I have commanded you. And behold, I am with you always, to the end of the age. (Matthew 28:19–20)

    God knows that our strongest memories combine multiple senses. Baptism taps into the visual, auditory, and tactile senses and sometimes even taste and smell. This is why long after we've forgotten what we said in the "sinner's prayer," we remember the date, time, place, and people of our baptism.

    Baptism is an enacted prayer. Peter called it "an appeal to God for a good conscience" (1 Peter 3:21). Furthermore, this enacted prayer is always perfectly articulated, since immersion reenacts exactly the right message. We all need this kind of memorable marker, especially when we endure times of trouble. If there were a symbol to capture the meaning of baptism, it would be something like a wedding ring—a tangible reminder of a lifelong commitment.
2. *Baptism connects us to God.* It's not merely a symbol. It's a sacrament. Symbols merely represent something; a sacrament *accomplishes* something. Sacraments connect us to heavenly realities.

    Though the water isn't magical, the obedient act is mystical. Something actually changes in baptism. In the words of Paul, through immersion we "put on Christ" (Galatians 3:27). Our old man is gone and the new has come. Furthermore, we receive the permanent indwelling of the Holy Spirit: "He saved us, not because of works done by us in righteousness, but according to his own mercy, by the washing of regeneration and renewal of the Holy Spirit, whom he poured out on us richly through Jesus Christ our Savior" (Titus 3:5–6). Obviously, the Spirit can indwell anyone he chooses at any time he deems right. Nonetheless, the Bible's promise of the Spirit is connected to the obedience of baptism.

Our status with God changes. If there were a symbol to capture this change in status, it would be circumcision:

> In him also you were circumcised with a circumcision made without hands, by putting off the body of the flesh, by the circumcision of Christ, having been buried with him in baptism, in which you were also raised with him through faith in the powerful working of God, who raised him from the dead. (Colossians 2:11–12)

3. *Baptism saves us through faith.* For many, this is too strong a statement. After all, we're saved by grace through faith *alone.*

We're certainly not saying that we're saved by performing some good work of baptism. What we're saying is that baptism is the appropriate biblical expression of real faith. In reality we're simply quoting Scripture itself: "Baptism, which corresponds to this, now saves you, not as a removal of dirt from the body but as an appeal to God for a good conscience, through the resurrection of Jesus Christ" (1 Peter 3:21). And, "Whoever believes and is baptized will be saved, but whoever does not believe will be condemned" (Mark 16:16).

Baptism is actually a brilliant religious ceremony. It's the only ritual in all the world's religions that deals adequately with both guilt and shame. Guilt is when we cross a line we know we shouldn't have crossed. It's an internal and individual feeling. Shame, on the other hand, is when we don't measure up to a line drawn for us by others—family, sports team, military unit. It's a public and social feeling. Baptism is an individual act that removes our guilt by forgiving our sins. At the same time, baptism is a public declaration that removes our shame by incorporating us into the body of Christ. It's pure genius—and one of the greatest invitations you'll ever get from God.

If there were a symbol to capture this concept, it would be Israel crossing the Red Sea on dry ground. It's God's extraordinary and miraculous act of salvation that creates a new people out of old slaves. In Paul's words,

> I do not want you to be unaware, brothers, that our fathers were all under the cloud, and all passed through the sea, and all were baptized into Moses in the cloud and in the sea, and all ate the same spiritual food, and all drank the same spiritual drink. For they drank from the spiritual Rock that followed them, and the Rock was Christ. (1 Corinthians 10:1–4)

Paul compared Israel's Exodus to Christian baptism. As Moses led Israel through the sea by the Spirit, so Christians pass through water by the Spirit to follow Jesus. God's invitation through baptism releases us from slavery to sin and gives us freedom as part of a new nation marching to the true promised land. Baptism is a gracious gift from God.

Key Points

- Baptism is a sacrament important to every church throughout history.
- Baptism is the proper response to faith in Jesus, marking our new life in Christ by imitating his death, burial, and resurrection.
- Baptism connects us to God through faith in Jesus Christ and through the indwelling of the Holy Spirit.

This Week

- ☐ **Day 1:** Read the essay.
- ☐ **Day 2:** Memorize Acts 2:38.
- ☐ **Day 3:** Read Exodus 14–15.
- ☐ **Day 4:** Meditate on Romans 6:3–6; Titus 3:5–6; 1 Peter 3:21.
- ☐ **Day 5:** If you haven't yet been baptized, then set up a time with your church to be baptized.

Overachiever Challenge: Memorize Romans 6:3–6.

Bonus Read: Jack Cottrell, *Baptism: A Biblical Study.*

40

God's Solution to Racism

> He made from one man every nation of mankind to live on all the face of the earth, having determined allotted periods and the boundaries of their dwelling place.
>
> —Acts 17:26

Question: What is the Christian solution to racism?

We recognize that we live in a nation with deep racial tensions. Yet this isn't merely a national crisis; it's a Christian crisis. Many churches are as deeply divided as their communities. For the children of God, this is a family affair. Our Father is being scandalized because his children are practicing the worst kind of sibling rivalry.

Racial Division in the Old Testament

There is only one human race; there are many nations. Why? According to the history of the Bible, there were two pivotal moments that drove a wedge between brothers, causing a division of languages, cultures, nations, and ethnicities. The first came right after the Flood, when Noah's three sons went their separate ways: "The sons of Noah who went forth from the ark were Shem, Ham, and Japheth. . . . These three were the sons of Noah, and from these the people of the whole earth were dispersed" (Genesis 9:18–19). Because of his sin, Ham was cursed and alienated from his brothers (verses 22–27).

The second moment was the Tower of Babel, when people said, "Come, let us build ourselves a city and a tower with its top in the heavens, and let us make a name for ourselves, lest we be dispersed over the face of the whole earth" (Genesis 11:4). Because of their arrogance, God confused their languages, causing separation among them (verses 6–8).

Because of human sin, people were dispersed. Dispersion is not the problem. God intended humans to rule the entire earth. Diversity is not the problem. God created us genetically to have all kinds of delightful differences. The problem is domination of one people group over others.

God chose the nation of Israel to be his people—not because they were the "best" but because they would be his means of reaching all people. Isaiah 49:6 says,

> It is too light a thing that you should be my servant
>   to raise up the tribes of Jacob
>   and to bring back the preserved of Israel;
> I will make you as a light for the nations,
>   that my salvation may reach to the end of the earth.

After all, by God's initial creative act, all people are his children: "He made from one man every nation of mankind" (Acts 17:26). Furthermore, God has embedded his own image in every human soul (Genesis 1:27).

Racial Reconciliation in the New Testament

Jesus seldom interacted with Gentiles (non-Jewish people), and when he did, it was always tentative. So it might be easy to imagine that Jesus didn't actively address racial reconciliation. However, you can't take Jesus seriously without moving outward toward others.

That's why the book of Acts has more to say about interethnic evangelism than anything else except salvation. Before Christians spread the gospel to all the world, they had to be convinced of the full humanity of other ethnic groups. That required more effort from God than one might expect. His slow yet purposeful progress was clear and deliberate.

Tracing the movement from Acts 6 through Acts 10 is instructive. In Acts 6 the disciples were forced to deal with the tension between Hebrew widows and those of a more Hellenistic background (verses 1–5). Granted, both were Jewish, but some weren't quite as kosher.

In Acts 8 Peter was sent with John to check out the newly founded Samaritan congregation—a blended people group of Jewish and other ethnicities (verse 14). These so-called half-breeds were soaking up God's grace (verses 5–13).

In Acts 9 we find Peter living at the home of Simon the tanner (verse 43). His occupation rendered him ritually unclean. This must have stretched Peter's comfort zone.

In Acts 10 Peter saw a vision of unclean animals. When God ordered him to eat, Peter objected to eating anything "unclean" (verses 10–14). God objected to Peter's objection. You see, this lesson was not about food but about Gentile inclusion. God punctuated the point with these memorable words: "What God has made clean, do not call common" (verse 15).

The vision was followed by a direct command of the Holy Spirit, who ordered Peter to follow three Gentiles who "coincidentally" arrived at Simon's gate at that precise moment (verses 19–20). Peter went with them to Cornelius's house, where he preached the good news of Jesus. The Holy Spirit made yet another appearance, and Cornelius and his household miraculously spoke in tongues. Peter baptized them into Jesus (verses 23–48).

We should learn two lessons from this. First, racism is a difficult hurdle for most of us. To deny that we have some prejudice is probably more arrogant than any of us can afford to be. Second, this is no small issue in the Bible because it's no small issue to God.

Interethnic evangelism is a key theme in Acts because it's key to the Great Commission. When Jesus said to make disciples of all *nations* (Matthew 28:19), the Greek wording literally means "all ethnic groups."

Racial reconciliation in Christ is a core principle in Paul's letters. Because racism is a consequence of sin, God is dead set on killing it through the sacrifice of Jesus Christ: "Now in Christ Jesus you who once were far off have been brought near by the blood of Christ. For he himself is our peace, who has made us both one and has broken down in his flesh the dividing wall of hostility" (Ephesians 2:13–14). This "dividing wall" was a literal barricade in the temple of Jerusalem barring Gentiles from entering. Archaeologists have found two segments of this wall with an inscription that reads, "No foreigner may enter within the balustrade around the sanctuary and the enclosure. Whoever is caught, on himself shall he put blame for the death which will ensue."[1] Jesus came to destroy every barrier that was keeping any person from coming to God.

God wants all people in his heaven but not just to gather a great crowd. Nor does God expect us to evangelize other groups because as good humanists we need to be nice to one another. It's not even simply that God values diversity or loves the whole world (which is, of course, true). The primary reason God wants all ethnic groups in heaven is because anything less is beneath his dignity. We evangelize the whole world because only then can our great God receive the praise he deserves from every people and tribe.

John put it this way in Revelation:

> After this I looked, and behold, a great multitude that no one could number, from every nation, from all tribes and peoples and languages, standing before the throne and before the Lamb, clothed in white robes, with palm branches in their hands, and crying out with a loud voice, "Salvation belongs to our God who sits on the throne, and to the Lamb!" (7:9–10)

Anyone irritated by multiculturalism will be miserable in heaven.

Racial Reconciliation in the Church

Every person has a heart language. Even those who learn multiple other languages will still pray in their heart language. This heart language involves not just vocabulary but also social values, body language, and traditions. Granted, we should all be flexible, especially for the sake of evangelism. However, it's unfair and probably unrealistic to ask culture groups to blend their heart languages in worship.

The bottom line is this: the path to ethnic unity is not through culturally combined services but through cooperative community service. Churches must begin partnering to pour God's love into specific geographic areas. Suburban churches with professional and financial resources could partner with inner-city churches whose experience and relationships could open doors to migrant workers, refugees, the generational poor, etc. This is only one example of literally thousands that could demonstrate racial reconciliation in view of the broader unchurched community.

In order for this to work, however, there needs to be a Barnabas (if you're unfamiliar with his story, it's recorded in Acts 11:19–30). This individual must be full of the Holy Spirit and respected in the communities that are serving together. And this person must be willing to risk his own reputation, as Barnabas did for the likes of Saul of Tarsus as well as for John Mark (9:26–27; 15:37–39).

Racial reconciliation is worth fighting for.

It has become apparent that racial reconciliation will not be brought about through government programs, humanistic propaganda, sensitivity training, or integrated education. In fact, our human efforts in recent decades have largely encouraged ethnic groups to protect their own turf and demand their own rights.

Jesus, however, calls for abandonment of self in the service of others. As long as we keep protecting our own interests, racial tensions will continue to fester.

There are two places where racism has failed to gain significant traction—the battlefield and the athletic field. Here the enemy is clearly identified. Our differences are insignificant compared with our shared goals. The key therefore to racial reconciliation is to gather diverse groups under a banner that's larger than themselves.

The good news for Christians is that Jesus is our banner. If we'll focus on him, we will inevitably be brought together. This is precisely why *only in the church of Jesus Christ will our culture find racial reconciliation.* There's simply no other banner large enough to encompass our diversity.

So we're morally obligated to use our influence, advantages, and resources to bring about racial reconciliation, especially in the body of Christ. Consider the exhortation of James 4:17: "Whoever knows the right thing to do and fails to do it, for him it is sin."

Key Points

- Global dispersion and diversity are healthy; domination because of prejudice is sin.
- The gospel message and the Great Commission are designed to overcome sin of all sorts, including racism. This is a clear emphasis throughout Acts and the epistles.
- The local church is the hope of the world, especially in overcoming racism.

This Week

- ☐ **Day 1:** Read the essay.
- ☐ **Day 2:** Memorize Acts 17:26.
- ☐ **Day 3:** Read Jonah 1–4.
- ☐ **Day 4:** Meditate on Isaiah 49:6; Ephesians 2:13–14; Revelation 7:9–10.
- ☐ **Day 5:** Have a meal with someone from a different ethnic or cultural background to learn about that person's story.

Overachiever Challenge: Memorize Isaiah 49:6.

Bonus Read: Christena Cleveland, *Disunity in Christ: Uncovering the Hidden Forces That Keep Us Apart.*

41

Freedom

There is therefore now no condemnation for those who are in Christ Jesus.

—Romans 8:1

Question: How can I experience freedom?

One of the greatest difficulties Christians face is accepting God's grace. We sense our own sin: "All have sinned and fall short of the glory of God" (Romans 3:23). Even though we know God forgives us, forgiving ourselves is difficult. Romans 8 will help. This is the single greatest chapter in the Bible for helping Christians move beyond the burden of judgment to the freedom of grace.

The Declaration of Freedom

"There is therefore now no condemnation for those who are in Christ Jesus" (Romans 8:1)—this single statement is a world-altering reality. Have we violated God's law? Yes. Are there clear consequences for transgressions? Yes. Nonetheless, in Christ all that is released.

This is not to deny the validity of God's law. There's still right and wrong. To get beyond the law, however, we need to know the limitations of the law.

The law can point out our failures, but it cannot build character. As Paul explained in Romans 7, the law actually increases violations. How? When the law says, "Don't covet," we ask, "What is coveting?" "Well," comes the answer, "coveting is when you want what others have." We reply, "Like what?" "Well, like your neighbor's house, wife, job, and toys." So we look across the fence, and we say, "Oh, I like that! Why can't *I* have that?" That's how the law increases transgression (verses 7–12). Whatever the law says no to suddenly becomes the very thing we want to say yes to.

Jesus freed us from this vicious cycle. Paul explained this early in Romans 8:

> The law of the Spirit of life has set you free in Christ Jesus from the law of sin and death. For God has done what the law, weakened by the flesh, could not do. By sending his own Son in the likeness of sinful flesh and for sin, he condemned sin in the flesh, in order that the righteous requirement of the law might be fulfilled in us, who walk not according to the flesh but according to the Spirit. (verses 2–4)

Notice that last phrase, describing believers "who walk not according to the flesh but according to the Spirit." The Spirit in us takes over where Jesus left off. Christ fully and finally freed us from the law—not just its penalty but its pull. He showed us a better way, a nobler path. Consequently, the penalty of the law is eradicated and the appeal of sin is curtailed.

So the only power the law has over us is what we give to it. That's where the Spirit steps in: "Where the Spirit of the Lord is, there is freedom" (2 Corinthians 3:17). He is the resource we need to fully appropriate the freedom we have in Christ.

The Spirit of Freedom

Being truly free starts with God forgiving our sin. *Done!* Or to quote Jesus, "It is finished" (John 19:30).

Our next step is to crucify our old selves. This happens through the slow and sometimes strenuous task of living by the Spirit rather than by the instincts of our old nature. This is also something Paul addressed in Romans 8:

> If the Spirit of him who raised Jesus from the dead dwells in you, he who raised Christ Jesus from the dead will also give life to your mortal bodies through his Spirit who dwells in you.
>
> So then, brothers, we are debtors, not to the flesh, to live according to the flesh. For if you live according to the flesh you will die, but if by the Spirit you put to death the deeds of the body, you will live. (verses 11–13)

That's true and straightforward. So why don't we just live it out?

There are probably many reasons, but the primary one is identity. We believe our deeds and desires determine our identity. We sinned, so we must be sinners. This is one of the most destructive lies of the Evil One. Our identity is in our created nature, not our fallen nature. We were created by God; therefore, we're his children. We were redeemed by Jesus; therefore, we're his possession. We were filled with the Holy Spirit; therefore, we're saints.

If we can believe what God says about us, we can better behave by the commands he gives us. This is precisely why one of the primary works of the Spirit within us is to convince us we're not who we think we are: "You did not receive the spirit of slavery to fall back into fear, but you have received the Spirit of adoption as sons, by whom we cry, 'Abba! Father!'" (verse 15). When we hear the Spirit's whisper, we can shout, "Abba! Father!"

While this may seem too good to be true, that's only the half of it. If God is our Father, we have all kinds of advantages in life. Two are worth special mention here.

First, our good Father wants to say yes to us. In fact, Jesus promised that every request of ours that aligns with his mission will be granted. He was actually pretty repetitive with this promise (Matthew 7:7–11; 18:19; 21:22; Luke 11:9–13; John 14:13–14; 15:7, 16; 16:23–24). Prayer is therefore a significant advantage for the Christian.

Second, we have hope that in heaven we'll share everything Jesus inherits from the Father because we're his children: "If children, then heirs—heirs of God and fellow heirs with Christ, provided we suffer with him in order that we may also be glorified with him" (Romans 8:17). His estate is substantial. You do *not* want to miss out.

The Plan for Freedom

This leads to another conclusion. If God is that invested in us, he'll protect his investment.

We certainly need God's protection in our current culture. We need protection from Satan, from society, and even from our own sin. We're under attack from every quarter.

Moreover, the earth itself labors under the crushing weight of sin. The physical creation shares the same curse as humanity (Romans 8:18–23). Creation groans, longing for the redemption of humanity (verses 19–22).

There'll come a day when all God's children will be fully redeemed. Indeed, today our souls are saved. Yet our bodies still show signs of the curse and decay. Someday, when Jesus returns, our mortal bodies will be transformed by the resurrection power of Jesus. As our physical bodies are fully redeemed, this physical earth will be also, giving way to a new heaven and a new earth. The coming attractions are bright indeed.

In the meantime, however, the Holy Spirit ensures that we make it to our destination. His invisible assistance is more vital than we could possibly imagine. He helps us in multiple ways, but one of the most powerful is prayer. Paul explained, "The Spirit helps us in our weakness. For we do not know what to pray for as we ought, but the Spirit himself intercedes for us with groanings too deep for words" (verse 26). When we lie breathless on our backs, unable to cobble words together into a prayer, the Holy Spirit intervenes with a wordless prayer. His groaning on our behalf says all that needs to be expressed to move God to action.

Even so, the groaning of the Spirit pales in comparison with his orchestration of the day-to-day events in our lives. He can take the worst of our suffering and weave it into a breathtaking tapestry. In the middle of our valley of the shadow of death, our lives may seem pointless, perhaps arbitrary. God may seem silent. Yet the Spirit journeys with us, guiding our destiny toward his purpose.

Paul attempted to capture all this in a single lofty sentence that has sustained countless Christians in their worst dark night of the soul: "We know that for those who love God all things work together for good, for those who are called according to his purpose" (verse 28). God never wastes pain—it's all used for his purpose. The events that shake your foundation are something God can use to build his kingdom.

Moreover, God isn't merely reacting to your life events. Rather, he preplanned your good, even before you were you. The Bible calls this predestination. Though this topic taxes the mental muscle of the finest thinkers, Paul's summary is enough to clarify all you need to know to survive today: "Those whom he predestined he also called, and those whom he called he also justified, and those whom he justified he also glorified" (verse 30). Put in our language, God planned for you, then chose you, then forgave you; hence, he will keep you.

The Fight for Freedom

God paid the ultimate price for you. His love for you knows no bounds. We can therefore rest assured that he'll never cease loving us, he'll never release us, nor will he allow anything to separate us from him.

Paul's crescendo in Romans 8 is one of the pinnacles in all God's revelation:

> If God is for us, who can be against us? . . . Who shall bring any charge against God's elect? It is God who justifies. Who is to condemn? Christ Jesus is the one who died—more than that, who was raised—who is at the right hand of God, who indeed is interceding for us. Who shall separate us from the love of Christ? Shall tribulation, or distress, or persecution, or famine, or nakedness, or danger, or sword? . . .

No, in all these things we are more than conquerors through him who loved us. For I am sure that neither death nor life, nor angels nor rulers, nor things present nor things to come, nor powers, nor height nor depth, nor anything else in all creation, will be able to separate us from the love of God in Christ Jesus our Lord. (verses 31, 33–35, 37–39)

Key Points

- Living in the freedom of grace is one of the biggest challenges most Christians face.
- In the Spirit we can experience full freedom.
- God, through Jesus, has provided everything necessary for our freedom.

This Week

- ☐ **Day 1:** Read the essay.
- ☐ **Day 2:** Memorize Romans 8:1.
- ☐ **Day 3:** Read John 8:1–11.
- ☐ **Day 4:** Meditate on Romans 8:15, 28, 37.
- ☐ **Day 5:** Write on a piece of paper every sin you keep holding against yourself, then burn the paper as a symbol of releasing it to God's grace.

Overachiever Challenge: Memorize Romans 8:28.

Bonus Read: Jerry Bridges, *Transforming Grace: Living Confidently in God's Unfailing Love.*

42

Radical Change

> Do not be conformed to this world, but be transformed by the renewal of your mind, that by testing you may discern what is the will of God, what is good and acceptable and perfect.
>
> —Romans 12:2

Question: How can I change?

Our biography doesn't have to determine our destiny. We can change.

Change isn't easy, but neither is it complicated. There are three simple steps to change: (1) believe the promise of change, (2) receive the power to change, and (3) accept the challenge to change.

You *can* change, and you already have all the resources you need.

Believe the Promise of Change

The ancient prophet Ezekiel recorded God's promise:

> I will give them one heart, and a new spirit I will put within them. I will remove the heart of stone from their flesh and give them a heart of flesh, that they may walk in my statutes and keep my rules and obey them.

> And they shall be my people, and I will be their God. (11:19–20, repeated almost verbatim in 36:26–28)

This prophetic promise looked forward to Jesus. His sacrifice frees us so his Spirit can deploy us.

No matter how dark your night, God can give you a new lease on life. If you believe the promise, confess your need.

It's easier than you might think: "If you confess with your mouth that Jesus is Lord and believe in your heart that God raised him from the dead, you will be saved. For with the heart one believes and is justified, and with the mouth one confesses and is saved" (Romans 10:9–10). Your past is no longer a barrier to your best future: "If we confess our sins, he is faithful and just to forgive us our sins and to cleanse us from all unrighteousness" (1 John 1:9). Belief and confession lead to transformation: "If anyone is in Christ, he is a new creation. The old has passed away; behold, the new has come" (2 Corinthians 5:17).

Receive the Power to Change

It may seem as if the odds are against us. We have internal impulses that feel too strong to master. We have a culture saturated with seduction. We have an invisible enemy who is ancient, crafty, and powerful. How can we possibly overcome these obstacles?

1. *God's love overcomes our internal impulses.* That's the promise God gave as far back as Ezekiel (quoted earlier): that he would give us a new heart and a new spirit. Anyone who has ever fallen in love knows this to be true. A guy who couldn't spell *potpourri* starts adorning his apartment with lavender, cinnamon, and honeysuckle. Conversely, a woman who never liked sports falls in love and suddenly finds herself accessorizing with her beau's favorite team jersey. Likewise, when we experience the transformational power of God's acceptance, it alters our interests.

2. *Our Christian community overcomes our culture.* God made us insatiably social. We just can't help ourselves—it's instinct. That can be a terrible thing (think middle school), causing us to follow fools into self-destructive behavior. Yet on the whole it's advantageous. Our commitment to family, team, unit, or community causes us to conform to the values of those we value. This instinctive conformity leads to a powerful synergy that allows us not only to accomplish more together but also to live healthier lives. (Fact: when my wife is out of town, I don't like the person I become. I eat junk, watch too much TV, stay up too late, and forget to take vitamins. I suspect you're smiling knowingly right now.)

   This is precisely why regular church attendance is so important. It reinforces the values that reinforce our lives. It's not just—or even primarily—the sermons. It's connecting with others we admire. We're better together.

   To really fast-track transformation, we need to be part of a small group. Why? Because crowds are great for inspiration, but groups are effective for transformation. At church we're hip to hip in rows. In homes we're face to face in circles.

   Small groups offer two things that cannot happen in large gatherings: the ability to talk personally and the accountability to apply the Bible practically. Preachers may be professional teachers, which is a good thing. Nonetheless, it's not simply knowing God's Word that changes lives; it's applying it in the rough-and-tumble of our personal relationships.
3. *God's Spirit in us overcomes the demons against us.* "Little children, you are from God and have overcome them, for he who is in you is greater than he who is in the world" (1 John 4:4). Is Satan powerful? Yes. Is he organized into a global force of destruction? Yes. It's likely that you have demons assigned to you right now who know your weaknesses and work to exploit them.

   It's also likely that you have angels assigned to you as a protective detail. More importantly, you have the Spirit of God inside you as an advocate. His presence is of inestimable value in your transformation. This truth should build confidence and grow grit in your soul.

Knowing now that you have all the necessary weapons and resources—will you accept the challenge to change?

Accept the Challenge to Change

All of us have areas of our lives not yet fully submitted to Jesus Christ. It might be an addiction to some substance. It could be an uncontrolled tongue (or texting). Perhaps it's self-deprecation or doubt. Undoubtedly, all these are rooted in some kind of pride attempting to displace God as sovereign. So before moving on, identify *one* practice (not three or five) that you'll commit to change. Pause and do this now before moving to the next paragraph.

Whatever you just identified will be difficult to change. Don't be naive and assume that because you're a Christian, you can just knock it out. Transformational change is tough, but as believers we have all the resources needed.

Let's look at two passages that are most instructive in making tactical, practical, and permanent changes. The first is our core verse:

> Do not be *conformed* to this world, but be *transformed* by the renewal of your mind, that by testing you may discern what is the will of God, what is good and acceptable and perfect. (Romans 12:2)

There are two words in this passage that offer keen insight into life transformation. The first is the word *conformed.* The Greek word is this: *syschēmatizō.* Can you see in the middle of that word the source of our English word *schematic*? This word carries the idea of a template. There are cultural schematics: materialism, entertainment, individualism, and sensuality. These are values that are "in the air," so to speak. The gravitational drift of culture will always pull toward these values, unless we deliberately counterbalance their effect. How do we do that?

There are four things God gives us to use against culture's influence.

1. *Scripture.* Studies like this help us think differently about life. If the Word of God isn't in you, the world around you will permeate you.
2. *Music.* Music bypasses the gatekeeper of the soul. Worship music exalts God, and we get caught in the upward draft. It lifts us to places we want to be. The heavier your past baggage, the more helium of worship you'll need to raise you where you want to be.
3. *Service.* Jesus still shows up among the disenfranchised—the orphan, the trafficked, the poor. When we take a stand where he is, we experience solidarity with him.
4. *Fellowship.* As we gather to worship, pray, and proclaim God's Word, the whole is greater than the sum of its parts. We're transformed simply by positioning ourselves amid the faithful.

The second word in Romans 12:2 that's so instructive is *transformed.* The Greek word is *metamorphoō.* You can see an English word in it: *metamorphosis.* This Greek word was borrowed in English to describe the transformation of caterpillars into butterflies and tadpoles into frogs. It carries the connotation of radical transformation.

We can be completely different people. How? By *not* conforming.

Bottom line: *transformation requires nonconformity.* If you want to change your life, you must first change your friends. Changing friends requires changing your environment. Changing your environment requires changing your priorities. For some this means a difficult breakup. For others it requires quitting a team or a job. For some it will even necessitate a move.

Is a new life worth the sacrifice of radical reorientation? This leads to our second passage that especially helps us in making tactical, practical, and permanent changes:

> If then you have been raised with Christ, seek the things that are above, where Christ is, seated at the right hand of God. . . .
>
> *Put to death* therefore what is earthly in you: sexual immorality, impurity, passion, evil desire, and covetousness, which is idolatry. . . .

> *Put on* then, as God's chosen ones, holy and beloved, compassionate hearts, kindness, humility, meekness, and patience, bearing with one another and, if one has a complaint against another, forgiving each other; as the Lord has forgiven you, so you also must forgive. (Colossians 3:1, 5, 12–13)

We must remove and replace. This is how transformation happens. We put to death old habits and adopt new ones.

According to Paul, here are two things that must go: sexual immorality and greed. Other things are on the list, but these two summarize a bunch of them. Money and sex are roadblocks to spiritual growth when they're out of bounds. If you say you want to change, change starts here. Rid yourself of habits and opportunities leading to these two social seductions.

Next, we must put into practice some key virtues. Paul listed them in the passage above. These three top the list: acts of kindness (being the hands of Christ), humility (adopting the mind of Christ), and forgiveness (practicing the heart of Christ).

There's no shortcut to radical transformation. The cost is high, often excruciating. But of this there's no doubt: the benefits are more gratifying than the sacrifice is difficult.

Key Points

- Radical transformation is possible—the Bible promises this.
- The power to change is found in God's love, God's people, and God's Spirit.
- Personal transformation may require changing friends, environments, and priorities in order to put off old practices and start new ones.

This Week

- ☐ **Day 1:** Read the essay.
- ☐ **Day 2:** Memorize Romans 12:2.
- ☐ **Day 3:** Read Matthew 17:1–20.
- ☐ **Day 4:** Meditate on Romans 10:9–10; 2 Corinthians 5:17; 1 John 4:4.
- ☐ **Day 5:** What is one thing you identified above that you need to put off and one thing you need to put into practice? Share this with an accountability partner to plan how to pull this off.

Overachiever Challenge: Memorize 1 John 4:4.

Bonus Read: Tim Chester, *You Can Change: God's Transforming Power for Our Sinful Behavior and Negative Emotions.*

43

Knowing God's Will

"Who has understood the mind of the Lord so as to instruct him?" But we have the mind of Christ.

—1 Corinthians 2:16

Question: Can I know God's will for my life?

The simple answer is yes. God is more interested in revealing his will to you than you are in receiving it. The Bible, in fact, makes a concerted effort to reveal God's general will.

First and foremost, he wants us to be saved. God "is patient toward you, not wishing that any should perish, but that all should reach repentance" (2 Peter 3:9). He desires that we live healthy and holy lives: "This is the will of God, your sanctification: that you abstain from sexual immorality" (1 Thessalonians 4:3). Sexual purity is just one example; God longs for your good in every area. Paul said, "Rejoice always, pray without ceasing, give thanks in all circumstances; for this is the will of God in Christ Jesus for you" (1 Thessalonians 5:16–18).

God desires you to do good so you can benefit others through an undeniable life witness: "This is the will of God, that by doing good you should put to silence the ignorance of foolish people" (1 Peter 2:15). In fact, God sometimes allows us to suffer so our witness can expand: "It is better to suffer for doing good, if that should be God's will, than for doing evil" (1 Peter 3:17).

There is therefore little question as to God's general will. Even so, for lots of daily decisions, as well as major life decisions, we just don't know what God wants us to do: how to counsel a friend, what job to take, or whom to marry. For example, Paul often didn't know God's will for where he should go (Acts 18:21; Romans 1:10; 15:32).

How can I know what God wants me to do in specific situations that the Bible doesn't address? Knowing God's will starts with something Jesus said: "If anyone's will is to do God's will, he will know whether the teaching is from God or whether I am speaking on my own authority" (John 7:17). If we do God's will that we *do* know, we can then discover his will for what we don't yet know.

We Have the Mind of Christ

Can you imagine being able to know what God is thinking? As you watch the news or enter a new relationship, wouldn't you love to have access to God's perspective and opinion? Paul said we can. We can know the deep and hidden thoughts of God. This is beyond extraordinary. How is that even possible? How could we ever get on the same cognitive wavelength as the Creator of the universe?

Paul wrote, "Who knows a person's thoughts except the spirit of that person, which is in him? So also no one comprehends the thoughts of God except the Spirit of God" (1 Corinthians 2:11). We all know that's true. That's what makes first dates so difficult. You're wondering what the other person is thinking. That's why job interviews are so intimidating. Interviewers smile and shake your hand, but you don't know whether they are impressed with you or think you're a knucklehead. That's why even the best friendships and the best marriages have conflict. We think we know what another person is thinking, but all too often we miss the mark entirely. In reality we cannot know with certainty what another person is thinking.

Yet listen to what Paul said next:

> We have received not the spirit of the world, but the Spirit who is from God, that we might understand the things freely given us by God. And we impart this in words not taught by human wisdom but taught by the Spirit, interpreting spiritual truths to those who are spiritual. (verses 12–13)

What in the world does this mean?

Two things stand out. First, this access isn't open equally to every Christian. There are some who are saved who don't have the capacity to think spiritually. They're still practicing a lifestyle that doesn't represent the priorities of God. The more entangled we are in habitual sin, the less we understand the Bible. Why? Because our pattern of reading Scripture allows us to justify our behavior. We've all done that. Greedy people ignore Jesus's advice on money. When you're in an inappropriate relationship, you skip over any passages on purity. When you're a gossip, you avoid the book of Proverbs.

Second, a problem that's probably more common is that we just don't know what the Scriptures teach. That's actually a preventable problem. This whole project of identifying fifty-two key texts is an attempt to help rectify biblical illiteracy in our churches. Knowing the basics of God's Word allows us to ask honestly whether our lives are in alignment with God's priorities. If we allow the Bible to massage our thinking and alter our habits, we have the very real possibility of having the mind of Christ.

It isn't natural for a fallen human being to think the thoughts of God: "The natural person does not accept the things of the Spirit of God, for they are folly to him, and he is not able to understand them because they are spiritually discerned" (1 Corinthians 2:14). We shouldn't be surprised when someone from the world, or even someone barely in the church, cannot make sense of the Bible. But that doesn't mean that God has no clear opinions or that a spiritually mature Christian doesn't have access to those opinions. You *can* know the thoughts of God. You *can* have the mind of Christ.

In verse 16 we come to one of the most stunning statements of the Bible (Paul was paraphrasing Isaiah 40:13): "Who has understood the mind of the

Lord so as to instruct him?" The answer is obvious: no one! No one can instruct God, as if he needed our opinion. We'll never make some observation that causes God to throw his head back and say, "I never knew that!"

Yet the verse isn't finished. In a breathtaking conclusion, Paul said, "But we have the mind of Christ."

Let me say this as simply as I can: if you're a Spirit-filled follower of Jesus Christ and you align your life with his priorities, the more Scripture you consume, the more potential you have to access the thoughts of God. Obedience to God's commands results in revelation of God's will. If we want to discover more of God's will, we must not only know God's Word but also align our lives with his will inscribed in his Word.

This is not to say we have to be perfect. Obviously, no one has achieved that, outside of Jesus. What it does mean is that the more we obey God's Word, the more we'll understand his will. Conversely, the more we know God's Word *and fail to obey,* the quicker we'll go spiritually blind and deaf.

How to Go Spiritually Blind and Deaf

It was about 740 BC. King Uzziah had just died, and the nation of Judah was in crisis. For generations God had called his people to repent. Their persistent rejection of Yahweh led to cultural chaos. God had had enough.

He appeared to the prophet Isaiah in an astonishing vision. The temple filled with smoke, while six-winged flaming angels flew about shouting, "Holy, holy, holy is the Lord of hosts; the whole earth is full of his glory!" (Isaiah 6:3). Yahweh himself showed up. There Isaiah heard God's call: "Who will go for us?" Isaiah replied, "Here I am! Send me" (verse 8).

God then commissioned Isaiah:

> Go, and say to this people:
>
> "Keep on hearing, but do not understand;
> keep on seeing, but do not perceive."

> Make the heart of this people dull,
>   and their ears heavy,
>   and blind their eyes;
> lest they see with their eyes,
>   and hear with their ears,
> and understand with their hearts,
>   and turn and be healed. (verses 9–10)

God's call to Isaiah was to blind Israel's eyes and dull their hearing. How? Through the continued preaching of God's call to repent.

In the New Testament, three people quote this passage: Jesus (Matthew 13:14–15), John (John 12:39–41), and Paul (Acts 28:25–27). Each time, it's the act of preaching that hardened people's hearts.

Preaching is incredibly dangerous because those who listen but don't obey become deaf. How? We all know people who sleep through an alarm clock or who live beside a landing strip but never hear a plane. Hearing without heeding leads to deafness. When we ignore God's warnings, he sends us further warnings that make us only harder of hearing.

God's will is clarified through obedience but obscured by disobedience. There comes a point when the disobedient no longer hear, no matter how loudly God shouts. Many of them go to church every Sunday.

Key Points

- God's general will is crystal clear, especially when it comes to morality.
- The Holy Spirit reveals God's will to those who obey his Word.
- Disobedience blinds us to God's will, even as preaching makes us deaf.

This Week

☐ **Day 1:** Read the essay.

☐ **Day 2:** Memorize 1 Corinthians 2:16.

☐ **Day 3:** Read Acts 17–18.

☐ **Day 4:** Meditate on Isaiah 6:9–10; John 7:17; Colossians 1:9.

☐ **Day 5:** Pray this for yourself: "We have not ceased to pray for you, asking that you may be filled with the knowledge of his will in all spiritual wisdom and understanding" (Colossians 1:9).

Overachiever Challenge: Memorize Isaiah 6:9–10.

Bonus Read: Henry Blackaby, Richard Blackaby, and Claude King, *Experiencing God: Knowing and Doing the Will of God.*

44

The Resurrection

If Christ has not been raised, then our preaching is in vain and your faith is in vain.

—1 Corinthians 15:14

Question: Did Jesus really rise from the dead?

The Resurrection is the bedrock of Christianity. If Jesus didn't rise from the dead, Christianity crumbles.

Paul said as much in our core verse. Thus, "Did Jesus rise from the dead?" is the central question we must answer to determine whether faith in Christ is well founded or only a farce.

To that end, we'll address two profoundly important questions: (1) Why should I believe Jesus rose from the dead? (2) If this is true, why does it matter?

Why Should I Believe Jesus Rose from the Dead?

These following four facts are affirmed by virtually every historian who has studied the first-century world. If the facts are all true, the resurrection of Jesus is the only explanation to account for all of them.

1. *Jesus of Nazareth was executed by crucifixion.* This is the unanimous testimony not only of the biblical authors (Matthew, Mark, Luke, John, Paul, Peter, and the author of Hebrews) but also of the ancient historians Josephus[1] and Tacitus.[2] If the Jewish leaders believed Jesus was a threat, they would certainly have handed him over to the Roman governor for execution.

   According to all four gospels, Joseph of Arimathea—a member of the Sanhedrin, the ruling council of Jews in Jerusalem—provided a tomb for Jesus's burial. This act of piety was later remembered by Paul (Acts 13:29; 1 Corinthians 15:4). If this story was fabricated, it was bold—even foolhardy—to claim that a Sanhedrin member had sympathized with Jesus and to make such a claim within a generation of the events. If Joseph of Arimathea didn't actually do what the Evangelists claimed, his family surely would have sought legal reparations.
2. *The tomb was empty.* A few critics attempt to deny the empty tomb, though the unanimous testimony of the Bible affirms it. Hence, those few detractors must explain why there was never any veneration of the tomb of Jesus. Considering the Jewish practice of honoring prophets' graves, this is incomprehensible without an empty tomb.

   Additionally, the central doctrine of the early church was the bodily resurrection of Jesus. It's inconceivable that the Christian church, which began in the very city of Jesus's execution, could have made any headway had his tomb still been occupied. Someone surely would have produced the body and squelched the emerging movement.

   Some may suggest that the apostles' experience was either a hallucination or a vision of some sort and didn't require the tomb to be empty. However, there's virtually no example of Jews, or anyone else for that matter, talking about any "spiritual" or "mystic" resurrection. Resurrection always referred to the raising of a dead body. Sure, people had visions and dreams, but they were identified as angelic visitations (compare Acts 12:14–15) and never as a resurrection. Simply put, the empty tomb is a prerequisite for any kind of belief in or proclamation of Jesus's resurrection.

Finally, the earliest argument against the Resurrection dealt with an empty tomb. Matthew recorded the story of the guards reporting that the disciples stole the body (28:11–15). The issue at this point is not which side was telling the truth but rather who started the rumor and why. This is hardly the kind of tale that Christians would have invented, since it needlessly implicated them in a crime. Furthermore, moving the body would desecrate Jesus's honorable burial, so no Christian would take credit for that. So what about the Roman soldiers? Considering that they could be killed for losing their "prisoner," it's implausible that they would have made up the story.

Matthew tells us that the story came from the chief priests and elders (verses 11–13). It's reasonable to conclude that the empty tomb is what motivated them to say such a thing; had there been no empty tomb, there would have been no need to accuse the disciples of stealing the body.

All indications are that the tomb was in fact empty.

3. *The apostles believed Jesus had appeared to them in a tangible body.* Perhaps the disciples were mistaken, but they were definitely convinced Jesus rose (Matthew 28:9; Luke 24:36–43; John 20:27). This belief transformed them.

Further points must be made here. First, Greeks and Romans never desired resurrection, since they considered the body a prison of the soul. Homer and Aeschylus denied the possibility of resurrection.[3] So in a world where resurrection was neither expected nor desired, Christians were preaching resurrection as their central doctrine (Acts 17:32; 1 Corinthians 1:22–23).

On the other hand, the Jews—many of whom did believe in resurrection—usually viewed it as physical and corporate and as something occurring at the end of time. Consequently, though the Christian view of resurrection could have developed only in a Jewish context, it was radically different from the prevailing concept in Judaism in a couple of significant ways: (1) it was an individual (Jesus) resurrected, not the nation; and (2) it was within time, not at the end of history. Resurrection thus became, for the first time, proof of the Messiah. As such, it was central to the church.

This radical new theology of resurrection requires explanation. The disciples couldn't just manufacture a new worldview without powerful grounds for doing so.

Furthermore, whatever experience the disciples had—or thought they had—that led them to conclude Jesus was resurrected, it was something that radically transformed them. Peter went from being a coward (Matthew 26:69–75) to being a bold preacher (Acts 2:14–40). James, the half-brother of Jesus, went from being a critic (John 7:1–9) to being the key leader of the Jerusalem church (Acts 15:13; 21:18; Galatians 2:9). Thomas went from being a skeptic to being a worshipper (John 20:24–28) with his profound declaration of Jesus's deity: "My Lord and my God!" (verse 28). Then there's Paul, who went from being the church's chief persecutor to being its most effective promoter (Galatians 1:11–16; 1 Corinthians 9:1; 15:8–10).

In short, something extraordinary happened to these men to cause their lives to be so radically transformed.

4. *The Christian church was founded.* Every Jewish movement in the first century died with its founder or continued only under the leadership of his next of kin. With Jesus, we have a messianic leader who was arrested and then crucified—the most ignominious punishment available. This destroyed all hope that Jesus was any kind of Messiah the Jewish leaders could have imagined (Luke 24:21). Yet fifty days later, the church exploded in the very city where Jesus had been executed. Moreover, the dreaded cross

> became the centerpiece of the entire movement. And how can one explain the celebration of communion, a ritual eating of Jesus's flesh and blood? Who would memorialize a dead Messiah with such cannibalistic symbolism?
>
> Likewise, the practice of baptism into the death, burial, and resurrection of Jesus (Romans 6:4–5) has to have some reasonable genesis. Not only does the form of this practice assume a belief in resurrection, but this particular rite also replaced circumcision (Colossians 2:11–12), one of the cherished marks of Judaism. It would be difficult to overstate the significance of such a shift. It would be akin to one of our churches putting an image of Buddha on the cross.
>
> Furthermore, what would cause a group of Jews to alter the deeply cherished and persistent practice of observing the Sabbath (Saturday) to institute a Sunday worship service? For a people steeped in tradition stretching back fifteen hundred years, such a change could be effected only by a spiritual tsunami.
>
> So there was massive, world-transforming, life-altering change. What could account for it?

Many have attempted alternative explanations for the bodily resurrection of Jesus. Nonetheless, these four facts defy any other explanation. You can rest assured in the reality of the Resurrection.

And if it's true—why does it matter?

Why Does It Matter That Jesus Rose from the Dead?

Though the cross is the central symbol of Christianity, the Resurrection is the core of biblical teaching (Acts 2:22–36; 4:2, 33; 23:6; Romans 1:4; 6:5; 1 Corinthians 15; Ephesians 1:20; 2:4–7; Philippians 3:10–11; 1 Thessalonians 4:13–18; 1 Peter 3:18–22). This is our creed: "If you confess with your mouth that

Jesus is Lord and believe in your heart that God raised him from the dead, you will be saved" (Romans 10:9). Paul proclaimed the account of the Resurrection that he inherited from his predecessors (1 Corinthians 15:3–4). Why is the Resurrection the central doctrine of Christianity?

1. Jesus had *completed* his work, fulfilling prophecy (Psalm 16:8–11; Isaiah 53:8–10; see also Hosea 6:2). We can believe his self-revelation and and obey his teachings because he defeated death (Romans 6:9; 1 Corinthians 15:20, 55–57) and established our justification (Romans 4:25).
2. Jesus is *exalted* to God's right hand (Acts 2:32–33; Ephesians 1:20–21), proving himself to be "both Lord and Christ" (Acts 2:36) and God's own son (Romans 1:4). Jesus is thus the cornerstone of the church and the exclusive source of eternal life (Acts 4:10–12).
3. We have an *advocate* at God's right hand, defending us before God (Romans 8:31–39). In this way Jesus grants repentance and forgiveness (Acts 5:30–31; 13:38). Thus, the judgment of God holds no dread for us (John 5:28–29; Acts 17:31).
4. We have *fellowship* with Jesus in his suffering and death (Romans 6:4–5; Colossians 2:12; Philippians 3:8–11). Therefore, we're dead to sin (Romans 6:6–14), to the law (Acts 13:37–39; Romans 7:1–5; 8:1–4), and to the thoughts and things of this world (Colossians 3:1–2; Romans 8:5).
5. We have *power* through the Holy Spirit (John 14:26; Acts 2:33, who gives us courage to proclaim the gospel (Acts 1:8; 4:31).
6. We have *hope* (1 Corinthians 15:19–20; 1 Peter 1:3). If Jesus was raised, we can be too—not merely from the dead but to the right hand of God (Ephesians 2:6). According to 1 Corinthians 15:40–54, our new bodies will be like the body of Jesus—heavenly, imperishable, glorified, powerful, spiritual, suddenly changed, and immortal. We become coheirs with Christ (Romans 8:17) and fellow rulers with him (Revelation 20:6).

Does it matter that Jesus rose from the dead? Nothing matters more! Moreover, our faith is founded on historical evidence, fulfilled prophecy, and the testimony of millions of transformed lives.

Key Points

- Christ's resurrection is the core of Christianity.
- There are four facts that become unexplainable without the Resurrection.
- Because of his resurrection, Jesus is enthroned and we are empowered.

This Week

- ☐ **Day 1:** Read the essay.
- ☐ **Day 2:** Memorize 1 Corinthians 15:14.
- ☐ **Day 3:** Read Mark 16; John 11.
- ☐ **Day 4:** Meditate on Ezekiel 37:1–14; John 11:25; 20:1–31.
- ☐ **Day 5:** Identify one of the six points above that should have a bigger impact on your life. How should this truth change your actions or thinking?

Overachiever Challenge: Memorize John 11:25.

Bonus Read: Gary R. Habermas and Michael R. Licona, *The Case for the Resurrection of Jesus.*

45

Grace

By grace you have been saved through faith. And this is not your own doing; it is the gift of God.

—Ephesians 2:8

Question: What do we have to do to be saved?

Every religion has its own answer to this question: What do we have to do to be saved? Some encourage sacrifice; others, service; others, rituals of purification or meditation. What all have in common is some human effort to achieve favor with God. This may include knocking on doors with pamphlets, giving away wealth, self-flagellation, or confession and restitution. The common thread, however, is human effort to reach God's height.

Grace Is God's Salvation

Christianity alone moves in the opposite direction. Rather than us climbing upward, Christianity asserts that God moved downward. Salvation is not accomplished through human effort but offered through God's sacrifice. Logically, this is the only way to be sure of salvation. After all, how can a human reach God?

Of all the New Testament authors, Paul was clearest on this point. Let's listen to a few excerpts from his most notable treatise on grace, the letter to the Romans: "All have sinned and fall short of the glory of God, and are justified by his grace as a gift, through the redemption that is in Christ Jesus" (3:23–24). "Since we have been justified by faith, we have peace with God through our Lord Jesus Christ. Through him we have also obtained access by faith into this grace in which we stand, and we rejoice in hope of the glory of God" (5:1–2). "Sin will have no dominion over you, since you are not under law but under grace" (6:14). "If it is by grace, it is no longer on the basis of works; otherwise grace would no longer be grace" (11:6).

With this brief flyover, we clearly see the core of Christianity: we're saved by God's grace, not our own effort.

Though Paul is the dominant voice for grace, he's no outlier. Peter said the same thing. During a debate with some Jewish Christians who attempted to impose circumcision as a prerequisite for conversion, Peter concluded his argument with these words: "We believe that we will be saved through the grace of the Lord Jesus, just as they will" (Acts 15:11). Jesus's brother, James, officiated the debate and concurred with Peter, stating that grace was the official stance of the church (verses 13–19).

Grace Is a Social System

The clearest statement of salvation by grace through faith comes from Paul's little letter to the Ephesians. It's one of those banner statements of the Bible:

> By grace you have been saved through faith. And this is not your own doing; it is the gift of God, not a result of works, so that no one may boast. For we are his workmanship, created in Christ Jesus for good works, which God prepared beforehand, that we should walk in them. (2:8–10)

While this description of salvation is the clearest on record, it also introduces a paradox. We're saved by grace through faith, yet this passage tells us that we're created for good works. So the question is this: What's the relationship between grace, faith, and works? In other words, if we're saved by grace, why are we expected to perform good works?

The simplest answer is that works are the consequence of our salvation, not the cause. What we accomplish for Christ is a by-product of our salvation, not the foundation of it.

There's a social setting for this description of salvation that paints a picture of the relationship between faith, grace, and works. In the economy of the ancient world, about 2 percent of the population controlled virtually all the goods and services. They were called patrons. These patrons hired employees (or slaves) in their homes, such as doctors, lawyers, teachers, and artists. These servants were called brokers, and they made up approximately 5 percent of the population. Meanwhile, those employed outside the home—day laborers, farmers, craftsmen, etc.—were called clients. This group made up the majority of the population (about three-quarters). This left the bottom 15 percent as "expendables" who served in the lowest occupations—miners, prostitutes, ditchdiggers—and who had very short life spans.

These patrons, brokers, and clients had clearly defined social roles and responsibilities. The patron's job was to provide the resources needed for his clients to survive, such as a job, home, land, medical care, and legal protection. The total of the gifts a patron provided was called "grace."

The broker's task was to expand the patron's influence. Brokers were evangelists responsible for acquiring more clients. But why would patrons want more clients if they constantly had to give them gifts? Wasn't it an economic liability to provide for clients? It certainly was. However, in the ancient world, wealth wasn't the most coveted commodity; *honor* was. The more clients a patron provided for, the more honored the patron was in the community.

The clients, on the other hand, had one primary purpose: to honor their patron. Their only job was to make him famous. If he was running for political office, they ran behind him, promoting his campaign. If he was harvesting a field, they would go work in the field. If he was addressing a crowd, they gathered to sing his praise. So while the patron would never mention his gifts again, the client was to never fail to mention every gift he gave as often as possible.

There was a word the Greeks used to describe this loyalty the clients offered their patron. That word was *faith,* perhaps better translated as "fidelity."

So Paul's statement "By grace you have been saved through faith [fidelity]" (verse 8) was a description of Jesus as the patron and us as his clients. Simply put, our role as Christians is to do whatever we can to make Jesus famous.

Grace Is Our Service

Our efforts to make Jesus famous extend God's grace to other potential clients. Our service is thus an act of grace. That's why our spiritual gifts are called grace: "Having gifts that differ according to the grace given to us, let us use them" (Romans 12:6). Peter said virtually the same thing: "As each has received a gift, use it to serve one another, as good stewards of God's varied grace" (1 Peter 4:10). Paul described his own ministry as an act of grace: "You have heard of the stewardship of God's grace that was given to me for you. . . . Of this gospel I was made a minister according to the gift of God's grace, which was given me by the working of his power" (Ephesians 3:2, 7).

One more thing. Grace is not merely our service to others. It's the very character of our lives that inevitably results in gracious acts toward others.

Here's how it works: God gives us grace so that we become grace-filled persons performing gracious acts toward others. Grace becomes our nature. It's not achieved through works but received through Jesus (2 Corinthians 12:9; 1 Peter 1:13).

Grace thus carries the connotation of "favor" or "blessing." Grace is what one person gives to another whom she accepts as a friend. In this way God has made us his friends and clients by bestowing on us his benefits (John 1:16–17; Acts 11:23; 15:40; 1 Corinthians 1:4; 2 Corinthians 8:1–2; 9:8; Ephesians 1:6–7; 2 Thessalonians 1:12; James 4:6; 1 Peter 5:5, 10). This grace indicates that we have a right relationship with God. As such, it's synonymous with "membership in the church" through a relationship with Jesus (Acts 13:43; Romans 5:2; 6:14–15; 1 Corinthians 15:10; 2 Corinthians 13:14; Galatians 5:4; 2 Thessalonians 2:16; 1 Timothy 1:14; 2 Peter 3:18). To this extent, grace has more to do with God's election than our effort (Romans 11:5–6; Galatians 1:15; Ephesians 4:7; 2 Timothy 1:9).

Grace Is a Greeting

There's a peculiarity in the New Testament that's easy to overlook. *Grace* became a Christian greeting so common that it begins and ends all the letters in the New Testament (with rare exceptions). Here's a typical rendition: "Grace and peace to you from God the Father and the Lord Jesus Christ." This combination of *grace* and *peace* is fascinating as a sociological artifact. You see, before *grace* became a theological term, a similar form of this word was used as a common greeting among the Romans and Greeks. In every public square of the Roman Empire, one could hear noble gentlemen greeting one another with this word. It was a wish of health and blessing, like our phrase "Have a nice day." *Peace,* on the other hand, was common fare among the Jews. It's a translation of the Hebrew word *shalom.* This rich word was a wish for health, wholeness, peace, and blessing. It was a theologically laden term heard in every synagogue.

The church of Jesus Christ combined the common greetings of these Jewish and Greco-Roman worlds precisely because they were two worlds united in Jesus. Furthermore, the full theological weight of both terms was brought to bear in the most common greeting of Christians.

There's a lesson here. Grace is so central to who we are as Christians that we incorporate it into our everyday speech. As followers of Jesus, we use common language in uncommon ways to make the extraordinary act of God's grace available to every person in our circle of influence. Grace as a greeting is a potent example of how Jesus can become an integral part of our everyday world. Language for Christians is sanctified for evangelism. We control words, opening the possibility of infusing every conversation with meaning that can alter eternity.

Key Points

- Grace is what distinguishes Christianity from every other religion.
- Salvation by grace through faith directly reflects the patron-client social system.
- Our good works flow from our fidelity that we offer Jesus, our patron of grace.

This Week

- ☐ **Day 1:** Read the essay.
- ☐ **Day 2:** Memorize Ephesians 2:8.
- ☐ **Day 3:** Read Luke 15.
- ☐ **Day 4:** Meditate on Acts 15:11; Romans 3:23–24; 10:13.
- ☐ **Day 5:** Identify one thing you could do this week in a thirty-minute time frame that would make Jesus more famous.

Overachiever Challenge: Memorize Romans 3:23.

Bonus Read: Philip Yancey, *What's So Amazing About Grace?*

46

Unity

There is one body and one Spirit—just as you were called to the one hope that belongs to your call—one Lord, one faith, one baptism, one God and Father of all, who is over all and through all and in all. But grace was given to each one of us according to the measure of Christ's gift.

—Ephesians 4:4–7

Question: What can possibly unify the church?

One of the very last things Jesus prayed for was unity for the church:

> I do not ask for these only, but also for those who will believe in me through their word, that they may all be one, just as you, Father, are in me, and I in you, that they also may be in us, so that the world may believe that you have sent me. (John 17:20–21)

Jesus's prayer has yet to be answered. There are literally hundreds of Christian denominations. It's actually a bit embarrassing. What can possibly unify the church?

The Means of Unity

Some will argue for organizational unity. Using leadership principles, they seek to unite the organizational structures of various denominations. Others attempt doctrinal unity through theological discussions. The idea is that if we agreed about the meaning of the Bible, we would align in ministry. Honestly, that has been a nonstarter. What Jesus appears to have been asking for is neither organizational unity nor ideological uniformity. Rather, in his prayer he sought our *relational* unity: "just as you, Father, are in me, and I in you" (verse 21). This unity can actually be achieved, and Ephesians 4 tells us how: spiritual gifts.

The early church sprang up within the Roman Empire, which was deeply divided across ethnic, geographic, gender, and political lines. The church of Jesus Christ was the only organization that crossed those lines. What seemed impossible became practical because Christians made Jesus Lord of all. As Paul said, "There is neither Jew nor Greek, there is neither slave nor free, there is no male and female, for you are all one in Christ Jesus" (Galatians 3:28). This was reality, not idealism. At the core of this reality was the distribution of spiritual gifts to each Christian that they might exercise them for the benefit of the body.

Spiritual Gifts in the New Testament

We've all heard about spiritual gifts. Did you realize that each passage that lists them appears in the context of unity in the church?

Romans 12:6–8; 1 Corinthians 12:4–10, 28; and Ephesians 4:11 are the primary passages listing a total of sixteen spiritual gifts. Each passage is an argument for the unity of the church through Christians using their godly gifts. The clearest statement is Ephesians 4:4–7, our core passage.

The primary purpose of spiritual gifts is to build a unified body of Christ. So what are these gifts?

Before listing the sixteen gifts mentioned in Scripture, let's lay down an important principle: *spiritual gifts are abilities given by the Holy Spirit that an individual can use to benefit the body of Christ.* Some of these gifts are miraculous, such as prophecy, miracles, healing, and tongues. Most of the gifts, however, are natural abilities, such as teaching, administration, giving, and mercy.

Though some gifts may be given after salvation, most are given at birth. They're innate abilities we have that become spiritual gifts not when the Spirit gives them to us but when we give them back to God in the service of his church. Again, our abilities become gifts when they're given away, not when they're initially obtained.

So here are the sixteen gifts listed in these passages. Read through this list to see whether you can identify abilities you have that could benefit the body of Christ:

1. *Teaching*—explanation and application of truth (Romans 12:7; 1 Corinthians 12:28; Ephesians 4:11).
2. *Ministering*—helping people by meeting their needs (Romans 12:7; 1 Corinthians 12:28).
3. *Administration*—oversight and execution of church affairs (Romans 12:8; 1 Corinthians 12:28).
4. *Evangelist*—one with special ability to present the gospel to the unsaved (Ephesians 4:11).
5. *Pastor*—a shepherd who cares for, protects, leads, and feeds the flock (Ephesians 4:11).
6. *Exhortation*—practical (sometimes private) preaching that calls for action (Romans 12:8).
7. *Giving*—ability and willingness to give resources for the good of the church (Romans 12:8).
8. *Mercy*—providing comfort for those who are sick, afflicted, or outcast (Romans 12:8).
9. *Faith*—ability to take God at his word and trust him in daily needs and trials (1 Corinthians 12:9).
10. *Discerning spirits*—insight into another person's motives, attitude, or purpose (1 Corinthians 12:10).

11. *Apostle*—one who is sent out with a commission (1 Corinthians 12:28; Ephesians 2:20; 4:11). Primarily, this was the Twelve for Israel (Matthew 10:2–4; Acts 1:20–26) and Paul for the Gentiles (Romans 11:13).
12. *Prophecy*—speaking forthrightly a revelation received directly from God (Romans 12:6; 1 Corinthians 12:10, 28; 14; Ephesians 4:11).
13. *Miracles*—ability to alter natural events or processes (1 Corinthians 12:10, 28).
14. *Healing*—ability to restore health to a person's body (1 Corinthians 12:9, 28).
15. *Tongues*—ability to speak in a language one has never learned or studied (1 Corinthians 12:10, 28; 14:1–27).
16. *Interpretation of tongues*—ability to translate an unlearned language into one's native language (1 Corinthians 12:10; 14:26–28).

Determining and Using Your Spiritual Gift

Did you find your gift on the list above? Many don't. If none of these sixteen gifts fit your personal profile, that doesn't mean you have no gifts to offer the body of Christ. The lists in the Bible are never comprehensive. They're representative lists that paint a portrait. Similarly, the lists of sins in Paul's epistles aren't *all* the sins, but they show the kinds of behavior that one should avoid. And the lists of qualifications for elders and deacons in 1 Timothy 3 and Titus 1 are not the *only* positive traits one might expect or seek, but they point to the kind of person who "fits the bill."

This principle suggests that some abilities the Spirit has given to benefit the church may not be on the list. For example, the very first recorded spiritual gift was given to a man named Bezalel, who was tasked with building the tabernacle:

> See, I have called by name Bezalel the son of Uri, son of Hur, of the tribe of Judah, and I have filled him with the Spirit of God, with ability and

> intelligence, with knowledge and all craftsmanship, to devise artistic designs, to work in gold, silver, and bronze, in cutting stones for setting, and in carving wood, to work in every craft. (Exodus 31:2–5)

If Bezalel were alive today, he would be on HGTV as an interior decorator. (Hey, it's a spiritual gift!)

Likewise, King David was gifted as a musician (1 Samuel 16:23), but that's not on any list in the New Testament. Solomon said in Proverbs that a joyful heart is good medicine (17:22), but humor isn't on any list. Counseling is an incredibly valuable skill in the church that never made the lists. Artists, plumbers, accountants, lawyers, HR, PR, IT—all are invaluable to the body of Christ, yet none are on the biblical lists. None of the gift lists are complete, yet they are comprehensive enough to inform us what could be on them.

This leads to an important point: How can I know what my spiritual gift is if it's not on the list? This may sound mysterious or complicated. It's not. Here is the answer in three simple steps: (1) walk into a room, (2) look around, and (3) identify what needs to be done that you would enjoy doing with excellence. *That is your spiritual gift.*

Or perhaps we should clarify: that *could be* your spiritual gift, if you gave it back to the Holy Spirit and let him guide you in using it to serve others. Spiritual gifts are spiritual only when they benefit someone else. We never see Paul healing himself, though he had the gift of healing. We never see generous givers giving to themselves as a spiritual gift. We don't find preachers or teachers alone in a room instructing themselves. Why? Because the purpose of every spiritual gift is for the benefit of others as a mechanism for unity.

Spiritual gifts are to be given away. Put another way, we're not buckets for God's blessings; we're conduits. God never gives a gift to a person merely because he loves that individual. He gives gifts to someone in order that through that person he can love someone else. His purpose for our gifts is not that we be blessed but that we become a blessing. This is a brilliant strategy that makes us interdependent, humble, and corporately strong.

This leads to one final point. Gifts are neither for the benefit of the gifted nor primarily for the benefit of the recipient. They're to benefit the *church* by building unassailable unity through mutual dependence.

This is why those with the gift of leadership serve rather than exercise authority. That's why not everyone who's sick gets healed in the New Testament. The point is not the miracle but the faith it builds into the Christian community.

It's our love and service that stun and attract the watching world. Go back to Jesus's prayer: "that they may all be one . . . so that the world may believe that you have sent me" (John 17:21). Gifts are to build unity, and unity is an apologetic to bring outsiders into the community. Our unity is as compelling as our preaching.

In a world torn by race, class, gender, and politics, people are looking for a place to belong, a place to be accepted, and a place that's safe to love and be loved. If you have a skill, make it spiritual by using it to serve someone in the church so someone outside the church can be drawn to Jesus.

Key Points

- Jesus's prayer in John 17 was for the unity of the church. It appears to be unanswered.
- We get to answer Jesus's prayer by exercising our spiritual gifts for the benefit of the body.
- Christian unity is a powerful apologetic for a watching world in desperate need of belonging.

This Week

☐ **Day 1:** Read the essay.

☐ **Day 2:** Memorize Ephesians 4:4–7.

☐ **Day 3:** Read Acts 15.

☐ **Day 4:** Meditate on John 17:20–21; Galatians 3:28; Ephesians 4:11–16.

☐ **Day 5:** Walk into a room. Look around. Identify what needs to be done that you would enjoy doing and would do with excellence. Now do that.

Overachiever Challenge: Memorize Galatians 3:28.

Bonus Read: C. Peter Wagner, *Discover Your Spiritual Gifts: The Easy-to-Use Guide That Helps You Identify and Understand Your Unique God-Given Spiritual Gifts.*

47

Humility

> Have this mind among yourselves, which is yours in Christ Jesus, who, though he was in the form of God, did not count equality with God a thing to be grasped, but emptied himself, by taking the form of a servant, being born in the likeness of men.
>
> —Philippians 2:5–7

Question: How does humility help you succeed?

Servant leadership is a buzzword. It gained traction back in the 1980s when corporate leaders and university researchers began to rethink the use of power in business and politics. They found that the most positive use of power was to help the powerless. When leaders used their influence and authority to benefit those who could not repay them, the leaders' respect, influence, and effectiveness grew far more than when they used their power for self-protection or self-promotion.

A leader's natural instinct is to protect his power. As it turns out, giving away power, honor, and influence is the secret sauce of becoming an effective leader.

Servant leadership was the brainchild of Jesus Christ. He was the first leader in history to advocate power moving downward rather than upward. He loved the least, recovered the lost, defended the defenseless, and included the outcast.

Servant leadership comes down to humility, an attribute honored in our culture. Yet in Jesus's day, humility was perceived as weakness. To call someone humble was to insult that person.

This is stunning for us, since humility is expected, even demanded, from everyone in our culture (except boxers and wide receivers). Jesus took the word *humility* and put it in the "W" column. The very way we use this word today pays tribute to Jesus's effectiveness as a social engineer.

Humility in Jesus

To say Jesus was humble hardly does him justice. He descended from heaven to earth to be born in a barn and killed on a cross. Paul used a particularly aggressive Greek word *kenoō* ("to empty" or "to abase"[1]) to capture the essence of Jesus's self-abnegation. Jesus "did not count equality with God a thing to be grasped, but *emptied* himself, by taking the form of a servant, being born in the likeness of men" (Philippians 2:6–7). This extraordinary sentence is breathtaking.

Jesus temporarily laid down divine rights of omnipresence, omnipotence, and omniscience so he could come to earth as one of us in order to lift us from our fallen state. Jesus descended from heaven to earth (a distance too great to measure) so in his ascension we could be lifted to our original creational dignity. This whole idea is expressed in the word *incarnation*. Jesus robed himself in flesh so we could participate in his divine nature.

Though this is the great mystery of Christianity, it's also a practical necessity. The kind of humility Jesus showed is precisely what makes good parents, good CEOs, good generals, and good coaches. This is a father on the floor wrestling with his boys. It's the CEO picking up trash. It's the general personally leading troops into battle. It's the coach running drills alongside her players.

None of this has to happen. Leaders can't be forced into it. Nonetheless, when it happens, followers are inflamed with loyalty and respect for one who walks in their shoes.

Leadership theory is finally catching up to Christian theology—the best leaders are servants of those they lead.

Humility in the Bible

Throughout the Bible, God commanded his people to be humble. The principle is simple and often repeated: God exalts the humble and humbles the haughty.

This divine reversal is a common thread in Scripture (1 Samuel 2:7–10; Job 40:11–12; Psalm 18:27; 147:6; Proverbs 18:12; 29:23; Isaiah 2:11–17; 57:15; Ezekiel 17:24; 21:26). For example, "Pride goes before destruction, and a haughty spirit before a fall" (Proverbs 16:18). Again, "When they are humbled you say, 'It is because of pride'; but he saves the lowly" (Job 22:29). God turns the totem pole of human values on its head. Those on top are pushed to the bottom, and those on the bottom are exalted to the highest place.

Jesus repeated this theme in his own preaching: "Whoever exalts himself will be humbled, and whoever humbles himself will be exalted" (Matthew 23:12; see also Luke 14:11; 18:14). Both James and Peter have their own rendition of the theme: "Humble yourselves before the Lord, and he will exalt you" (James 4:10) and "Clothe yourselves, all of you, with humility toward one another, for 'God opposes the proud but gives grace to the humble.' Humble yourselves, therefore, under the mighty hand of God so that at the proper time he may exalt you" (1 Peter 5:5–6).

As if this wasn't enough, Jesus also had a whole series of sayings about "the first will be last and the last will be first" (Matthew 19:30; 20:8, 16; Mark 9:35; Luke 13:30). This repetition is needed for all of us who seek advancement in our careers, recognition from our peers, and affection from our followers.

This leadership lesson was lost on James and John, who were audacious enough to ask for chief seats. Jesus offered this rebuke to them (and to us): "Whoever would be first among you must be slave of all. For even the Son of Man came not to be served but to serve, and to give his life as a ransom for many" (Mark 10:44–45).

Likewise, in the upper room, after washing their feet, Jesus again had to settle his disciples' dispute about who was the greatest: "The kings of the Gentiles exercise lordship over them, and those in authority over them are called benefactors. But not so with you. Rather, let the greatest among you become as the youngest, and the leader as one who serves" (Luke 22:25–26).

Jesus was hardly a solitary voice advocating humility. Other teachers were known to say similar things. Jesus was, however, a singular figure modeling humility. No other leaders washed their followers' feet, touched lepers and bleeding women, honored children, included the poor and outsiders, and gave prostitutes an audience.

Humility is not just a philosophical ideal or even an ethical principle from God. Humility is an actionable practice modeled by Jesus. His ministry (and death) exemplified his expectations of how we should posture ourselves for influence and leadership. Even pinned to a bloodied cross, Jesus's first statement reverberated with humility: "Father, forgive them, for they know not what they do" (Luke 23:34).

Humility in Action

When we think of humility, what most often comes to mind is an emotional posture or self-assessment. It's a kind of "aw, shucks" attitude: *I'm really no better than anyone else.* Humility, in our vernacular, is an attitude about yourself. That's well and good. After all, arrogance is seldom attractive. But biblical humility is not so much about how you feel about yourself; it has much more to do with how you treat others.

To that end, we want to identify some actions to implement and thereby more consistently model humility. After all, nothing reflects the life of Jesus more than using power for the powerless. So here are four suggestions. You may not be able to implement them all, at least not immediately. So choose just one to practice this week in a thirty-minute block.

1. *Associate with the lowly as if they were dignitaries.* Paul said, "Live in harmony with one another. Do not be haughty, but associate with the lowly. Never be wise in your own sight" (Romans 12:16). Likewise, James warned us not to give preferential treatment to those with wealth (James 2:1–9) and asked this question: "Has not

God chosen those who are poor in the world to be rich in faith and heirs of the kingdom, which he has promised to those who love him?" (verse 5). God doesn't look at someone's face before he determines that person's treatment. Neither should we. Nor should we look at their wallet, popularity, or prestige.

2. *Prioritize children.* One frenzied day Jesus's disciples blocked a group of people who wanted Jesus to bless their babies (Mark 10:13). The disciples were looking out for Jesus's interests, trying to keep his agenda clear for the highest priorities. Their motive was good. But they didn't realize that Jesus always prioritized children and those of low estate. This is the only time Jesus was incensed with his disciples: "He was indignant and said to them, 'Let the children come to me; do not hinder them, for to such belongs the kingdom of God'" (verse 14).
3. *Purposely put yourself in a humble place.* In Jesus's context that meant deliberately taking a lower seat at a banquet (Luke 14:10). In our context that might mean parking farther from the office so others have a shorter walk. It could mean you never walk past trash without picking it up. It might mean (quoting the title of an excellent book) that *leaders eat last.* It could be letting someone go ahead of you in line, emptying the dishwasher at home, or filling the Keurig at work. Whatever it looks like, it means deliberately giving up your right to privileges. Those who notice will actually respect you more. Not everyone will notice. However, everyone will hear of it. Those who see will spread positive gossip that PR could never purchase.
4. *Serve.* Jesus modeled this by washing his disciples' feet (John 13:1–20). One of the greatest surgeons in our city flips burgers at our church. A woman who worked in President Bush's cabinet holds two-year-olds every Sunday morning in our church nursery. It's imperative that the highest leaders master the humblest service, because if service is beneath you, leadership is beyond you.

Key Points

- The doctrine of the Incarnation is couched in terms of humility.
- The entire Bible reiterates the principle of humility—that God deposes the proud and exalts the humble.
- We can practice specific actions to implement humility in our own leadership.

This Week

- ☐ **Day 1:** Read the essay.
- ☐ **Day 2:** Memorize Philippians 2:5–7.
- ☐ **Day 3:** Read Genesis 37; 39–41.
- ☐ **Day 4:** Meditate on Proverbs 29:23; John 3:30; 1 Peter 5:5–7.
- ☐ **Day 5:** Choose one of the above action items to implement this week.

Overachiever Challenge: Memorize John 3:30.

Bonus Read: Robert K. Greenleaf, *Servant Leadership: A Journey into the Nature of Legitimate Power and Greatness.*

48

Overwhelming Worry

Do not be anxious about anything, but in everything by prayer and supplication with thanksgiving let your requests be made known to God.

—Philippians 4:6

Question: How can I reduce worry?

Few behaviors sabotage our effectiveness more than worry.

But this pandemic is treatable. After all, worry is internal. No one forces you to do it, no one but you can fix it, and no one but you is fully aware of the extent of it. Our worry is precisely that: *ours.*

It's triggered by circumstances but not caused by them. For example, worry isn't isolated to a specific economic group we call "poor." In fact, the economic poor often worry less about money than the economically advantaged. Our greatest worry is often caused by comparison, not need. On paper this makes no sense.

Worry is seldom reserved for the most likely immediate possibilities. In fact, most of our worries are about terrorists, tumors, kidnappings, and such. Our imaginations run amok. Why do we do this?

Worry stems from poor mental habits. It's unnecessary, unproductive, and unrealistic. As the wise King Solomon said, "Anxiety in a man's heart weighs him down, but a good word makes him glad" (Proverbs 12:25).

Worry Is Bad Theology

Worry isn't merely a psychological problem; it's a theological problem. The origin of worry is Genesis 3, which takes us back to the primordial sin in the garden. Eve determined to be "like God" (verse 5). She and Adam decided to run the world on their own. Rather than living under God's authority, they chose to take on his status and responsibilities. They asserted themselves as rulers of their own universe. Consequently, they learned the stress of trying to control time, destiny, and morality.

No human being is capable of exercising such control. Yet all of us try. We play God and find ourselves overwhelmed by the pressure.

Worry is toxic to our souls because it blinds us to what God has done and blocks us from what he could do—all because we focus on ourselves rather than God. Our craving for self-sufficiency disables trust.

Jesus diagnosed our condition in a simple parable about soil and seeds. One of the soils he identified was thorny. This, Jesus said, is like a life choked by worry. You may make temporary spiritual progress, but soon your growth is choked by the weeds—those cares of life that consume our nutrients and leave us fruitless (Matthew 13:22).

All this is neutralized by faith. Both the Old and the New Testaments have a simple solution: trust God. This is not blind trust as much as trusting God's track record. He has proved himself faithful. Jesus said as much:

> Do not be anxious, saying, "What shall we eat?" or "What shall we drink?" or "What shall we wear?" For the Gentiles seek after all these things, and your heavenly Father knows that you need them all. But seek first the kingdom of God and his righteousness, and all these things will be added to you. (Matthew 6:31–33)

Jesus is, of course, only echoing the ancient hymn: "Cast your burden on the LORD, and he will sustain you; he will never permit the righteous to be moved" (Psalm 55:22). Peter later reiterated the idea: "Cast all your anxiety on him because he cares for you" (1 Peter 5:7, NIV).

That's easier said than done. For the essential steps we can turn to Jesus. The Gospels have more to say about eliminating worry than almost all other books of the Bible combined.

Practical Steps to Minimize Worry

It's unlikely that many of us will completely overcome worry. Nonetheless, we can make progress. Jesus gave us practical advice. We'll start there and allow the apostle Paul to add a couple of exclamation points at the end.

1. *Look at the world.* The first step to minimize worry is to just look around at the natural world. In the Sermon on the Mount, Jesus gave the longest address on worry in Scripture. He gave two tangible illustrations.

   First, "Look at the birds of the air: they neither sow nor reap nor gather into barns, and yet your heavenly Father feeds them. Are you not of more value than they?" (Matthew 6:26). If you've ever questioned God's goodness, go outside and look around; there are always birds somewhere. Where is their worry? In the heat of summer or the dead of winter, they always find food. The Sonoran Desert of Arizona (where I live) receives a sparse seven inches of rain a year.[1] How anything in nature survives is astounding. Yet every day there's the chatter of quail, the strut of a roadrunner, the flitting of sparrows, the hum of hummingbirds, the proud soaring of the hawk, and the call of the majestic owl at twilight. The birds of the air are proof of the absurdity of worry. Even in a desert, they thrive. Do you really imagine God is less concerned with you? Even in your own desert, your God is an oasis where life can flourish.

   Likewise, Jesus directed our attention to a field in bloom:

> Why are you anxious about clothing? Consider the lilies of the field, how they grow: they neither toil nor spin, yet I tell you, even Solomon in all his glory was not arrayed like one of these. But if God so clothes the grass of the field, which today is alive and tomorrow is thrown into the oven, will he not much more clothe you, O you of little faith? (verses 28–30)

Flowering fields are fleeting. Yet hardly anything compares to the beauty of a field in full bloom. It's a display of epic extravagance. The golden poppies of California or the bluebonnets of Texas, the columbines of the Rockies or the sunflowers of Kansas, the violets of Illinois or the black-eyed Susans of Maryland. All are breathtaking, inspiring—and fleeting. Their beauty is unrivaled by the best wardrobe on any red carpet. A mere glance should silence the silliness of worry. God graces his creation with extravagance. Will he not cover you more carefully than a field of grass?

2. *Listen to God's Word.* Luke alone recorded the interaction between Mary, Martha, and Jesus over a meal in their home (Luke 10:38–42). Martha dutifully prepared the matzah and hummus. She wanted the meal to be perfect. After all, she was hosting the Lord of hosts. One would assume you would want to get that right. Mary, like a younger sister, acted irresponsibly by neglecting her duties in order to sit at Jesus's feet. How dare she!

As the evening rolled on, Martha rolled her eyes with every plate she brought from the kitchen. Finally, fed up with her sister's negligence, Martha exploded from the kitchen, her apron all in a bunch. Her frustration burst into a fury: "Tell her then to help me!" (verse 40).

One would expect Jesus to have replied by affirming a good Judeo-Christian work ethic: "Mary, do your part." Nope. He rebuked Martha instead: "Martha, Martha, you are anxious and troubled about many things, but one thing is necessary. Mary has chosen the good portion, which will not be taken away from her" (verses 41–42).

3. *Conquer your thoughts.* Worry is a battle of the mind. What we focus on will determine the direction our thoughts go. Neuroscientific research has given us the fascinating insight that protein branches hold our thoughts. In a real sense, thoughts create real estate in our brains. The more we dwell on a thought, the larger the constellation of proteins becomes.[2] We give over space and place to the thoughts we allow to dominate our minds.

   This modern insight sheds light on the ancient advice of Paul:

> Do not be anxious about anything, but in everything by prayer and supplication with thanksgiving let your requests be made known to God. And the peace of God, which surpasses all understanding, will guard your hearts and your minds in Christ Jesus.
>
> Finally, brothers, whatever is true, whatever is honorable, whatever is just, whatever is pure, whatever is lovely, whatever is commendable, if there is any excellence, if there is anything worthy of praise, *think about these things.* (Philippians 4:6–9)

Paul elsewhere wrote, "We destroy arguments and every lofty opinion raised against the knowledge of God, and take every thought captive to obey Christ" (2 Corinthians 10:5). This isn't just about defending Christianity. It's about mental, emotional, and spiritual health. When Satan accosts us with negative thoughts, we wrestle those to the ground and expel them from our minds.

The trick is that we can't just rid ourselves of a thought. That leaves a vacuum in its place, and the negativity gets sucked right back in. We must replace negative thoughts with God's truth.

Scripture, sermons, and Christian music are powerful resources for mental transformation. The space and place you give to thoughts will grow roots in your brain. What we fertilize most will win the battle for our brains.

Worry is the result of feeding the wrong thoughts. Since negativity is the default in our world, only diligence will posture us to take every thought captive for Christ.

Key Points

- Worry is negative psychology. It's under our control, and it only hinders our effectiveness.
- Worry is bad theology. It started with sin in the Garden of Eden, and it always minimizes our trust and joy in God.
- Jesus (along with Paul) offered several insightful steps for controlling our thoughts.

This Week

☐ **Day 1:** Read the essay.

☐ **Day 2:** Memorize Philippians 4:6.

☐ **Day 3:** Read Genesis 42–45.

☐ **Day 4:** Meditate on Matthew 6:33; Luke 10:41–42; 2 Corinthians 10:5.

☐ **Day 5:** Do a media audit this week. Each day, simply record the amount of time you spend with TV, social media posts, and radio. Compare that with time spent listening to Christian music, going to church, and reading your Bible. According to that analysis, which side has the advantage over your mind?

Overachiever Challenge: Memorize Matthew 6:33.

Bonus Read: David A. Carbonell, *The Worry Trick: How Your Brain Tricks You into Expecting the Worst and What You Can Do About It.*

49

Mentoring

What you have heard from me in the presence of many witnesses entrust to faithful men, who will be able to teach others also.

—2 Timothy 2:2

Question: How can I find a mentor and be a mentor?

The word *mentor* is never found in the Bible. It actually comes from the *Odyssey*. Mentor was a friend of King Odysseus. When the king took off for the Trojan War, he left his son, Telemachus, and his house in Mentor's care. The goddess Athena took the form of Mentor, becoming Telemachus's teacher, counselor, and coach.[1] Since she was the goddess of war, the implication is that a mentor is one who represents the divine, preparing a young person for the battles ahead.

This became true of a string of mentors in the Bible. Jethro mentored Moses, who had to face Pharaoh. Moses, in turn, mentored Joshua, who led the conquest of the promised land. Eli mentored Samuel, who then guided Saul and David, the first kings of Israel. Elijah mentored Elisha, who confronted wayward kings. Mordecai mentored Esther, who intervened with King Xerxes, saving her nation from extinction. Jesus mentored his twelve apostles. Barnabas mentored Paul, who paid it forward to Timothy, Titus, and many others. Mentoring was so important to Paul's ministry that in his final letter to young Timothy he pleaded with him to continue this tradition (2 Timothy 2:2).

The majority of the leaders in the Bible were mentored by someone who came before him (with rare exceptions like Abraham, Elijah, and Jesus). So we'd all better take seriously this responsibility of being mentored and mentoring others.

Five Simple Steps to Finding a Mentor

If we're going to be serious about making a serious impact, we would do well to ensure that we have a coach who can help maximize our influence, regardless of our age or stage of life. Many young people want a mentor as a kind of personal counselor. They want someone they can "do life with." You do *not* need another sympathetic support system. You need someone who can sharpen your vision and push you forward in uncomfortable but essential ways.

Here are five steps that will help you secure a mentor.

1. *Small favors will prime big commitment.* Do not walk up to potential mentors and say, "Hey, would you mentor me?" You'll scare them off. They have no clear idea what kind of time commitment that requires. They'll say no before finding out. The only people you want to mentor you are people who don't have time to invest in you.

   So here's your strategy. Ask a potential mentor for fifteen minutes. You can meet for coffee (you buy!) or arrange a time at his or her office. Here is your request: "I've been watching you [identify here a specific behavior], and I have three coaching questions I'd like to ask, if we could schedule fifteen minutes at your convenience." You start out honoring the potential mentor by identifying his or her specific skills that could help you get better. All leaders crave influence. Play into this craving to get to a yes.
2. *Be deliberate with questions.* Prepare and write out your three questions beforehand. Ask specific coaching questions that will allow the mentor to help you achieve a measure of what he or she

has achieved. (You might want to run the questions by an adviser in advance to make sure they're clear and insightful.)

Arrive at your designated meeting place ten to fifteen minutes before your scheduled time. Trust me—you want to be sitting there waiting on the mentor, not vice versa. Ask your three questions, and follow up each one with this: "What is one action step I could take to carry this out?"

3. *Be respectful of the mentor's time.* At the fifteen-minute mark, thank your mentor for his or her time and excuse yourself. Even if you are invited to stay longer, respectfully decline (unless the mentor insists) by saying, "I'm so grateful for your time and honored that you would extend yourself to me, but I take seriously my responsibility to respect our agreed-upon time."
4. *Follow up.* After you've completed the action step, contact the mentor again. Ask for another fifteen minutes: "I want to thank you for those action steps you suggested. I've completed them and I've found them helpful. However, they led me to a couple more questions. Would you be willing to meet again for a follow-up assessment?"

   After the third or fourth meeting—assuming things go well—you then could ask for a once-a-month meeting for a six-month period. If you're showing promise, few leaders could refuse to invest in a potential disciple who is actually proving to be a good investment.
5. *Have multiple mentors.* Repeat this process for three or four major areas of your life. No one person will have all the wisdom for every area you want to excel in. It's appropriate to have a mentor for marriage, another for work, another for finances, another for overcoming any addiction, another for spiritual growth.

As we now turn our attention to being a mentor, you will also want to be clear on the role you'll play in the lives of your disciples.

Five Simple Steps to Being a Mentor

Few of us feel competent to shape the destiny of another human being. Yet where would you be if others hadn't overcome their own sense of inadequacy in order to invest in your life?

In at least one area of life, each of us should be able to say to others, "Be imitators of me, as I am of Christ" (1 Corinthians 11:1). If we can say that, the next logical statement is this: "What you have learned and received and heard and seen in me—practice these things, and the God of peace will be with you" (Philippians 4:9).

This isn't just advice to men. One of the great deficits of the modern church is godly mentors for younger women. Though women often are more reticent than men about mentoring, Paul made it clear that their model is equally important:

> Older women likewise are to be reverent in behavior, not slanderers or slaves to much wine. They are to teach what is good, and so train the young women to love their husbands and children, to be self-controlled, pure, working at home, kind, and submissive to their own husbands, that the word of God may not be reviled. (Titus 2:3–5)

So whether male or female, what action steps can you take to mentor younger Christians?

1. *Be a coach, not a teacher.* Often potential mentors fear they won't know enough Scripture. Your role is not to teach the Bible. There are pastors and teachers whom God has gifted for that. Your most valuable asset is life experience in marriage, work, parenting, or overcoming addictions. Moreover, what disciples need most is confidence. The fact that they respect you empowers you to raise their self-respect by simply respecting them. This alone can be transformational.

Most of us see ourselves in the rearview mirror. Mentors enable disciples to see themselves through the windshield. Your greatest gift is to help your disciples see their best future selves and bravely move forward to realize that vision.

This is so important that the command for courage is given four times in Joshua 1: "Be strong and courageous" (verses 6–7, 9, 18). They're the same words Moses had spoken to Joshua when he commissioned him (Deuteronomy 31:7).

2. *Create a circle of disciples.* The optimal number for a group of disciples seems to be five at a time. In almost every meeting, one will be absent, leaving a four-to-one ratio. This allows conversation to flow without any individual remaining anonymous or dominating. It typically takes six months to fill your circle, so be patient. You'll find that the circle of disciples is more powerful than the single mentor-disciple relationship. The group's shared wisdom, relationships, accountability, and encouragement will do far more than your personal pearls of wisdom.
3. *Involve your family.* The greatest lessons disciples learn are through their eyes, not their ears. Most young adults have had pretty poor models of marriage and parenting. What is caught has a greater impact than what is taught. To his disciples in Ephesus, Paul said this: "You yourselves know how I lived among you the whole time from the first day that I set foot in Asia, serving the Lord with all humility and with tears and with trials that happened to me" (Acts 20:18–19).

Most of your meetings will be just you and the disciples. However, at least once in your season of mentoring, you should do three things that will give your disciples access to your family: (1) Have them to your home for a meal. (2) Go out for a social event to play together. (3) Work together as a group in the community. Eating, playing, and working will reveal character in your disciples that will help you guide them with wisdom.

4. *Give practical assignments that stretch them.* Mentoring is about coaching, not counseling. People grow through accomplishing their mission, not revealing their pain. When Paul mentored Timothy, he sent him on one difficult mission after another, long before he ever allowed Timothy to preach, teach, or exercise authority in a church. When you demand that they go beyond their own borders, you'll prove to them that they're capable of more than they imagine.
5. *Minimize the conversations about sex and dating.* Someone needing accountability for addiction needs an expert, not a mentor. Sure, there are times to deal with failure. Yet that must not dominate the mentoring relationship. Your role is to push them up the ladder, not raise them from the gutter. Likewise, women mentoring women shouldn't allow too much talk about their dating relationships. Young women often deal with envy, dependence on men, and materialism. Raise them to higher levels of thinking and purpose.
6. *Rebuke.* When disciples disappoint, rebuke them—hard. You've earned that right. You should fear their future failure more than their hurt feelings. You're not their friend; you're their future.

Key Points

- Almost every great leader of the Bible was mentored, and many in turn mentored others.
- There are practical steps to finding a mentor; we all need this.
- There are practical steps to mentoring; we all owe this to others.

This Week

- ☐ **Day 1:** Read the essay.
- ☐ **Day 2:** Memorize 2 Timothy 2:2.
- ☐ **Day 3:** Read Ruth 1–4.
- ☐ **Day 4:** Meditate on Joshua 1:7; 1 Corinthians 11:1; Philippians 4:9.
- ☐ **Day 5:** Follow these steps to find a mentor or to become a mentor.

Overachiever Challenge: Memorize Joshua 1:7.

Bonus Read: John C. Maxwell, *Mentoring 101: What Every Leader Needs to Know.*

50

Scripture

> All Scripture is breathed out by God and profitable for teaching, for reproof, for correction, and for training in righteousness, that the man of God may be complete, equipped for every good work.
>
> —2 Timothy 3:16–17

Question: How do I get something out of the Bible?

Reading and applying the Bible are the most important skills for spiritual growth. Research has shown that those who engage the Bible four times a week or more have stronger marriages, healthier habits, and better self-esteem.[1] So how do I get something out of the Bible on my own?

We'll look at two skills: navigating the Bible and digging into a specific passage.

How to Navigate the Bible

The Bible is a collection of sixty-six books organized into two parts known as the Old Testament and the New Testament. The word *testament* simply means "contract" or "covenant." The Old Testament tells of God's first covenant with the nation of Israel. It's the story of God choosing Israel, rescuing them from slavery in Egypt, and establishing them in the promised land. The New Testament describes God's second covenant with all mankind. It's the story of God choosing us and rescuing us from slavery to sin through the sacrifice of Jesus Christ.

The thirty-nine books of the Old Testament were written between 1400 and 450 BC, but they aren't arranged chronologically. Rather, they're organized into five categories, as you can see in the following chart:

Law	History	Poetry	Major Prophets	Minor Prophets
Genesis	Joshua	Job	Isaiah	Hosea
Exodus	Judges	Psalms	Jeremiah	Joel
Leviticus	Ruth	Proverbs	Lamentations	Amos
Numbers	1 & 2 Samuel	Ecclesiastes	Ezekiel	Obadiah
Deuteronomy	1 & 2 Kings	Song of Solomon	Daniel	Jonah
	1 & 2 Chronicles			Micah
	Ezra			Nahum
	Nehemiah			Habakkuk
	Esther			Zephaniah
				Haggai
				Zechariah
				Malachi

The books of the Law were written by Moses. They trace God's covenant from Creation through the founding of the nation of Israel. The books of Genesis and Exodus are the essential background for the story of Jesus.

The history books recount the rise, fall, judgment, and restoration of Israel. The names and places are foreign, but the struggles and victories are familiar. We see the life of King David narrated in 1 and 2 Samuel, and we better understand how Jesus fulfilled his legacy as our king.

The poetry books contain wisdom and worship of the Jewish people in ancient times. Interestingly, they express the same yearnings we have for God today. Many people read or even sing the psalms for worship and inspiration. Proverbs is especially valuable for life wisdom and for raising children.

The books of prophecy were written by men chosen by God to proclaim his word. The major prophets aren't more important than the minor prophets; they're just longer. They are concerned with the spiritual health of Israel (with the rare exception of Jonah, reluctantly preaching to Ninevites), calling God's people to abandon their sin and live wholeheartedly by his principles. Many people find the prophets the most difficult books to understand in the Old Testament; their language and history can seem so foreign. But they are critical for understanding the message of the New Testament. This is especially true of Isaiah, which is quoted more than any other prophetic book.

The twenty-seven books of the New Testament (written between about AD 45 and 95) are arranged under three major categories of Gospels, History, and Letters:

Gospels	History	Letters from Paul to Churches	Letters from Paul to Individuals	Other Letters
Matthew	Acts	Romans	1 & 2 Timothy	Hebrews
Mark		1 & 2 Corinthians	Titus	James
Luke		Galatians	Philemon	1 & 2 Peter
John		Ephesians		1, 2, & 3 John
		Philippians		Jude
		Colossians		Revelation
		1 & 2 Thessalonians		

The Gospels are the primary accounts of the life and teachings of Jesus. Matthew and John were among Jesus's twelve apostles and were important eyewitnesses. Mark was a young man who lived in Jerusalem and later followed both Paul and Peter on their preaching tours. Church tradition tells us that Mark wrote down Peter's account in his gospel. John was arguably Jesus's best friend. He wrote a simple yet profound account of Jesus's life, which makes it a great place to start reading Scripture. Luke, the only non-Jewish author of the Bible, never personally met Jesus, but he wrote both Luke and Acts, which together amount to more than a quarter of the New Testament (actually more words than any other New Testament author, including Paul).

The book of Acts is a must-read because it records the founding and expansion of the Christian church, a period spanning from about AD 30 to 62.

The New Testament letters (also called epistles) were written to provide guidance, encouragement, and warnings about specific challenges individuals or churches were facing. Romans is one of the longest and most important of these letters. However, Ephesians, Philippians, and Colossians also have a majesty and power that are quickly apparent. The letter from James, Jesus's half-brother, is also a great place to start reading the Bible because of its densely packed practical wisdom.

How to Dig into a Specific Passage

The goal of reading the Bible is not information but transformation. Hebrews 4:12 is true: "The word of God is living and active, sharper than any two-edged sword, piercing to the division of soul and of spirit, of joints and of marrow, and discerning the thoughts and intentions of the heart." God's Word has a way of penetrating our deepest secrets and greatest dreams.

With that in mind, the following steps will help you move from information to transformation.

1. *Pick a Bible you're comfortable with.* There isn't one right Bible. Just find one you can read and are comfortable carrying with you. You can't go wrong with a *New International Version Study Bible.* It's a bit more expensive, but it has a tremendous number of helpful study tools. Here are five features that can be particularly helpful:
   - *A table of contents* lists every Bible book and the page it starts on. Each book is also divided into chapters and verses.
   - *Time lines* list Bible events in chronological order to help you see when they took place.

- *Maps* help you find the geographic location where events took place.
- *Introductions* to each Bible book offer "CliffsNotes" about the book's author, purpose, time, themes, and outline.
- *Footnotes* give brief explanations about the historical background, social values, and important words.
- On each page are *cross-references* to several other Bible passages that will augment your understanding of the particular verse they're linked to. (Here's how to read those references: the chapter is the number before the colon, and the verse is the number after it. So *John 3:16* means "the book of John, chapter 3, verse 16.")

While there's no replacement for an actual Bible you can hold in your hands, many people also use the free YouVersion app for reading on the run. It includes many Scripture versions, including several audio versions you can listen to on your commute.

The endgame is to get a Bible you enjoy reading and look forward to spending time with each day.

2. *Read it.* You need three things in order to get the most out of reading the Bible:
   - *A place.* Choose a quiet place and a consistent time for reading your Bible. Turn your phone off and dig in. Ten to fifteen minutes is probably a good target at first.
   - *A plan.* Some people like to read straight through from Genesis to Revelation. Others want to read more chronologically, which requires jumping from book to book. The YouVersion app has a number of reading plans ranging from a single book up to the entire Bible. Perhaps the best starting place for beginners is to read from these four books: Genesis, John, Acts, and Romans. They'll provide a strong foundation for reading the whole Bible.

- *A pen.* As you read, if there's something you don't understand, simply jot down a question in the margin of your Bible or in a journal. Curiosity is the greatest tool for Bible study. Your pastor or study group leader can help you find resources to answer many of your questions.

  Remember, however, that the goal is not information but transformation. So your questions shouldn't reflect mere curiosity. Rather, keep asking how you can apply these principles and teachings at home, at work or school, and in your neighborhood. Also, many find that journaling a prayer about the text is a great way to grow in your awareness of how to apply the passage. A simple strategy is to answer two questions each day:

  1) What stood out to me in this passage?
  2) How will I live that out practically today?

James 1:22 says it well: "Do not merely listen to the word, and so deceive yourselves. Do what it says" (NIV).

The very best tool for application is memorization. Identify a single verse you need to live out and say it aloud until you know it by heart. This becomes a crowbar for the Holy Spirit to use in applying that passage to specific situations in your life.

Don't lose heart. Growing in the knowledge of God's Word is like any other exercise or skill. The more you do it, the more you get from it.

There'll be times when you won't feel like reading the Bible or applying it to your life. This happens to everyone. Don't be discouraged if you miss a day. Pick up right where you left off.

God has promised blessing and success to those who diligently seek him in his Word:

> Keep this Book of the Law always on your lips; meditate on it day and night, so that you may be careful to do everything written in it. Then you will be prosperous and successful. (Joshua 1:8, NIV)

Follow the example given in the prayer of Psalm 119:11: "I have stored up your word in my heart, that I might not sin against you."

Key Points

- The Bible is God's authoritative Word. When you apply its principles to your life, you will be transformed.
- A study Bible provides a number of tools to help you engage the Bible.
- To get the most from your daily reading, you'll need a place, plan, and pen.

This Week

- ☐ **Day 1:** Read the essay.
- ☐ **Day 2:** Memorize 2 Timothy 3:16–17.
- ☐ **Day 3:** Read Mark 4:35–5:43.
- ☐ **Day 4:** Meditate on Psalm 119:11; Hebrews 4:12; James 1:22.
- ☐ **Day 5:**
    - ☐ Purchase (or pull out) a Bible you'll read.
    - ☐ Identify a regular place and time to read your Bible throughout the week (aim for at least four days).
    - ☐ Choose a reading plan; it could cover anywhere from one book to the whole Bible.
    - ☐ Find a blank journal to record three things as you read: (1) any questions you have about each reading; (2) one thing that stands out to you from each reading; and (3) one way you'll apply the teaching to your life. You might also choose a verse to memorize.

Overachiever Challenge: Memorize Hebrews 4:12.

Bonus Read: Mark Moore, *Seeing God in HD: God's Word in Today's World.*

51

Gaining Grit

Since we are surrounded by so great a cloud of witnesses, let us also lay aside every weight, and sin which clings so closely, and let us run with endurance the race that is set before us, looking to Jesus, the founder and perfecter of our faith, who for the joy that was set before him endured the cross, despising the shame, and is seated at the right hand of the throne of God.

—Hebrews 12:1–2

Question: How do we gain grit?

Psychologist Angela Duckworth has done extensive research on what determines success. She studied thousands of individuals at the US Military Academy at West Point and at the National Spelling Bee as well as salespeople and rookie teachers in tough neighborhoods.

The answer she discovered is not IQ. Nor is it wealth, race, or physical prowess. The answer is *grit,* defined as "passion and perseverance for very long-term goals." It's the ability to stick with a difficult task not for weeks or months but for years. Grit empowers you to live life "like it's a marathon, not a sprint."[1] It's the single most important factor in success.

We know this to be true. So how can we apply it to our spiritual lives? How do we gain grit?

Two keys for gaining grit are embedded in our core passage. First, you look around to others you're responsible to and responsible for. Second, you look ahead at the reward you'll reap through perseverance. To quote Jesus, "By your endurance you will gain your lives" (Luke 21:19).

So who are these witnesses around us? They are described in Hebrews 11, which traces our spiritual heritage from Abel to Abraham and on through Moses, David, and the prophets. Though they may seem far way, this passage appeals to us to keep them in mind: "All these, though commended through their faith, did not receive what was promised, since God had provided something better for us, that apart from us they should not be made perfect" (verses 39–40). In light of their sacrifice, we run our own races. They're not the beer-bellied fans in the stands. They're the weatherworn champions who finished their races and now stand beside our lanes, cheering us on. They know well the sacrifice and suffering we're going through.

At the head of them all is Jesus Christ. It's his sacrifice that elicits our own. Our endurance flows from his example and his presence with us.

Aside from Jesus, there may be no better example of suffering nobly than the apostle Paul. He cataloged his suffering in 2 Corinthians 11:24–28:

> Five times I received at the hands of the Jews the forty lashes less one. Three times I was beaten with rods. Once I was stoned. Three times I was shipwrecked; a night and a day I was adrift at sea; on frequent journeys, in danger from rivers, danger from robbers, danger from my own people, danger from Gentiles, danger in the city, danger in the wilderness, danger at sea, danger from false brothers; in toil and hardship, through many a sleepless night, in hunger and thirst, often without food, in cold and exposure. And, apart from other things, there is the daily pressure on me of my anxiety for all the churches.

Why was Paul able to endure so much? Remember the two things that grow grit: Paul looked around to others he was responsible to and responsible for. And he looked ahead at the reward he would reap through perseverance. He put it this way:

> Whatever gain I had, I counted as loss for the sake of Christ. Indeed, I count everything as loss because of the surpassing worth of knowing Christ Jesus my Lord. For his sake I have suffered the loss of all things and count them as rubbish, in order that I may gain Christ and be found in him, not having a righteousness of my own that comes from the law, but that which comes through faith in Christ, the righteousness from God that depends on faith—that I may know him and the power of his resurrection, and may share his sufferings, becoming like him in his death, that by any means possible I may attain the resurrection from the dead. (Philippians 3:7–11)

Paul never changed his tune. In his final letter, endurance was the refrain. He used six Greek words to emphasize endurance; they're translated in English as "share in suffering" (2 Timothy 1:8; 2:3), "am suffering" (2:9); "endure suffering" (4:5); "endure" (2:10, 12); "patiently enduring evil" (2:24); "patience" (3:10; 4:2); "steadfastness" (3:10); and "endured" (3:11).

In the end, here's Paul's conclusion:

> I have fought the good fight, I have finished the race, I have kept the faith. Henceforth there is laid up for me the crown of righteousness, which the Lord, the righteous judge, will award to me on that day, and not only to me but also to all who have loved his appearing. (4:7–8)

With that, he signed off on his letter penned in a dungeon in Rome. The next time he saw the sun, he walked the Ostian Road, just outside the city, to the place where he would be beheaded.

How to Train Grit

We've already identified from Hebrews 12 two foundations of grit. First, you look around to others you're responsible to and responsible for. Second, you look ahead at the reward you'll reap through perseverance. In that light, how can we gain grit?

While there's no magic wand or silver bullet for growing grit, here are five suggestions:

1. *Accept delayed gratification.* Forgoing present pleasure for long-term gain is the starting point for any gritty person. The spiritual disciplines of fasting and prayer are practical exercises that enable this skill to spill over into all areas of your life.
2. *Recognize consequences.* The spiritual disciplines of reading and memorizing the Bible will develop this skill. A good starting point is the book of Proverbs. Read one chapter a day for a month. Each day, select and memorize a verse that addresses a potential deficit in your character.
3. *Get over yourself.* The best spiritual discipline for this life skill is service—doing something for another who cannot pay you back. A second skill is active listening. You could google a number of simple exercises to practice active listening. The Bible itself advocates meditation on Scripture (Psalm 1:2)—sitting quietly and envisioning a passage's implications for your life.
4. *Be accountable.* Gritty people don't do life alone. They submit their dreams and disciplines to others who can hold them accountable, critiquing their performance and celebrating their successes. The circle you choose to surround yourself with will determine your success. We all need a circle below us for service, a circle around us for encouragement, and a circle above us for mentoring—what the Bible calls *discipleship.*

5. *Cultivate optimism.* This can include humor, positive thinking, joy, etc. Two critical spiritual disciplines that build optimism are worship and the Sabbath. These often work in tandem. Worship is showing honor to God, especially through corporate singing, communion, and preaching. Observing the Sabbath is resting from work, which rejuvenates our bodies, minds, and spirits. Together they create space for optimism to flourish.

If you're honored by God to be a parent, coach, teacher, or mentor, here are five tips for growing grit in others:

1. *Set and communicate high expectations.* In a society saturated with accommodation, excuses, and tender feelings, many find this difficult. We want to be everybody's buddy. Yet what people need is not another pal but a spiritual parent who will push them beyond their barriers of comfort. "Average" never grows grit.
2. *Provide clear structure and boundaries.* It's difficult for most to become self-starters if they don't begin with rigid routine. Good character doesn't foster good habits. Rather, good habits foster good character.
3. *Increase their responsibility over time.* This fosters a sense of obligation to others and respect for their mentor. Focus on performance; reward performance with responsibility; respond to responsibility with respect.
4. *Demand that your disciples respect their peers.* This means zero tolerance for gossip, laziness, sloppiness, or tardiness. Things to watch out for here are excuses and finger-pointing. Grit demands that you take responsibility for your own course. For gritty leaders, failure is never someone else's fault.
5. *Show you care.* People tend to live up to the expectations of those who love them. When you show you care by investing time, attention, and rebuke, you earn the right to raise expectations. People tend to believe about themselves what you give them the right to believe. Be as lavish with praise as you are quick with criticism—both are within bounds.

There's more to say on growing grit, but those five suggestions will give us a good start.

Key Points

- Grit is the key to success in life.
- Grit grows when you look around to others you're responsible to and responsible for, as well as when you look ahead at the reward you'll reap through perseverance.
- You can follow practical steps for growing grit in yourself and in others.

This Week

- ☐ **Day 1:** Read the essay.
- ☐ **Day 2:** Memorize Hebrews 12:1–2.
- ☐ **Day 3:** Read Nehemiah 1–2.
- ☐ **Day 4:** Meditate on Luke 21:19; Philippians 3:7–11; 2 Timothy 4:7.
- ☐ **Day 5:** Write out an action plan for growing grit in yourself or in someone else.

Overachiever Challenge: Memorize 2 Timothy 4:7.

Bonus Read: Caroline Adams Miller, *Getting Grit: The Evidence-Based Approach to Cultivating Passion, Perseverance, and Purpose.*

52

Heaven

I saw a new heaven and a new earth, for the first heaven and the first earth had passed away, and the sea was no more. And I saw the holy city, new Jerusalem, coming down out of heaven from God, prepared as a bride adorned for her husband. And I heard a loud voice from the throne saying, "Behold, the dwelling place of God is with man. He will dwell with them, and they will be his people, and God himself will be with them as their God."

—Revelation 21:1–3

Question: What will heaven be like?

News flash: we're not going to heaven. According to Revelation 21:1–3, the New Jerusalem is coming down from the new heaven to the new earth, where we will dwell with God for eternity.

That's actually good news. The portrait of the New Jerusalem in Revelation 21–22 tells of a city on a physical earth. We go there in resurrected bodies, still physical but without the limitations of aging, illness, or aches (1 Corinthians 15:35–49). According to Philippians 3:21, our resurrected bodies will be like Jesus's resurrected body. In his new body, he walked through walls and defied gravity (John 20:19; Acts 1:9).

The implications are extraordinary. Imagine it: living with perfected bodies in a restored Eden. There'll be agriculture and architecture, culture and art, plants, animals, and entertainment—and all without sin. That's what the new earth will be like.

Imagine how technologically advanced we would be if we weren't distracted by war, disease, crime, and disorder. We may well have technological advancements in the New Jerusalem that far exceed anything we have here. God isn't opposed to our curiosity or creativity; he actually gave us both. As Solomon said, "It is the glory of God to conceal a matter; to search out a matter is the glory of kings" (Proverbs 25:2, NIV).

Our eternal praise will be not merely singing but producing new acts of art, work, accomplishment, and learning. Jesus, in fact, is preparing that place for us as we speak: "I have told you that I go to prepare a place for you" (John 14:2).

So what will the New Jerusalem be like? Revelation describes it in terms of both what isn't there and what is there.

What Isn't There

In the New Jerusalem, there'll be no unemployment, picket lines, police, politicians, doctors, lawyers, preachers, prisons, hospitals, IRS, ICE, CIA, FBI, mothballs, locks, Kleenex, light bulbs, weddings, funerals, or armies, just to name a few.

The last two chapters of Revelation get even more specific:

1. There'll no longer be any sea (21:1). On this earth, seas separate people. In the new earth, there will finally be no separation of nations, peoples, tongues, or tribes. There'll be diversity but without division, racism, or nationalism.
2. There'll be no more tears or death, no crying or pain (verse 4). No funerals, divorces, murders, thefts, gossip, broken dreams, unresolved anger, haunting memories, or lifelong regrets.
3. We won't need churches or temples because we'll perpetually be in God's presence (verse 22). We won't have to chase after him through priests or programs.

4. There will be no sun or moon (verse 23). God himself will provide all the light we need.
5. There will be no curse (22:3), meaning we won't be earning a living by the sweat of our brows. For women, there'll be no more painful childbirth.

   For both men and women, the battle between the sexes will be over. Christians currently have the responsibility to mitigate this curse of gender conflict (Galatians 3:28). Though there may still be differentiated roles for men and women, there should be little left of the curse in Christian homes today. Yet it's still primarily women who get lower-paying jobs, who get raped, who are beaten by husbands, who are saddled with domestic responsibilities that they often bear alone.

   On the new earth, all this will change. There'll be no more competition, fighting, or cruelty between male and female—and none of the resultant suffering. God will put an end to the inequity between the sexes.
6. Nothing impure will enter the New Jerusalem (Revelation 21:27). Including you and me? Yes! You'll be in heaven, but you'll no longer have any sin.

   That sounds like a fairy tale. The reality is that Jesus's work of redemption will finally be complete with our physical transformation. The impulses of our new bodies will match the intentions of our saved souls.

   Consider this: those things that cause me to sin now will not be present in heaven. First, Satan and his cronies don't get guest passes. They're out. Therefore, they can no longer put ideas in my mind and opportunities in my path. Granted, I'm perfectly capable of sinning all by myself. But God's enemies prod me along. Without them, I'd be a lot closer to perfection.

   Second, I won't live in a society where sin prevails and is promoted. There'll be no lewd billboards or aggressive drivers with fingers flying out their windows. No red-light districts or adult bookstores, no materialistic malls or Hollywood productions to promote sensuality. My environment will be purified and my mind transformed.

Third, there'll be no marriage or giving in marriage. Our sexuality will be transformed. The Bible never says we'll be asexual in heaven, but we can be certain that whatever sexuality looks like, it won't be the source of sensual entrapment that it is here and now.

Fourth, there'll be no competition in heaven. So my need to best others will be obliterated. Since we'll be dwelling perpetually in the presence of God, our thoughts will be high; our motives, noble; our spirits, humble.

7. There's one last thing to mention. It's time. Often we prioritize projects rather than people. We listen poorly and work haphazardly because we're pressed by a clock. In eternity, what's the rush? We'll always have time to listen to a child's story, to hold a loved one's hand, to sit quietly and watch the world. There'll be no deadlines to meet, no traffic jams to beat, no lines to rush.

It sounds too good to be true. Nevertheless, the New Jerusalem will lack everything that hinders us from full righteousness. We can therefore be sinless.

What Is There

In light of what *isn't* there, heaven will be a wonderful place. But our hearts truly yearn for heaven because of what *is* there.

There'll be saints of old in heaven: Abraham, Isaac, Jacob, Peter, James, and John. Oh, the conversations we'll have!

Perhaps personally more important, our loved ones will be there. Wives will be reunited with husbands, and children, with parents. Granted, the nature of the relationships will change, but how sweet it still will be! Parents will see children who died in their cribs. Grandparents will introduce themselves to grandchildren who knew them only through stories.

As sweet as these reunions will be, that's not why we want to go there.

There'll also be unimaginable wealth. John described the New Jerusalem as a city of vast proportions with stunning treasure (Revelation 21:18–21). Even the pavement is twenty-four-karat gold.

The new earth will surely put this earth to shame (and God didn't do half-bad here!). No one will lack for food. Everyone will be a prince or princess in the kingdom of God.

We all dream of such luxury and comfort, but that's not, however, why we want to go to heaven.

We'll have new bodies. No more arthritis, no more physical limitations, no more looking in the mirror and asking "Why?" We'll have energy to work and play, time to rest and worship.

As wonderful as that sounds—this, too, is not why we want to go there.

We want to go there because *he* is there. *He is there.* The one we've talked about, sung to, read of, and written for. He's waiting with outstretched arms and these words: "Well done, good and faithful servant. . . . Enter into the joy of your master" (Matthew 25:21).

I can't help but think that one glimpse of his person will make all our words irrelevant. He's so much grander than we've described, so much more glorious than we've imagined. Our impulse will be not to embrace him as a buddy but to fall down at his feet, awestruck and overwhelmed in the majesty of the moment. I suspect that it will be only his immense love that draws us to our feet to receive his embrace.

Better Than You Imagine and Sooner Than You Think

Three times Jesus repeated: "I am coming soon" (Revelation 22:7, 12, 20). His impassioned plea is that we come to him: "The Spirit and the bride say, 'Come!' And let the one who hears say, 'Come!' Let the one who is thirsty come; and let the one who wishes take the free gift of the water of life" (verse 17, NIV).

Here, then, is the most amazing truth of all eternity: *God loves you.* In fact, he doesn't just love you; he really, really likes you. He invites you to him because he craves your presence (21:3).

So what can we say in reply to the God of the universe, who invites us to come? Here's the biblical script (in 22:20):

Jesus says, "Surely I am coming soon."

And we say, "Amen. Come, Lord Jesus!"

Key Points

- We're going not to heaven but to the New Jerusalem on the new earth, in physical yet glorified bodies.
- This new earth will not have sickness, death, division, decay, or anything that could bring tears to our eyes.
- This New Jerusalem will have all sorts of comfort and beauty but mostly Jesus—in person and present for eternity.

This Week

- ☐ **Day 1:** Read the essay.
- ☐ **Day 2:** Memorize Revelation 21:1–3.
- ☐ **Day 3:** Read Revelation 21–22.
- ☐ **Day 4:** Meditate on John 14:2; Philippians 3:21; Revelation 22:20.
- ☐ **Day 5:** Ask someone you have a relationship with to describe to you what heaven will be like. If appropriate, ask whether that person has confidence he or she is going there.

Overachiever Challenge: Memorize John 14:2.

Bonus Read: Randy Alcorn, *Heaven.*

Notes

Introduction

1. Arnold Cole and Pamela Caudill Ovwigho, *Bible Engagement as the Key to Spiritual Growth: A Research Synthesis* (Center for Bible Engagement, 2012), 4–5, www.backtothebible.org/files/web/docs/cbe/Research_Synthesis_Bible_Engagement_and_Spiritual_Growth_Aug2012.pdf.
2. Cole and Ovwigho, *Bible Engagement,* i.

Chapter 4: Covenant

1. Conrad Hackett and David McClendon, "Christians Remain World's Largest Religious Group, but They Are Declining in Europe," Pew Research Center, April 5, 2017, www.pewresearch.org/fact-tank/2017/04/05/christians-remain-worlds-largest-religious-group-but-they-are-declining-in-europe.
2. Though we know less about these ancient covenants than we would like, there does appear to be a parallel in ancient Assyria, a treaty between Ashurnirari V and Mati'ilu: "If Mati'ilu sins against (this) treaty made under oath by the gods, then, just as this spring lamb, brought from its fold, will not return to its fold, . . . alas, Mati'ilu . . . will not return to his country." James B. Pritchard, ed., *The Ancient Near East: An Anthology of Texts and Pictures* (New Jersey: Princeton, 2011), 210.

Chapter 8: Jesus and David

1. Psalms of Solomon 17:5, in R. H. Charles, ed., *The Apocrypha and Pseudepigrapha of the Old Testament in English,* vol. 2, *Pseudepigrapha* (Oxford: Clarendon, 1913), 648. This is an ancient collection of poetry attributed to King Solomon but likely not written earlier than the first century BC.

2. 4Q174, in Florentino García Martínez and Eibert J. C. Tigchelaar, eds., *The Dead Sea Scrolls: Study Edition,* vol. 1, *1Q1–4Q273* (Grand Rapids, MI: Eerdmans, 2000), 353.
3. Jacob Neusner, ed., *The Babylonian Talmud: A Translation and Commentary,* vol. 7b (Peabody, MA: Hendrickson, 2011), 92. The Babylonian Talmud is the most important body of teaching outside the Bible for the Jewish faith.

Chapter 9: Finding Happiness

1. Philip Brickman, Dan Coates, and Ronnie Janoff-Bulman, "Lottery Winners and Accident Victims: Is Happiness Relative?," *Journal of Personality and Social Psychology* 36, no. 8 (1978): 920–21.
2. Sonja Lyubomirsky, *The How of Happiness: A Scientific Approach to Getting the Life You Want* (New York: Penguin, 2007), 20.
3. Caroline Leaf, *Switch On Your Brain: The Key to Peak Happiness, Thinking, and Health* (Grand Rapids, MI: Baker, 2015), 50, 64.

Chapter 10: Prophecy

1. Flavius Josephus, *The Wars of the Jews,* in *The Works of Josephus: Complete and Unabridged,* trans. William Whiston (Peabody, MA: Hendrickson, 1987), 743.
2. *Encyclopaedia Britannica,* s.v. "Bar Kokhba," www.britannica.com/biography/Bar-Kokhba-Jewish-leader.
3. Peter W. Stoner and Robert C. Newman, *Science Speaks: Scientific Proof of the Accuracy of Prophecy and the Bible,* rev. ed. (Chicago: Moody, 1976), 101–6.
4. Stoner and Newman, *Science Speaks,* 107.
5. Josh McDowell and Sean McDowell, *Evidence That Demands a Verdict: Life-Changing Truth for a Skeptical World* (Nashville: Thomas Nelson, 2017), 231.

Chapter 12: Messiah

1. Craig A. Evans, "The Messiah in the Dead Sea Scrolls," in *Israel's Messiah in the Bible and the Dead Sea Scrolls,* ed. Richard S. Hess and Daniel Carroll (Grand Rapids, MI: Baker Academic, 2003), 86.
2. Author's translation of Isaiah 10:27, in *Targum Jonathan to the Prophets* (Cincinnati, OH: Hebrew Union College, 2005).
3. 2 Esdras 12:33, in Michael D. Coogan et al., eds., *The New Oxford Annotated Bible: New Revised Standard Version with the Apocrypha,* 4th ed. (New York: Oxford University Press, 2010), 1706. The Apocrypha is a collection of ancient books valued by the early church. Catholic Bibles include these with the sixty-six books of the Old and New Testaments.
4. 2 Baruch 40:1, in R. H. Charles, ed., *The Apocrypha and Pseudepigrapha of the Old Testament in English,* vol. 2, *Pseudepigrapha* (Oxford: Clarendon, 1913), 501.
5. 11Q13, in Florentino García Martínez and Eibert J. C. Tigchelaar, eds., *The Dead Sea Scrolls: Study Edition,* vol. 2, *4Q274–11Q31* (Grand Rapids, MI: Eerdmans, 2000), 1207, brackets in the original.

Chapter 13: Jesus Rejected

1. "Psalm 118:22," Sefaria, www.sefaria.org/Psalms.118.22?lang=bi&with=Targum&lang2=bi, emphasis added.

Chapter 15: Atonement

1. A. Cohen, trans., Sotah, *The Babylonian Talmud,* ed. I. Epstein (London: Soncino, 1936), 73–74.
2. To illustrate the upside-downness of the suffering-servant idea, compare an ancient Jewish paraphrase (Targum) of two verses from Isaiah 53 with Isaiah's original. Verse 4 reads, "Surely he has borne our griefs and carried our sorrows; yet we esteemed him stricken, smitten by God, and afflicted." The Targum rewords this as "Therefore He shall pray for our sins, and our iniquities for His sake shall be forgiven us; for we are considered crushed,

smitten of the Lord, and afflicted." And in verse 5 Isaiah stated, "He was pierced for our transgressions; he was crushed for our iniquities; upon him was the chastisement that brought us peace, and with his wounds we are healed." The Targum interprets the verse this way: "He shall build the house of the sanctuary, which has been profaned on account of our sins; He was delivered over on account of our iniquities, and through His doctrine peace shall be multiplied upon us, and through the teaching of His words our sins shall be forgiven us." See Jonathan Ben Uziel, *The Chaldee Paraphrase on the Prophet Isaiah,* trans. C. W. H. Pauli (London: London Society's House, 1871), 183.

Chapter 16: New Covenant

1. Similar sentiments were found in various Jewish scrolls written between the Old and New Testaments (Jubilees 1:21–25; Testament of Judah 24:2–3; Testament of Levi 18:11). These documents were not included in the Jewish Bible but were part of the historical record of the Jews.

Chapter 18: Blessedness

1. Aristotle, *Nicomachean Ethics,* trans. and ed. Robert Crisp, rev. ed. (Cambridge: Cambridge University Press, 2014), 1098b–1099b.
2. Sirach 25:8–9; 26:1, in Michael D. Coogan et al., eds., *The New Oxford Annotated Bible: New Revised Standard Version with the Apocrypha,* 4th ed. (New York: Oxford University Press, 2010), 1490–91. The book of Sirach is a wisdom book written in the era between the Testaments and is included in the Apocrypha.
3. Tosefta 9:30, in *A History of the Mishnaic Law of Damages,* ed. Jacob Neusner, vol. 1, *Baba Qamma: Translation and Explanation* (Eugene, OR: Wipf and Stock, 2007), 126.
4. 4 Maccabees 10:15, in Bruce M. Metzger and Roland E. Murphy, eds., *The New Oxford Annotated Apocrypha: The Apocryphal/Deuterocanonical Books of the Old Testament* (New York: Oxford University Press, 1991),

353. *The* fourth book of Maccabees is a philosophical discourse using examples from around the time of the famous Maccabean revolt.

5. 4 Maccabees 5:16, in Bruce M. Metzger and Roland E. Murphy, eds., *The New Oxford Annotated Apocrypha: The Apocryphal/Deuterocanonical Books of the Old Testament* (New York: Oxford University Press, 1991), 347.
6. 2 Maccabees 7:9, in Michael D. Coogan et al., eds., *The New Oxford Annotated Bible: New Revised Standard Version with the Apocrypha*, 4th ed. (New York: Oxford University Press, 2010), 1613.

Chapter 21: Money

1. Howard L. Dayton Jr., "Statistic: Jesus' Teaching on Money," *Christianity Today,* www.preachingtoday.com/illustrations/1996/december/410.html.

Chapter 22: The Golden Rule

1. Bruce M. Metzger and Roland E. Murphy, eds., *The New Oxford Annotated Apocrypha: The Apocryphal/Deuterocanonical Books of the Old Testament* (New York: Oxford University Press, 1991), 7. The book of Tobit records a Jewish legend from the time between the Testaments and is included in the Apocrypha.
2. H. Freedman, trans., Shabbath, vol. 1, T*he Babylonian Talmud,* ed. I. Epstein (London: Soncino, 1938), 140.

Chapter 27: The Gospel

1. Craig Evans, "Mark's Incipit and the Priene Calendar Inscription: From Jewish Gospel to Greco-Roman Gospel," *Journal of Greco-Roman Christianity and Judaism* 1 (2000): 67–81.
2. *The International Standard Bible Encyclopedia,* ed. Geoffrey W. Bromiley, vol. 2, rev. ed. (Grand Rapids, MI: Eerdmans, 1982), 529.
3. Translation is from Ben Witherington III, *The Gospel of Mark: A Socio-Rhetorical Commentary* (Grand Rapids, MI: Eerdmans, 2001), 69.

Chapter 28: Faith

1. Flavius Josephus, *The Life of Flavius Josephus,* in *The Works of Josephus: Complete and Unabridged,* trans. William Whiston, rev. ed. (Peabody, MA: Hendrickson, 1987), 7, emphasis added.

Chapter 29: Rest

1. Bob Sullivan, "Memo to Work Martyrs: Long Hours Make You Less Productive," CNBC, January 26, 2015, www.cnbc.com/2015/01/26/working-more-than-50-hours-makes-you-less-productive.html.

Chapter 34: Worship

1. Watchman Nee, *The Release of the Spirit* (New York: Christian Fellowship, 2000), 12.

Chapter 35: Communion

1. Brant Pitre, *Jesus and the Jewish Roots of the Eucharist: Unlocking the Secrets of the Last Supper* (New York: Doubleday, 2011), 160.

Chapter 40: God's Solution to Racism

1. Ilan Ben Zion, "Ancient Temple Mount 'Warning' Stone Is 'Closest Thing We Have to the Temple,'" *Times of Israel,* October 22, 2015, www.timesofisrael.com/ancient-temple-mount-warning-stone-is-closest-thing-we-have-to-the-temple.

Chapter 44: The Resurrection

1. Flavius Josephus, *The Antiquities of the Jews,* in *The Works of Josephus: Complete and Unabridged,* trans. William Whiston, rev. ed. (Peabody, MA: Hendrickson, 1987), 480.
2. P. Cornelius Tacitus, *The Annals,* in *The Annals and the Histories,* Great Books of the Western World, ed. Robert Maynard Hutchins, vol. 15 (Chicago: Encyclopaedia Britannica, 1952), 15.44.
3. Homer, *Iliad,* 24.549–51; Aeschylus, *Eumenides,* 645.

Chapter 47: Humility

1. "Strong's G2758—Kenoō," Blue Letter Bible, www.blueletterbible.org/lang/lexicon/lexicon.cfm?t=kjv&strongs=g2758.

Chapter 48: Overwhelming Worry

1. Kevin Hultine, "The Secret Life of the Sonoran Desert," interview by Ira Flow, NPR, March 29, 2013, www.npr.org/2013/03/29/175741691/segment-1.
2. Caroline Leaf, *Switch On Your Brain: The Key to Peak Happiness, Thinking, and Health* (Grand Rapids, MI: Baker, 2015), 50.

Chapter 49: Mentoring

1. Homer, *Odyssey,* trans. Robert Fitzgerald (New York: Farrar, Straus and Giroux, 1998), 2.235–38, 2.282–312, 2.424–29, 3.26–33.

Chapter 50: Scripture

1. Arnold Cole and Pamela Caudill Ovwigho, *Bible Engagement as the Key to Spiritual Growth: A Research Synthesis* (Center for Bible Engagement, 2012), 4–5, www.backtothebible.org/files/web/docs/cbe/Research_Synthesis_Bible_Engagement_and_Spiritual_Growth_Aug2012.pdf.

Chapter 51: Gaining Grit

1. Angela Lee Duckworth, "Grit: The Power of Passion and Perseverance," TED video, 2:49, www.ted.com/talks/angela_lee_duckworth_grit_the_power_of_passion_and_perseverance.